No Life
Without
Roots

No Life Without Roots

Culture and Development

Thierry G. Verhelst

Translated by Bob Cumming

Zed Books Ltd
London and New Jersey

No Life Without Roots was first published in French under the title
Des racines pour vivre by Editions Duculot, Paris Gembloux, in 1987.
It was first published in English by Zed Books Ltd, 57 Caledonian Road,
London N1 9BU, UK and 165 First Avenue, Atlantic Highlands,
New Jersey 07716, USA, in 1990.

Cover designed by Andrew Corbett.
Cover photograph from *Guinea-Bissau alfabeto*, by courtesy of the
authors, Giuseppe Lodi, Carlos Lopes, Luisa Sabadini.
Typeset by EMS Photosetters, Thorpe Bay, Essex.
Printed and bound in the United Kingdom
by Biddles Ltd, Guildford and King's Lynn.

Second impression, 1992.

British Library Cataloguing in Publication Data

Verhelst, Thierry
   No life without roots : culture and development
   1. Developing countries. Economic development.
   Social aspects
   I. Title
   330.9172'4

   ISBN 0-86232-848-9
   ISBN 0-86232-849-7 pbk

Library of Congress Cataloging-in-Publication Data

Verhelst, Thierry G.
   [Des racines pour vivre. English]
   No life without roots ; culture and development/
Thierry Verhelst; translated by Bob Cumming.
     p.   cm.
   Translation of: Des racines pour vivre.
   Includes bibliographical references.
   ISBN 0-86232-848-9 (U.S.)
   ISBN 0-86232-849-7 (pbk.)
   1. Developing countries—Social conditions.
   2. Economic development—Social aspects.
   3. Technical assistance—Social aspects. I. Title.
HN980.V4413   1989
330.9172'4——dc20   89-39009
                               CIP

Contents

Foreword   1

Part One: Cultural Imperialism and Cultural Resistance   7
1. **The Collapse of Development Models**   9
   The failure of Western development policies   10
   Development as liberation: strengths and weaknesses   13
2. **Culture: The Forgotten Dimension**   17
   Development: a white man's dream   20
3. **Indigenous Cultures as Foundations for Alternatives**   24
   Economics: *homo economicus* and the others   25
   Technology: taking a short cut   32
   Politics: stateless nations and nationless states   38
4. **Indigenous Cultures as Sources of Social Struggle**   43
   Non-conventional types of struggle   43
   Religion: opium or liberation   45
5. **Development: A Trojan Horse?**   52
   Acculturation–inculturation   53
   Cultural resistance   55

Part Two: Underdevelopment and Overdevelopment   59
6. **The Withering Away of People's Identity**   61
   Development, a term to be discarded?   62
7. **Alienation Amidst Plenty**   65
   Crisis within crisis   67
   A cultural winter   70
8. **Third World Aid to the West**   72
   An embodied spirituality for activists   75
   NGOs: struggle and contemplation   77
9. **Intercultural solidarity**   79
   Delinking   80
   A deeper understanding of indigenous cultures   83
   New criteria for development projects   84
   Beyond 'development pornography'   86
   A touch of modesty for Western donors   88

Part Three: A New Generation of Projects   89
    Introduction   91
10. **Research and Participatory Observation**   93
11. **Safeguard and Adapt**   102
12. **From Solidarity to Perplexity**   113
13. **Getting Off the Beaten Track**   117
    Vademecum for the presentation of a project   119

Part Four: The Right to be Different   121
14. **A View from the Ashram**   123
15. **Lomé III – a New Approach?**   147
16. **Summary and Conclusions**   156

    Notes   163
    Bibliography   179
    Index   183

'*So many state offices, so many development agencies are well meaning but destroy us nonetheless. They have taught us to beg but we want liberation by our own means. Our Inca ancestors were our pioneers. Their gold drove the white man mad and cruel, but they themselves only used it to make jewellery. Theirs was the right attitude. Wealth is not our goal. What is important is the spiritual element, and economic, cultural and political independence.*'

Anamaria Guacho,
Quechua peasant,
General Secretary
of the *Movimiento Indigena del Chimborazo*,
Ecuador.

'*Divesting our relations of any hint of racism means affirming: we are different, and we are going to stay different.*'

Edgar Pisani,
former European Commissioner
responsible for questions of development.

Foreword

Is development like some Trojan Horse, introducing Westernization into the Third World? There are those who say so and who claim that development constitutes a rape, whether by coercion or by seduction. That assertion is the starting point of the present book.

Innumerable organizations of international co-operation, both public and private, have taken on the role of champions, promoters and financiers of development, progress and the socio-economic advancement of the peoples of the South. In reality, these initiatives often mean projecting into culturally alien ground, ideas, aspirations and experiences that are tied to a specific situation, to a particular history, to a well defined *Weltanschauung*, namely that of the modern Western world. Yet other peoples, or other cultural communities within them, have quite different social, economic and political aspirations, or similar aspirations but different ways of attaining them. In short, happiness does not have a universal flavour and the means of pursuing it may vary. International development co-operation often sets out to transform the mentality and traditions of human communities referred to as underdeveloped. Is it not a mistake as fatal as it is crass to see only the negative or backward aspects of indigenous traditions? Such traditions, long considered mere 'obstacles to development', might well constitute an ultimately beneficial force of resistance to a foreign model of society whose effects are undesirable. Furthermore, indigenous values and the religions which uphold them offer alternative social models as well as different forms of action to implement such models.

'Development' is a vast topic. The aim of this book is therefore delimited as follows. On the one hand, it deals with what is often referred to as 'the cultural dimension of development'. On the other, it describes, for the most part, the activities of private development organizations and international solidarity movements. The setting of these limits calls for a certain clarification.

It is obvious that economic exploitation and political oppression are amongst the basic causes of the Third World's problems. There is no question here of passing over this fact in silence on the pretext of concentrating on culture. Any consideration of the cultural dimension of development must take into account the external and internal mechanisms of economic and political domination. The domination exercised by countries of the North over those of the Third World is an undeniable historical reality. Thus, 'agro-business' imposes monocultures which rapidly impoverish tropical soils. The transnational companies enforce the cultivation, heavily backed by capital and machines, of agricultural products destined for external markets at the expense of food crops, thereby spreading famine and malnutrition. Factory-ships exhaust entire coasts of their fish, creating underwater deserts and depriving local fishermen of their traditional livelihood. Primeval forests are uprooted at a senseless rate, with catastrophic results for the ecological balance. The North profits from the ever-increasing prices of its own products while the prices of the agricultural and mineral raw materials, on whose sale the Third World depends, are usually in decline. The industrialized countries diffuse an ideology of development, modernization and progress which serves specific interests. It consists of such ideas as the international division of labour, economic *laissez-faire* and political control of peasant and workers' organizations, often backed by more or less overt state violence. The International Monetary Fund imposes social and economic conditions which are nothing less than political decrees whose social impact is disastrous. The North is instrumental in plunging Third World states into chronic debt. It applies irresistible pressure to certain governments to maintain economic policies which drag their peoples down into the abyss of dependence and impoverishment. This kind of economy is tolerated, even encouraged, by the local middle class who profit from it. North–South relations are thus further complicated by the mechanisms of internal domination specific to each country. It is, therefore, not simply a matter of blaming the white man for all the sins of the world and wallowing in self-hatred. Neither geography nor race primarily determine responsibility. It is a question of mechanisms of domination. The North has no monopoly on this, even if it is the most powerful centre. This book will touch only briefly on the phenomenon of economic and political imperialism whose driving forces are the financial centres and governments of the northern hemisphere. Nor will it deal at length with the mechanisms of internal domination within each country. Such problems are not the subject of the present study. They are, however, a determining factor in the current world situation and the reader is advised to bear them in mind while reading this book. If necessary, reference may be made to the work of such writers as Celso Furtado, André Gunder Frank, Samir Amin, Pierre Jalée, Jean Ziegler, Claude Julien, René Dumont, Susan George and many others who have made definitive studies of imperialism, although most of them — and this is significant — mainly stress economic and political aspects and pay far less attention to the effects on the cultural identities of the peoples concerned. The first chapter of this book refers to certain of these works, along with Rostow's 'catching-up' theory and the ensuing dependence on the West, which they seek to combat. It gives only a necessarily brief summary of development theories which may make difficult reading for those who are completely unfamiliar with the material. If need be, the reader may skim these pages and move on to tackle the essence of the subject in Chapter 2. These opening pages merely sketch in the background. But, as in the theatre, this is important since it helps to place the drama in context.

As a further clarification of the subject matter, this work will deal mainly with the practices of non-governmental aid development organizations, the NGOs. Relatively less attention will be paid to state organizations and the specialized international organizations such as UNDP, FAO, the World Bank and its affiliates, the European Development Fund, and so on. The havoc and waste brought about by certain major projects and programmes of these technocratic organizations is well known. Already denounced by many experts and by the grass-roots communities who bear the brunt of them, the practices of the great bureaucracies of development will be only briefly touched on here. An analysis will, however, be made of the last Lomé Convention, signed by the EEC with Third World states, since it is indicative of a new outlook and offers interesting scope to NGOs in particular. Since this book deals mainly with the practices of NGOs, it is to them that questions and challenges are addressed. The challenge will be mainly aimed at the Third World solidarity movement in general and at progressive funding agencies, to which I belong, in particular. Having an insider's view of the latter, I think I am in a position to assess some of their limitations, even though I may share their basic convictions. If the practices of progressive NGOs are described and questioned here, it is largely because it is they who have best analysed the intricate machinery of the systematic underdevelopment of the Third World. It is they who have succeeded in establishing new, better adapted guidelines for solidarity in both political and economic terms. What many of them currently refer to as 'partnership' relations between Western NGOs and grass-roots communities in the Third World adequately illustrates their capacity for dialogue, for self-criticism and for changes in strategies and attitudes. They are closer to the everyday reality of the countries in question than many other authorities and more paternalistic donor agencies. It is perhaps above all to these NGOs that we must look to take up this new challenge resulting from recent changes in consciousness regarding the cultural dimension of development.

In this book I will present the current position in the debate as expressed by a growing number of experts and local communities. The questions are urgent. The answers, unfortunately — or should one say fortunately, since it is so important to avoid yet more standardization in cultural matters? — are uncertain and sometimes contradictory. These pages will also attempt to make their own contribution to the debate. It is no easy task. The relationship between culture and development is complex. Indeed, it has been said that culture is 'the aporia of development', in other words a problem that leaves anyone who tackles it confused and surrounded by contradictions.

This book is also a means of bringing the great wealth of information and contacts at the disposal of most NGOs to a wider audience. Those involved in development work sometimes have the feeling they are like sponges, soaking up the immense contribution of the Third World, but sadly unable fully to convey to others all its richness and diversity. This impotence is due to the fact that NGOs do not have at their disposal adequate means to reach the general public, and to the fact that the most liberating and inspiring things witnessed in the

Third World are often difficult to describe. Real development is not photogenic, since, above all, it takes place in people's hearts and minds.

The present work fits into no single scientific discipline. It is not a study in cultural anthropology. Nor is it the work of a researcher in the human sciences writing from the tranquillity of a university library. Rather, it was written in the field, amidst the hubbub of the daily activities of an NGO actively involved in almost every country of the Third World, plied with demands from all quarters, facing innumerable challenges, responding to countless cases of human suffering and hope. If this book is the fruit of lengthy contemplation, it is also the result of a personal commitment. These pages grew out of a set of experiences and convictions acquired over a period of twenty years of contact with the reality of the Third World, sometimes as a legal adviser and teacher in Africa but, in my turn, learning from it in a million ways, sometimes as an NGO representative in Asia and nourished in return by eastern spirituality, sometimes as project officer in South America and comforted there by the life-enhancing hope of its basic Christian communities. This present work was also inspired by countless partners, colleagues and friends. Their experience and their suggestions form the fabric of this book. I take this opportunity to thank them. My thanks go in particular to Kalpana Das, Yaya Diallo, Robert Vachon and Raimundo Panikkar who organized, at La Marlagne in Belgium, an extraordinarily productive conference on international co-operation and culture. Organized by the Monchanin Intercultural Centre (Montreal) in collaboration with the Peace University (Namur), with the participation of a few anthropologists, philosophers, economists, jurists and activists from both North and South, this conference marked, for me, the beginning of a profound questioning of the subject. I owe a great deal to Étienne Le Roy, Georges Anglade, René Bureau, Denis Goulet and all those who attended the conference and whose contributions helped to spark off the present work. My grateful thanks also go to Sulak Sivaraksa of Thailand, Yvon Ambroise, as well as Siddharta and Alida of India, Jean-Marc Ela of the Cameroons, Oscar Bimwenji of Zaire, Maria Angelina de Oliveira and Alfredinho Kunz of Brazil, Anamaria Guacho of Ecuador, Franklin Armand and Rénald Clérismé of Haiti, Marc Luyckx of Belgium, Alistair and Fiona Hulbert of Scotland, to my colleagues in *Broederlijk Delen, Entraide et Fraternité* and APHD (Asia Partnership for Human Development) without whose encouragement and criticisms this book would never have seen the light of day. Lastly, my thanks go above all to the grass-roots communities I met all over the world. They inspired the best of this book.

In these pages, the reader will come upon the expression 'Third World'. The term has, justifiably, been frequently criticized. In the first place, one ought to speak of 'Third Worlds', so diverse are the countries of the southern hemisphere in terms of geographic location, economic conditions and specific socio-cultural characters. To this diversity between countries must be added the fundamental difference that exists between their citizens. Depending on their social class, they find themselves very differently affected by problems, from which some benefit rather than suffer. In actual fact, lumping together everything that is different from ourselves is a particularly Eurocentric trait. (Moreover, the term 'Third World' refers not only to the three great continents of Africa, America and Asia, but also to a fourth area whose economic and strategic importance is enormous, namely Australasia, which is frequently overlooked.) The term 'Third World' must also be questioned on the grounds that it will soon be three quarters of humanity whom we continue to diminish by means of this misleading mathematical term. So why use the term here? Because it is brief and understood by everyone. But also because it has the advantage of calling to mind the injustice denounced by the French revolutionaries of 1789: the Third Estate represented the majority of the French people although the *Ancien Régime* accorded them no power. Similarly today, there is no common measure, if only on a numerical basis, between the population of the Third World and the influence it wields. This is certainly true from the economic and political points of view. From the cultural point of view, which concerns us here, the impact of the peoples of the South on the Western world remains very much less than it might and should be. Ethnocentrism, at once engendered and reinforced by our position of economic dominance, has impeded the process of mutual enrichment which normally accompanies contact between peoples. Today, however, the Europe of old, returning to its humanist traditions, has become aware of this and is now engaged in a dialogue which is both productive and full of promise. A large international network is gradually developing, composed of committed devlopment activists and academics anxious to deepen their understanding of this complex but vitally important theme. It is called 'South–North Network on Cultures and Development'. (For further information, write to the Secretariat of the Network, provisional address: 23, Avenue d'Anderghem, 1040, Brussels, Belgium.) The debate has been opened. It promises to be lively. I hope here not so much to supply answers as to encourage each reader to embark on the exciting adventure of intercultural dialogue.

Thierry Verhelst

Part One:
Cultural Imperialism and Cultural Resistance

1.   The Collapse of Development Models

As everyone knows, none of the major objectives of the last two 'Development Decades' declared by the United Nations have been attained. Today, poverty and malnutrition are more prevalent than they were twenty-five years ago. The greater part of humanity is currently experiencing a deterioration in the quality of life, on the social and political as much as the economic level. In Africa, food production goes down each year by one per cent. Countries in the process of industrialization, such as Mexico, are crippled by debts. Life-skills are disintegrating only to be replaced by alienation, as can be seen from the moral impoverishment and growing crime rate in the major cities of the South. Dictatorships reign in many places and human rights are violated almost everywhere.

The much acclaimed experiments of the Ivory Coast and Brazil now seem more like mirages than miracles. The neo-liberalism to which the 'Chicago boys' have given free rein in Pinochet's Chile has drained the country's economy dry. Poverty and intolerable inequality have increased in most countries whose regimes — politically oppressive for the most part — have opted for liberal capitalism. Those countries not on the brink of social and economic disaster are often bogged down in various forms of dependence that disrupt their societies and stifle their capacity to fight back and make innovations.

For their part, the revolutionary socialist experiments which had raised so much hope have given rise to too much political repression and economic failure for us to continue seeing them as the obvious solution for those peoples dominated by Western imperialism. Within 'actually-existing socialism', agriculture appears to be congenitally sick. Peasants prefer to limit their crops or consume them themselves, rather than have to sell them at imposed prices and be reduced to the role of underpaid producers for the benefit of a privileged class of bureaucrats and an urban proletariat which, though often greatly in the minority, is constantly referred to as the 'avant-garde'. Admittedly, a few exemplary experiments have been successful. Many countries could learn from the policy of health care in Vietnam or the literacy programme set up in Ethiopia. But good individual programmes alone are not enough to make models of these countries (nor can they bring about socialism on their own). Too often, things have been botched, as the self-criticisms made on numerous occasion by, amongst others, Pham van Dong, Samora Machel, Mengistu Haile Mariam and Fidel Castro clearly show. The evils they denounce are almost identical and no one seems able to eradicate them. Apart from the classic shortcomings in agriculture, industry and distribution, there are the problems of cumbersome bureaucracies, of the repressive authoritarianism of civil servants, their shirking of responsibility, their arrogance, which reveals a lack of respect — paradoxical but all too real — for the common people, and the widespread corruption that results from this.

But it is not only Soviet-inspired models that are being called into question. The appalling results of the Khmer Rouge revolution under Pol Pot, who had hoped to introduce a radical Maoist 'socialism' as quickly as possible, will never be forgotten.

Even one-time model experiments like those of Tanzania and the People's Republic of China no longer fascinate the experts or mobilize Third World activists. Today, only Nicaragua and Zimbabwe still attract some attention. But, as well as the policies of destabilization which their neighbours direct at them, these countries have to contend with serious internal contradictions. In fact, at the present moment, there are no valid development models.

Nowadays, everyone is ready to admit that attempts at global development, in its many guises, have ended in failure. They represent 'the bankruptcy of the paradigm of development' for, on four essential fronts, the Third World has suffered setbacks: the equitable distribution of available goods and services; the creation of jobs; the increase in economic independence; and the social cost of investment.[1]

Such a negative assertion calls for a critical examination of the theories and strategies employed so far in matters of development. There is no space here to go into the details of these doctrines. It may, however, be useful to recall their main features and underline their fundamental differences, so as to be in a better position to determine where the seed of the vital alternative might lie.

The failure of Western development policies

The oldest and still the most widespread theory, if not in all the international organizations at least with the general public, is what I would call the 'catching-up theory' (often referred to as the 'trickle-down theory'): underdeveloped countries (nowadays tactfully, if often wrongly, referred to as 'developing countries) display a 'backwardness' in comparison with the rich countries. All that is necessary for the countries of the South is to go through the various 'stages of growth', which W. W. Rostow described with an optimism equalled only by his ethnocentrism.[2] In fact, his conception of the matter was based on a unilinear view of history, according to which the modern West is at once the goal to be reached and the example to be followed. This conception, which gave birth to a veritable 'ideology of development',[3] stems from the somewhat simplistic perspective of the evolutionism that marked science in the last century.

According to the social Darwinism that characterizes this approach, societies evolve from lower to higher forms. Cultural differences, according to this theory, are merely a question of backwardness. Modernization will bring about the universalization of the culture peculiar to modern industrial society. Thus, modernization simply means Westernization. Note that Rostow, who saw his work as a 'non-communist manifesto', merely echoes here the Eurocentrism of Marx and Engels[4] who, products of their age, believed that progress and civilization were synonymous with Westernization. Although anti-imperialist, they believed the French annexation of Algeria and the collapse of Indian civilization beneath the iron hand of British conquest to be necessary evils. It is this same social Darwinism that serves to justify the notion of hierarchies of cultures, which in turn legitimizes the hierarchization of societies, and hence colonialism. The ideology of development shares the same logic and thus facilitates neo-colonialism. Any idea of cultural difference is denied by the evolutionist theory. Societies are doomed to extinction if they do not go through the different stages of 'growth'.

The 'catching-up' theory was often to take the form of ambitious five-year plans, many of which promoted industry at the expense of agriculture (this was particularly true in Algeria under Colonel Boumedienne). Huge projects were undertaken, notably those of the World Bank, as well as the setting up of extremely ambitious infrastructures: transcontinental roads, enormous hydro-electric dams (Inga, Itaipu, Aswan), ultra-modern university hospitals, harbour installations and other projects which, in Brazil, the opposition rather neatly and aptly label 'Pharaonic'. The transnationals discover fabulous new markets and a cheap, docile workforce. They promptly set up shop all over the Third World, using as bait the transfer of technology, the creation of jobs and other advantages often as deceptive and dubious as they are grandiose. A sort of triumphalism based on productivity and technology monopolized the speeches of governments, as well as experts and spokespersons of bilateral and multilateral aid organizations. A similar optimism was rife in the private 'aid development' organizations, whom the UNO and the World Bank recognized as playing an increasingly important complementary role. As the experts became aware that the 'target populations' (!) were less than enthusiastic about their programmes, they increasingly called upon organizations working in closer contact with local communities, namely the NGOs (non-governmental organizations).

It is a fact that NGOs are in a position to work more easily at grass-roots level. But, even they must listen closely to people in order truly to comprehend their needs and correctly evaluate their potential will to change, to 'progress'. The NGOs of the 1960s were generally dependent on the prevailing ideology and therefore believed they had to help the Third World to modernize itself so as to close the gap between it and the West. Having a preconceived notion, therefore, of the desired future of the countries where they would be working, these NGOs could afford to listen to the 'target populations' only in so far as the latter agreed to fall into line with the projects designed for them. Any discordant observations or behaviour on their part was seen as some kind of deviance, or attributed to ancestral tradition whose paralysing influence on progress had already been denounced by Rostow and others. Projects aimed at increasing agricultural production, at improvements in housing conditions, health and education were conceived and planned in Europe and America, then carried out on site. More often than not, the participation of the local population was limited to a small financial contribution or to voluntary work, and did not extend to the conception of the project itself. Other NGOs, more concerned to involve local people in the process of development, now refuse to foist on to some Third World region a project conceived thousands of miles away. They give their support only to projects planned locally.[5] The aim is excellent, but achieving it can pose problems, for those who initiate and direct such projects are often foreigners, either missionaries or voluntary workers. This has been particularly true in Black Africa.

The countless projects, large and small, which have been set up in the hope of ushering in modernization have not all been crowned by success, to put it mildly. Many were more or less abandoned by the local populations, who were supposed to benefit from them. Others succeeded on the material and technical level but ended up enriching local dignitaries without alleviating the poverty of those most in need. Due to lack of space here, I will mention only the particularly striking example of small and medium-sized co-operatives, so many of which have ended in failure.[6]

Whether its origins are state-funded, multilateral or private, aid organized according to the 'catching-up' theory revolves around concepts of modernization and technical and material development. In the specialized literature of Latin America, this *desarrollismo* (from *desarrollo*, development: therefore literally 'developmentalism') has become a pejorative term. The results of so much financial and human effort are in fact disappointing. Few countries or local communities have succeeded in breaking the circle of poverty because of such interventions. Certain projects have even had harmful effects, in some cases due to their creating a 'mentality of dependence', in others because they have reinforced the concentration of money and power in the hands of a privileged few. What is more, many projects have exacerbated cultural alienation. This is the subject of the present study. Aid has often increased dependence on the exterior. 'From aid to recolonisation, the lessons of failure'; such was the conclusion rightly drawn by a highly placed United Nations official after the first Development Decade.[7]

The 'pillage of the Third World', far from ending with the formal declarations of independence, has increased. And with it, the inequality between the North and the South as well as, inside each country, between the elite in power and the mass of the urban and peasant population. Even in certain newly industrialized countries where often impressive rates of economic growth have been recorded, it has been demonstrated that such growth has brought about neither automatic political democratization nor social improvement. The Algerian economist, Abdellatif Benachenou, himself from a country whose 'industrializing industries' once gave great rise for hope, now declares that 'democracy is not an inevitable product of the factory' and that 'industrialization does not solve the problem of the socialization of development'.[8] The cases of Singapore, Iran under the Shah, and South Africa confirm his conclusions (although recent developments in South Korea and Taiwan offer perspectives which may be somewhat more hopeful). The overall conclusion is so true that some experts, who have become aware of the social effects of policies of industrial development, have evolved new strategies called 'growth with equity'. Alas, with the rarest of exceptions, they have had little more success.

Development as liberation: strengths and weaknesses

The second 'Development Decade' (1970–80) was the time of a renewal of analyses and strategies, led by progressive economists such as Raúl Prebisch, Samir Amin and André Gunder Frank, who developed the theory of dependence. According to them, the poverty of the Third World was not due to a historical backwardness that could be eliminated by the simple process of modernizing the economy. Rather, it was the result of a systematic process of exploitation of the countries of the South by those of the North: world economy was characterized by relationships of dependence between the 'centres' and the 'peripheries'. Upholders of this theory also claim that the centre–periphery schema is reproduced inside each of the countries in question. The national elite represents an economic and political centre which marginalizes the peasant and urban masses. The latter are therefore doubly exploited, on an international level and within their own country.[9] When they have broken away from this dependence, Third World countries must base their development on their own needs. This means self-development based on collective self-reliance.[10]

Very few Western states have acknowledged the validity of this theory. They speak more readily of 'interdependence', as does the Brandt Commission. In contrast the demands of 'The Group of 77' within the UNCTAD, and the major conferences which, from 1974 onwards, were devoted to the 'New International Economic Order', concentrate on precisely this theme. With few exceptions,[11] the conferences, negotiations and other North–South dialogues have brought little change except in sectors, such as oil, where the balance of power can be reversed in favour of the South. If the strategies of the donor states have simply become improved versions of those of the first Development Decade, the states of the South, such as Tanzania under Julius Nyerere, Jamaica under Michael Manley, Allende's Chile, and Peru under its left-wing military leadership, have taken steps inspired by the new analysis. For a while, Colonel Boumedienne's Algeria played the role of precursor, as much by its enterprise on the international front as by its efforts to extricate the Algerian economy from Western domination. Its vast financial means allowed it to follow an ambitious and voluntarist policy of overall industrialization. Alas, the bill has been high, and dependence is no less than it was during the post-colonial period. All that has changed is the type of dependence; the present sort is more sophisticated (international financing, foreign licences and imported technology, international experts, etc). In South America, the industrialization envisaged by the United Nations Economic Commission for Latin America, spearhead of the dependence theory, ended up with the countries of this sub-continent paying three times as much money to import technology and expertise than they had thitherto done to import ready-made goods.[12]

As for the non-governmental organizations (unions, solidarity groups and funding agencies), the growing understanding of dependence as the cause of underdevelopment spread rapidly and brought with it major changes. The catch phrases of a certain number of them[13] have ceased to be 'aid towards socio-economic development' or 'technical co-operation'. Their thinking is now more in terms of partnerships and solidarity with the peoples of the Third World in their struggle for political independence (for example, supporting SWAPO, Namibia's liberation movement) as well as socio-economic self-reliance.[14] Poverty is no longer seen as simply caused by backwardness. Neither is it attributed to fate or to demographic and climatic factors alone, but rather to local, national and international economic structures. Since poverty is partly man-made, it ought to be eradicable by political means. A critical analysis of international economic relations and the socio-economic structures of each individual country of the Third World, as well as the study of their needs and potential, has therefore replaced the paternalistic gestures of assistance of the past. A development project is no longer judged without having been seen in its specific context and is supported only if it helps to free men and women from the structures that exploit and oppress them.[15]

In concrete terms, a well in the Sahel, a clinic in India or a rural extension programme in Peru will, in theory at least, have a relatively better chance of being financed if the project grew out of local awareness and is in keeping with a process that liberates people from the mechanisms that cause and perpetuate underdevelopment. Ideally, a project should be a local enterprise undertaken by a group of the indigenous population trying to put an end to the situation of dependence which keeps them in a state of poverty and oppression. For this reason, funding agencies who uphold this progressive view rarely initiate any projects from their own countries. They try instead to support local enterprises, believing that the peoples of the Third World must become the subjects rather than the objects of development. Since the whole world is in a state of crisis, it is necessary, say these NGOs, to change structures and attitudes in the North as well as in the South. This is the aim of the campaigns they mount to spread information and increase public awareness within their respective countries.

Today, the theory of dependence and self-reliant development, along with the support of projects geared to liberation, still forms the more or less explicit basis of the operations of many NGOs. It has the great advantage of revealing, with concrete data and information, some of the fundamental causes of the growing poverty rife in the countries of the 'periphery'. It shows that this poverty is not a question of backwardness, but rather of systematic retardation and destructuralization, in other words of clearly identifiable mechanisms that cause poverty.[16] The aim of this book is not to cast doubts on the validity of this analysis, but to point out a major deficiency in it. But it has first to be admitted that the liberation approach, ushered in during the 1970s by the theory of dependence and class analysis, has brought about undeniable improvement in solidarity work with the peoples of the Third World. Numerous 'consciousness-raising' projects based on the 'pedagogy of the oppressed' (formulated by the Brazilian educationalist Paulo Freire)[17] have helped to give marginalized rural and urban communities an understanding of the causes of their deplorable socio-economic situation and the determination to fight it. 'Conscientization' and literacy programmes have undoubtedly helped many communities to rid themselves of their fear of the violent repression of the rich and to cease to see their poverty as a question of fate. They not only eliminated illiteracy, but taught people to 'read', in other words to decipher, their own history and to 'write' it, in other words to create it themselves.[18] All over the world, NGOs have facilitated the work of community organizers employing a liberating pedagogy. These initiatives have given rise to all sorts of promising local enterprises: peasant associations in Burkina Faso; urban and rural unions in India; basic Christian communities in Brazil; women's groups in Jamaica; neighbourhood committees in the Philippines; among others.[19] When they had become aware of the causes of their poverty, many groups were effectively able to put an end to local corruption and to initiate micro-projects improving their incomes or standard of living. It has been possible to curtail or put an end to the extortion of some sub-prefect in the Cameroons, or to the commercial monopoly of some Thai money-lender.[20] Valid socio-economic projects can then be instigated. Even in a country as crushed by fear as Haiti, peasants dared to assert their rights and confront the Duvalier dictatorship. In the Philippines, NGOs have played an important role in raising consciousness among the most poverty-stricken. They played their part in this way in the overthrowing of the Marcos regime. In certain countries, peasant mobilization has been able to decrease their exploitation and curb violations of their basic rights, such as arbitrary imprisonment and eviction without due process of law. This whole process is important and constitutes 'seeds of hope'.[21]

The limitations of such projects are equally obvious. Wherever groups are effectively involved in social struggle and in changing the social and economic conditions that impoverish them, they are resisted by the determined, often violent, opposition of those in power. Admittedly, they may succeed in raising consciousness, in curbing local corruption or in raising the standard of living of certain communities, but they do not always bring about, at least in the short term, changes at a regional or national level, so that the regimes in power usually retain control and the overall situation is barely changed. The work of foreign NGOs, trade unions and civil rights groups working alongside local movements has, however, sometimes effectively helped to oust an oppressive regime. Nicaragua and Zimbabwe are cases in point. Exploitative dictatorships have been overthrown in these countries, opening up better prospects for the poorest. Similar efforts contributed to the overthrow of dictatorships in such countries as Haiti, Brazil, Argentina and the Philippines . . . As these pages are being written, the situation in South Africa is changing rapidly. If the Pretoria regime, long considered impregnable, is currently shaky, it is due to a persistent, subversive campaign in favour of democracy. Numerous, apparently innocuous, local operations, disseminating information, giving training, raising consciousness and mobilizing the people, have contributed greatly to this. These operations have often been made possible, or have at least been greatly strengthened, by the support of foreign NGOs.

To the often too fragmentary nature of the initiatives undertaken or supported by NGOs and popular liberation movements must be added another drawback, which ties in with the aims of the present work. It concerns the fact that these projects are insufficiently rooted in the local culture or cultures. There appears to be, in the minds of many Third World communities, a kind of resistance to the process of development which is being imposed on them and even to that which, in all good faith, is proposed to them. There is a resistance not only to development in the sense of dependence and imitation, but also regarding Western-style social analyses and strategies proposed by the upholders of the liberation thesis based on consciousness-raising, grass-roots organization and struggle for justice and economic self-reliance.

The aim of what follows is to point out that the failures and limitations of the development strategies and projects (such as modernization and Westernization, or conscientization and grass-roots organization) cannot be entirely explained by the socio-economic and political factors generally advanced. Are there perhaps obstacles to development and resistance to the spread of social consciousness which are beyond the tools of analysis of economists and political scientists and which baffle the understanding of social activists and NGOs? The origins of this kind of resistance may well lie in the cultural uniqueness of each of the populations in question and in their need to safeguard their identity.

2. Culture: The Forgotten Dimension

Insistence on the cultural uniqueness of different peoples is beset by dangers. It has been used to legitimize an unjust international division of labour and to maintain the current international economic (dis)order. Furthermore, it has often been used to disguise reactionary aims, based on the age-old strategy of *divide et impera*. The fate of the mountain people of Vietnam and the Miskitos of Nicaragua, whose legitimate demands were manipulated by the CIA (the US Central Intelligence Agency) attests to this. Similarly, in South Africa, ethnicity is being treacherously invoked by the Pretoria regime to justify the ideology of *apartheid*, misleadingly presented as 'separate development'. The history of the Third World is full of examples that should inspire the greatest caution in those who call for the respect of specific cultures. This may explain progressive circles' relative silence on the topic.[1] But being sensitive to the dangers of a particular position can mean one runs the risk of not acknowledging its intrinsic validity. This frequently happens with the question that concerns us here. Let us therefore tackle it, trying above all to define the term 'culture', whose very ambiguity reveals its extremely polysemic nature. This is vital, since the argument of the present book relies essentially on a broad definition of culture. We must, therefore, as *the starting point of our inquiry*, take the following comments on culture made by Roger Garaudy, following in the steps of Paulo Freire: '. . . not a luxury nor a simple aesthetic appreciation but the sum total of the solutions supplied by human beings to the problems environment sets them . . .'.[2] It is, therefore, not a question of culture in the narrow sense of the word, seen as a prestige commodity often reserved for an elite, nor as a more or less folkloric epiphenomenon, but of culture in the wider sense of the word. Let us, then, adopt, from amongst the many possibilities, the following definition: 'Culture is the sum total of the original solutions that a group of human beings invent to adapt to their natural and social environment'.[3]

By culture is meant, therefore, every aspect of life: know-how, technical knowledge, customs of food and dress, religion, mentality, values, language, symbols, socio-political and economic behaviour, indigenous methods of taking decisions and exercising power, methods of production and economic relations, and so on.

It is worth bearing in mind this wider conception of culture, for the theories of development employed up till now often presuppose a much narrower notion. Official statements by international organizations and development agencies and the publications of certain NGOs give the appearance of being aware of this problem; they stress the need to respect 'the local culture'. But a closer look shows that what they mean by this is merely art, music, dance and literature. Their efforts are often limited to the inclusion of a little local colour in the process of development-cum-Westernization, rather like those international hotels whose restaurants serve, all over the world, the same aseptic breakfast but do so in a picturesque setting with the staff dressed in traditional costume. 'Developers' do not really acknowledge that each people might have, as Robert Vachon puts it, a technical, socio-economic and juridico-political culture which is peculiar to them and which it is wrong to suppress, even in the name of development. Yet this is precisely what happens. Employing a caustic style intended to rouse readers from their ethnocentric lethargy, Robert Vachon, director of the Canadian review, *Interculture*, has rocked the boat of official 'developers' and NGOs involved with the Third World, although continuing to share their commitment to justice. He writes:

> our sanctimonious missions of civilization, development, conscientization, modernization, social change, democratization, liberation, social justice, and even of co-operation and international solidarity, are often Trojan horses *vis-à-vis* the traditions of Africa, Asia and the Americas. It is in this sense that, in the name of literacy, the oral traditions of the local people are destroyed; in the name of agricultural reform, of the best distribution of the land, wages and full employment, we destroy their original, non-monetary economic culture which is bound in a co-operative partnership with Mother Earth; in the name of our democracies we destroy their *dharma*-cracies; in the name of the acquisition of national sovereignty and the Nation State, we destroy their anti-state organizations; in the name of a democratic taking of power, we destroy their original consensual political culture of leaders without power; that finally, in the name of human rights, we destroy their traditional judicial world which sees man not as a subject of rights but primarily as a subject of acts of grace, of gratitude and cosmic responsibility. Certainly, we must make people aware of the structures of dependence and of the external domination exercised by multinationals and governments. But the heart of the problem will remain untouched unless we are aware of the network of internal dependence and domination exercised by modern Western culture itself. Indeed, the dominating factor is not primarily the multinationals, national and international governments or even capitalist, marxist or socialist ideologies, but our modern Western culture itself. And our international solidarity and co-operation movements are often, unconsciously, its first more or less voluntary slaves and its first more or less conscious ambassadors abroad.[4]

Not everyone would go as far as Vachon, but the sort of sensibility for which he is the passionate spokesman and which others have developed on a more academic level (Roy Preiswerk, Denis Goulet, Gilbert Rist, Abdu Rahman

Wahid, Ashis Nandy, Hassan Nawal, Alain Birou, Raimundo Panikkar, Ivan Illich, Rajni Kothari, Joseph Ki-Zerbo, among others),[5] is gradually spreading in contemporary writing and consciousness as well as in the practices of grass-roots communities. An Afro-Arab intellectual, Ahmet Baba Miske, claims that the basic cause of the crisis of the Third World is internal, psychological, spiritual.

> Humanity's basic problem, the fundamental cause of its current misfortunes and of the deadly catastrophes which threaten it, is not, in our opinion, underdevelopment, which is the result rather than the cause, just like the energy crisis and the inadequacies of the international co-operation network, etc. The basic problem is the assassination of civilizations whose societies remain in a state of shock, like a body without a soul, even if one last impulse of self-preservation means a sort of vegetable existence is maintained. . . . It is time that our elites, torn between their original society, often experienced as a ball-and-chain, and another mirage-society which they have sampled to varying degrees and towards which they are irresistibly attracted, it is time that these elites ask themselves certain questions; they who make absolute decisions in the name of their people, it is time they asked themselves if their choices are more valid than the profound needs and aspirations of the vast majority of their populations (even 'illiterate', 'unaware', etc).[6]

The challenge has been laid down and the ripples are being felt in various circles. Edgar Pisani, one-time EEC Commissioner of Development, now stresses the importance of 'taking into account the cultural dimension of development'.[7] During the negotiations of the third Lomé Convention, the Mauritian Ambassador, Raymond Chasle, became the eloquent champion of a new approach, placing the accent on the necessity for cultural diversity in the face of the unicity of the development concept.[8] At the request of the UN Director-General for International Development and International Economic Cooperation, a symposium on 'new strategies' was organized, with the collaboration of the International Foundation for Development Alternatives (IFDA). This meeting, attended by more than twenty distinguished representatives of the South (the respresentatives of the countries of the North were in the minority), concluded above all that current development policies lead to the destruction of the personality and integrity of peoples which, in certain aspects, is even more serious than that brought about by colonization.[9] Let us also quote an extract from the Declaration of Bellagio, produced by a workshop organized by the International Federation of Institutes for Advanced Study:

> All over the planet, the cultural integrity and vitality of the different human groups find themselves threatened by development strategies which stress economic growth and institutional efficiency at all cost. . . . Too often the values of the Third World are irredeemably damaged by models of social change based on consumption, competition, acquisition and on the manipulation of human aspirations.[10]

UNESCO in its turn is seeking a new approach, and launched, at the request of the General Assembly of the United Nations (Resolution 41/187 of 8/12/1986), a World Decade for Cultural Development 1988–97, to try to promote a 'global approach to development'. Mention should also be made, among the numerous recent declarations and studies, of the excellent dossier published by the Society for International Development to mark the Cancun Summit and very aptly entitled 'Culture, the Forgotten Dimension',[11] and the report of the Monrovia Symposium held under the auspices of the Organisation of African Unity.[12]

Development: a white man's dream

After twenty-five years of 'mis-development', open-minded people are becoming aware that the catching-up theory of development is guilty of excessive Eurocentrism. It is unnecessary here to reiterate this theory of development-as-Westernization, which has not only failed in its ambition to rescue the Third World from poverty, but also dangerously increased the latter's dependence in economic, political and cultural terms and, in certain cases, has accelerated the disturbing depletion of its natural resources and quality of life.

What is less obvious is that the theory of dependence and the practice of self-development resulting from a process of liberation are also tainted by a kind of cultural imperialism which is all the more persistent for being unconscious in the minds of activists who believe themselves to be anti-imperialist. Jean Ziegler has criticized the blindness of many progressives regarding the cultural factor. The Swiss Marxist sociologist warns against the often crude utilization of historical materialism:

> Materialist and dialectical sociology has long been guilty of wilful blindness. Fascinated by the practical aspects of class struggle, by the numerous conflicts men experience on the material production front, it has neglected another battle-field: the one where wars are fought for control of the imaginary.[13]

Groups and individuals from amongst the common people, belonging to various cultural worlds, have been sounding the alarm with increasing frequency. Not only do they feel their cultural identity threatened by the ideology and the alienating mechanisms of international capitalism, but also by left-wing parties and movements and by progressive NGOs who often deny or neglect the people's cultural and spiritual heritage.[14]

Paulo Freire's method of consciousness-raising literacy programmes, when rigorously applied in its pure form, clearly ought not to lead to the compulsory introduction of foreign ideas. According to Freire, conscientization is meant to allow the unconscious surfacing of the 'key words' which are problematic for the members of a given community, and the use of these words to awaken a critical, militant awareness regarding the alienation and exploitation to which they are subjected. In practice, however, the impatience of animators may well lead them to choose or even provoke the 'key words' which best fit their own progressive 'keyholes'! Often these activists do not share (or scarcely) the culture of the groups in question. One might well ask if the result is not the imposition of a new 'depository' of concepts whose contents are meant to be liberating but whose origins are foreign. One falls back into a 'bank account' perspective, where one gives and the other receives, one thinks and the other is thought. Although Paulo Freire has warned us that 'no one can free anyone else', the temptation for the would-be avant-garde is great.[15] Although understandable, it is nevertheless doomed to failure, as an experienced ex-minister of Salvador reminds us.[16]

How many conscientization projects backed by progressive NGOs in Asia, Black Africa and amongst American Indians are not guilty of this failing?

In Tamil Nadu (India), the author of the present work has personally witnessed leaders of a consciouness-raising programme who, although themselves Indians, were so ignorant of the local culture that the Hindu temples were as mystifying and exotic to them as they were to transient tourists! We must question the high number of organizers of social projects and activities who belong to a philosophical or religious world that is different from those of the people for whose benefit they claim to be working. Even those Western and Asian NGOs who sincerely try to support Buddhist, Hindu or tribal organizers, finance in practice too high a percentage of projects devised and directed by partners who are atheist or Christian. The statistics on this point are very revealing.[17]

In so-called Latin America, groups of Amerindians reject the analyses and projects of some left-wing parties who reduce their ethnic demands to a reactionary impulse. They demand the right to cultural pluralism.[18]

The failure of so many rural extension programmes in Africa is also a cause for concern. The cases are rare, too rare in terms of the efforts expended, of peasant or urban groups genuinely engaged in a radical process aimed at liberation in the long term. At the macro-social level, results are even poorer. What Ait Ahmed has called Afro-Fascism is no longer a haphazard phenomenon. There have been too many Bokassas, Amin Dadas, Macias Nguemas. Africa's position, from both the economic and socio-political points of view, is deplorable. Without underestimating the responsiblity of imperialism in the situation, one is forced to acknowledge that attempts to resolve the problem — independent trade unionism, militant peasant movements, civil rights committees, liberation projects — are both rare and precarious.[19] It must be admitted that solidarity work and NGO projects in Africa (with the notable exception of South Africa) seldom arouse much enthusiasm. So many failures baffle those who would like to see the African masses liberate themselves from exploitation, hunger and sickness.

Of course there have been successful struggles for national liberation. In Guinea-Bissau, Amilcar Cabral accorded great importance to 'cultural factors' on the grounds that, in the course of the struggle, these factors grow out of a dialectical relationship with the vestiges of traditional culture. He saw them as the womb from which the first resistance would emerge. Acknowledging this affirmation made by the great Guinean leader, Jean Ziegler considers liberation movements capable of shaping a nationalist feeling and of setting the liberated countries on the path to self-development.[20] Recent history appears to have proved him wrong. That the activists of PAIGC, FRELIMO and MPLA or the 'Ethiopia Tikdem' movement were true progressive nationalists is indisputable, but for all that, the facts show that they were unable to arouse their 'fellow-citizens'. The meagre results obtained in these countries in terms of socio-economic development, the breakdown of the PAIGC, the extraversion of Guinea-Bissau, the successes in Angola of the ethnic party UNITA and, in Mozambique, of the armed bands of MNR (supported by South Africa) all betray the fragility of nationalism and of the social and political consciousness required by the revolutionary avant-garde. Nor has the Ethiopian revolution exactly been a hotbed of nationalism, as demonstrated by the revolutionary Eritrean and Tigrean movements and the existence of secessions among the Somali and the Oromo.

So many blighted hopes in Africa and elsewhere call for a critical look at the attempts at development and conscientization undertaken so far, and a deeper examination of the extent to which the revolutions that have taken place, the regimes that have resulted from them and the programmes launched by those regimes have been of a truly indigenous, and therefore popular, nature. For Westerners and the Westernized elites of the Third World, this critical appraisal also involves a personal examination of conscience. Should they not admit, respectively, to Eurocentrism and mimicry?

The theory and practice of development as modernization and catching-up have mainly failed in their bid to help the masses of the Third World. On the contrary, they have helped to maintain and even aggravate the often appalling social conditions in which they find themselves. Nor have those approaches resulting from analyses and strategies of development as liberation, and the revolutions resulting from them, brought the peoples of the Third World all one might have hoped. In both cases, the failures and shortcomings are partly due to Eurocentrism. All the models, whether left-wing or right-wing, have been based on Western preconceptions. The indigenous cultures of the peoples of the Third World have been largely neglected. There is an urgent need to pay much greater attention to these than we have in the past. They must be studied much more closely.

This means, first of all, recognizing the enduring quality of indigenous cultures and discovering their vitality. Without this, we will be unable to appreciate the extent to which they succeed in putting up a fearful resistance to development projects conceived in the West, a resistance which often explains the mishaps that befall such projects. Resistance to be feared, admittedly, only by the promoters of these projects, and not by the local populations in question, for they manage, by the setbacks inflicted on the alien development, to safeguard their own identity. But indigenous cultures are more than just obstacles to a development that tries to impose cultural alienation. They are also economic, social and political sources of life. As such they can be matrixes of endogenous development in every aspect of life.

We shall look here at their powers of resistance and creative vitality in the realms of economy ('*Homo economicus* and the others . . .'), social life ('Taking a short-cut') and the juridico-political ('Stateless nations and nationless states'). In the vast area of social life, a choice had to be made, since it is impossible to deal with everything here. The choice fell on traditional forms of practical know-how as an aspect of social life. As such, it is extremely important. It may well be that people's capacity to ensure their self-development and, particularly, their self-sufficiency in food, may depend on recognizing this know-how.

3. Indigenous Cultures as Foundations for Alternatives

Indigenous cultures contain within them the seeds necessary to give birth to societies which differ from the standardized and devitalized model that has spread over the world. But what exactly are these differences?

In defining what characterized non-Western peoples and distinguishes them from whatever constitutes both the beauty and the deficiencies of the European spirit, the Indian philosopher Panikkar has used the terms 'anthropocentric' and 'cosmocentric'.[1] The distinction is a useful one since from it derives everything one can say of Western man when, embarking on the great adventure of Promethean individualism, he places himself at the centre of the universe: his linear as opposed to cyclic conception of the universe; his need to conquer nature and others as opposed to a taste for harmony with the environment; the priority accorded to doing and having as opposed to a sense of being. For some, it all began with the Sophists, the Greek philosophers of the 4th century BC who propounded the following: have the strongest possible desires and find the means to satisfy them. Since then, growth and progress have never stopped, along with material consumption.

> Henceforth, unlike the cultures of other continents, the only relationship man will envisage with nature is that of domination, and he will never cease to aspire to and covet the omnipotence of the gods.[2]

This is what Garaudy calls the 'secession of the West', implying by this that the other peoples of the world possess a set of common values different from those now prevailing in the West.[3] It is these people who inhabit what is nowadays called the Third World.

Hindu and Buddhist models, to mention but two, are imbued with a perception of reality as non-duality. Whereas the scientific and technological West tends to reduce the world to a collection of objects to be mastered, the Oriental world sees it as a single body to which it itself belongs. In harmonious partnership with the universe, the Oriental world has a fundamentally different conception of the human body and nature, of development and history. People do not look so much to the future as to the past or rather the present in all its profundity.[4] Hence the absence in the 'underdeveloped' person of that 'anxiety about the future'. An absence that irritates the Western developer.

Anyone who has come in contact with African, Polynesian or Amerindian populations will have noticed striking resemblances amongst them with what has just been said about the Orient. The West is therefore very different[5] from the rest of the world which it has come to colonize and 'develop' in the belief that it is bringing 'civilization'. Nowadays we are realizing that, although there has certainly been intense cultural deracination and a great deal of borrowing, there has been, for all that, no real process of Westernization in depth.

Economics: *homo economicus* and the others

That non-Western peoples possess specific preconceptions and methods of economic organization is beyond doubt. The anthropology of economics convincingly demonstrates this. What is less clear and much more problematic is the way values and patterns of traditional economic behaviour have endured in their complex modern societies.

In Africa, failures to increase productivity are countless. One African in two suffers from hunger. A recent study devoted to Zaire, but which is relevant to all sub-Saharan Africa, shows that the situation has greatly deteriorated in the last twenty years.[6] The real value of Zaire's Gross National Product now reaches only one-third of that of 1960. The agricultural sector has regressed in absolute figures and in relation to other sectors of the economy, especially the non-productive ones. Employment has increased in a public sector (39% of the total salaried work force) that is less and less effective, but has diminished in productive activities.[7] The average worker's wage is now worth less than 10% of its value in 1960. Transport and marketing systems have been disarticulated. Hence the importance of unofficial, alternative channels of income and provisioning, especially since the cost price of food products is too low to be an incentive for farmers. The disparity between town and country, between certain advantaged regions and the rest of Zaire and between the privileged minority and the masses has been accentuated. Vast areas of the interior have been virtually excluded. The same study is crammed with negative examples: the deforestation of increasingly large areas outside the towns, the 'de-electrification' of the urban centres of the interior, the 'de-equipping' of rural areas, and so on. Africa has not taken well to the system and mentality brought in by Western productivism. To be sure, one must not ignore the very real successes of certain commercial and even industrial enterprises, as well as those of some go-ahead peasants. Nor should we overlook the calm efficiency of African women, or Nigerian businessmen, Zimbabwean farmers and various other trades-people. But for all that, Africa has not 'taken off' and 'developers' still stumble over a rationality which is not that of their programmes. The growth in productivity that Africa so urgently needs has therefore not been achieved. It is this which absolves the cultural question of any accusation of being academic or irrelevant, whatever the 'realists' may think. In reality, instead of progress in Africa, there often seems to have been deterioration, regression with regard to the imported economic model and, notably, a return to an economy of self-subsistence.[8] Some private companies employ their staff for only a few hours a day so as to allow them to work the family land or kitchen garden, which often seems to be the only sure source of subsistence. Thus, monetary economy is losing ground and in some places one witnesses the partial return of the barter system. The African peasant's economic behaviour patterns seem to involve a delicate balancing act between the economic rationality prevalent in the West and certain non-rational social pressures or even beliefs which escape the more utilitarian, materialist and individualistic logic of Western capitalism. Understanding this rationality from outside poses two problems: one has to abandon a technico-rational view of the world, meanwhile avoiding the pitfall of the myth of paradise lost that ignores the harsh reality of the power relationships in play (mechanisms of exploitation and domination, and so on). Obviously, the recession witnessed in Africa cannot be exclusively attributed to non-progressive rationality. If peasants return to self-subsistence, it is also due to the fact that galloping inflation has eroded the value of money and that the continual exploitation of the peasantry by the towns has ended by making them 'delink'.[9] But recognizing these factors does not allow us to dismiss certain alternative socio-economic patterns of behaviour.

One cannot, therefore, claim on the strength of this that the African is indifferent to progress or to profit. But it is obvious that such values do not hold the same attraction for the as yet non-accultured[10] African as for the Westerner. It is a question of relative values, tempered by other equally important, even essential, judgements. Amongst these is the sense of community. This was how a preacher from an African religious movement expressed it to René Bureau, to make him understand the essential difference between Blacks and Whites:

> In the past, he told me, in your European villages, all the houses were single storey. Then, one day, a man more ambitious than others added another storey to his house; he invented the stairway and used more durable materials. His neighbours became jealous. They said: 'Who is this who wants to put himself above others?' Then they decided: 'If that's the way things are, we'll put two storeys on to our houses.' Later, other neighbours built three storeys. And thus your towns go on climbing to the skies. Well, with us it's the same. In a village, a man buys cement, a machine for making bricks and some corrugated iron for a roof. He builds a two-storeyed house. The neighbours get jealous: 'Who is this upstart who wants to be above other people?' But now comes the difference between us and the whites; the man is prevented from occupying his house or even from finishing it. Often, he will be forced to leave the village. That is why you can see so many ruins of stone houses overgrown by weeds, in many villages.[11]

Such is the price attached in Africa to social equality and a sense of community. The attitude evoked here may well touch on two other important concepts: that of the hierarchy — one must not raise oneself above the legitimate chief recognized by the group — and that of the limits to be respected in all technological undertakings — one must not challenge nature.

The African is so anxious to maintain the harmony of the social group to which he belongs that he brings into play a series of subtle behaviour patterns whose aim is to avoid excelling or being superior, which would endanger the coherence of the group. Those who have worked in the field have observed this attitude, whether it be in matters of economic production or in any other domain. While conducting seminars for common law judges in Rwanda, the author of the present book personally observed that, although they were perfectly capable of replying to the questions put to them, none of them dared give the correct answer before assuring themselves that several fellow-students were ready to do likewise. One must avoid seeming to be more learned or competent than others. The sense of community takes precedence over individualism and the competitive spirit.

This same sense of community plays a decisive role in the success or failure of certain co-operatives, tontine societies (mutual savings societies) and other groups who, developers hope, will take charge of local economic activities. The Zairean study mentioned earlier explains that collaboration does not function well unless it is based on traditional solidarity and not simply on economic profit. This is why so many co-operatives have failed in Africa. They are not natural extensions of traditional mutual aid. They differ fundamentally from the latter in that they aim to introduce a solidarity based on mere material interests and not on natural solidarity. Such natural solidarity may be based on birth, on co-residence, or on membership of the same religious movement.[12] Development projects in Black Africa often fail because they set up exogenous structures and try to introduce goals which are alien to tradition and to the local perception of needs. The economic successes of ethnic groups like the Bamileke confirms the above. The basis of their success appears to have been their powerful tradition and an extremely close-knit kinship system.[13]

Another subject that demands consideration: the attitude towards money. The number of treasurers who have disappeared with the funds of their co-operative, the high prevalence of corruption, the extent to which public funds are misappropriated, all these reveal an attitude so widespread that it cannot be analysed in ethical terms alone, nor can it be solved solely by repressive measures. Surely it calls for consideration of the cultural aspect of the traditional African attitude to money. Are we not forced to see here a kind of non-cooperation with the monetary system, or, at least, a very different perception of it? Otherwise, how are we to explain that the values of honesty and responsibility, so deeply rooted in tradition, become blunted or disappear altogether? Money, like other printed matter (contracts, newspapers, the law, etc.), exists as though in a moral vacuum, on offer to the most quick-witted and the least scrupulous. All of which has no connection with the original culture, and frequently proves to be an incitement to domination and exploitation. Moreover, anyone who has access to money comes under great social pressure. He is obliged to share the benefits with his innumerable and less fortunate 'brothers' and 'cousins'. Misappropriation of funds is, therefore, not entirely a question of personal enrichment as in the West, but is rather a question of obligations of social solidarity deeply rooted in tradition. Loyalty to the clan is seen as more important than loyalty to the employer, whether it be the State, the capitalist boss or a development project.

The question of a truly African conception of economy has yet to be established. Jean-Marc Ela[14] rightly warns African intellectuals against 'culturism' and merely looking to the past for solutions to Africa's current problems. He reminds them that whatever remains alive of African culture is in actual fact upheld by a people oppressed and exploited by a system as modern as it is familiar, which must be resisted.[15] While warning against romantic dreams about economics in the abstract, Ela himself, nevertheless, reports that in his own village of Tokombere in the Cameroons, the population (animists) resorts each year to the destruction of goods imported by Muslim merchants, as a protest against a type of economy they refuse.[16]

Jean-Marc Ela believes that every African, man or woman, can make very good use of Western rationality.[17] They are not indifferent to it as long as they do not feel their identity is being threatened. Having a long history of being plundered, they want to be sure of the path on which they are embarking, otherwise they prefer to stick to familiar things. It is their very survival that is at stake! Each time the meaning of life is brought into question, the African will turn to traditional references. Ela, whom one could hardly accuse of being obsessed with the past, thus recognizes the importance and the persistence of tradition.

This survival instinct is coupled with the great African myths and archetypes whose wisdom Europeans can vaguely perceive. But to do so, they must remove their blinkers. It is only thus that white people will cease to reproach so-called underdeveloped people of their notorious 'lack of initiative and responsibility'. For their part, white people have paid a terrible price for progress. Sigmund Freud has given it a name: anxiety. Now, it must be pointed out that certain prohibitions peculiar to the West have no currency in the African village. There, the infant is king. The mother's breast is always nearby and available; the warm, constant presence of the mother gives the child a feeling of total security. To survive, it has only to melt into the maternal bosom represented by the group, the community. But the penalty to be paid for not making one's children unhappy, for not living under constant stress, is low yield per hectare, insufficient speed on the assembly line, both mortal sins *vis-à-vis* 'the demands of development'.[18]

Traditional patterns of economic behaviour in Africa, and in many populations in Asia and America, survive and resist. Renouncing the accumulation of possessions, these communities esteem harmony above wealth, intuitively feeling that such accumulation will bring in its wake jealousy, conflict and fragmentation of the social body. This is not necessarily an idyllic attitude. The retaliatory measures taken in Africa against personal ambition are well known, as well as against creative imagination and originality. In this domain, accusations of sorcery play an effective and formidable role. It is not a question of idealizing traditional reality, but of finally recognizing it as such, different, disturbing and often full of a wisdom that the modern world could well use.

Reacting to the tendency of 'developers' to confuse poverty and misery, some people have tried to revalorize simple means and modest goals.

In *Small is Beautiful, a Study of Economics as if People Mattered*, the British economist E. F. Schumacher writes that a Buddhist life-style demands a Buddhist economy, just as the materialist conception of life gave birth to modern economy. Traditional Buddhism sees the essence of civilization not as a multiplication of needs, but as the purification of man's and woman's personality.[19] After having deplored the 'metaphysical blindness' of many of his colleagues, the author goes on:

> He [the modern economist] is used to measuring the 'standard of living' by the amount of annual consumption, assuming all the time that a man who consumes more is 'better off' than a man who consumes less. A Buddhist economist would consider this approach excessively irrational: since consumption is merely a means to human well-being, the aim should be to obtain the maximum of well-being with the minimum of consumption. Thus, if the purpose of clothing is a certain amount of temperature comfort and an attractive appearance, the task is to attain this purpose with the smallest possible effort, that is, with the smallest annual destruction of cloth and with the help of designs that involve the smallest possible input of toil . . . The same applies to all other human requirements. The ownership and the consumption of goods are means to an end.[20]

Obviously, not all Buddhists in modern Asia live by these principles. The progressive Thai Buddhist, Sulak Sivaraksa, deplores what his co-religionists have done to Bangkok, one of the most polluted cities in the world, where the rich flaunt their squandering in the faces of the poor who live in sub-human conditions. He attributes this to the 'satanic development model which nowadays predominates everywhere' and which exacerbates what he calls the Western 'think big syndrome': the fascination with everything over-sized, expensive and powerful at 'the expense of little people, animals and plants'.[21] That the views of the authors quoted here are not mere abstract speculation seems proven by a survey carried out in 1978 among peasants in Sri Lanka: it transpires that the rural groups interviewed give value to non-material needs and have only a modest desire to raise their standard of living. Villages envisage their futures in terms of their own, non-urban criteria.[22] Thus, the Buddhist system of values concretely influences economic organization and behaviour at the present time. Asia has many other spokespersons with more austere, frugal visions of life. Gandhi and Vinoba Bhave are perhaps the most revered embodiments of such visions. Other Indians (amongst them the followers of the late J. P. Narayan) are currently engaged in research and practical experiments in this field, though their observations on the subject rarely meet with any understanding on the part of the planners and 'developers', whether right- or left-wing. Mao, too, exhorted the Chinese to embrace austerity. His intention, like that of 'Che' Guevara, was to give priority to moral as opposed to material incentives to increase the productivity of workers and peasants. His famous *Little Red Book* states that the reconstruction of China must take place in an atmosphere of 'diligence and frugality'.[23]

There are peoples' movements in Asia that try to put into practice the teachings of traditional religion. The Sarvodaya Movement, founded in 1958, is active in over 2,300 villages in Sri Lanka.[24] It is solidly rooted in Buddhist beliefs and practices. The fundamental goal of Sarvodaya is the total awakening of the personality based on the four Buddhist virtues: *Metta* (goodwill towards all living things); *Karuna* (compassion aimed at averting the causes of human suffering and thus of poverty); *Mudhita* (the altruistic pleasure of rejoicing in one's neighbour's happiness); and *Upekkha* (equanimity, indifference to success, prestige and wealth). For this movement, *shramadana* (the sharing of one's time, thoughts and energy) is the central element. By means of *shramadana*, the movement tries to create a social and economic infrastructure based on a strong sense of community. A. T. Ariyaratne, the founder of the movement, strongly believes that in matters of personal relations, communal organization and education, many experiences based on Sarvodaya could be of benefit to other Third World societies as well as to those of industrialized countries.[25] It could help the latter in their search for a simple life-style and the alleviation of the tensions caused by industrialization.

The Benin writer, Tevoedjre, wrote a book that has attracted considerable attention, whose title alone gives some idea of its importance: *Poverty, the Wealth of Peoples*.[26] Basing himself on the one hand on the prophetic tradition of the Bible, acquired through his faith, and on the other hand on his own African tradition, he argues for a model of society not centred on the race for power and profit, but on a frugal well-being, incorporating the values of local culture. Recently, a geographer, Georges Anglade, has echoed him from the point of view of the Americas. A Haitian, now in exile, he has written *In Praise of Poverty*[27] to show that poverty can conceal 'know-how for survival'. Why, he asks, cling to wealth, its techniques and methods, hoping to eradicate its corollary, destitution, when a 'fruitful poverty' is available, able to innovate and bring about an alternative approach? There is no question of denying the need to combat dire poverty of the kind that destroys body and soul, but of throwing new light on ways of life which, although not Western, are nonetheless far from worthless. On the contrary, such ways of life constitute the expression of peoples' culture and of their real aspirations. They are, therefore, apt to be more efficient, as is evidenced by the growing importance of the 'informal sectors' in the economics of Third World countries. For his part, Ivan Illich champions the 'right to poverty' as the right to protection from the market economy and obligatory consumption, the right to survival according to a concept of *homo habilis* and *homo poeticus* as opposed to *homo economicus*.[28]

The definition of basic needs and deficiencies is less obvious than is generally supposed.[29] The West and its inhabitants, whose *malaise* has become evident, is discovering its own poverty in the midst of affluence and power. Is it not high time the West realized that there are some forms of struggle against poverty which are really refusals to accept difference? Such a realization is not just the lamentation of the guilt-ridden white man but is an acknowledgment of the existence of broader horizons which are far from unknown in the European tradition, notably in monastic Christian life. Eminent spokesperson for this wisdom, which is both old and new in the West, Illich states that 'the convivial society' will be made up of 'austere' people.[30]

What conclusions can we reach from these observations on the 'convivial economies' of the Third World? Basically, that there are other economic cultures than those of capitalism or Marxist–Leninist socialism. Non-Western cultures perceive economy in their own ways, which vary according to the nature of each individual people and the extent of its acculturation to the productivist, individualistic, materialistic mentality. Such cultures are based on values of conviviality, sobriety and mutual aid, on mechanisms aimed at maintaining social stability at all cost, on acceptance of hierarchies and respect for the natural order, on a sense of solidarity reinforced by (and also frequently limited to) adherence to a particular lineal, residential or religious group. At times, these cultures are vehicles for an acute sense of equality, at other times for acts of jealous repression of any expression of individual success. They foster loyalty and sacrifice to other ideals than those propounded by Western ethics.

They reject large-scale agricultural and industrial enterprises, as well as superficial, ostentatious life-styles. Finally, they make their own set of judgements regarding the relative merits of profit, free time and social harmony. Generally speaking, survival, subsistence, and what in the West is referred to as 'filling the housewife's basket', are seen as more important than profit with the material and spiritual dangers it generates. In many cultural communities, rational man is not necessarily *homo economicus*, in other words someone who assesses the cost/profit equation using criteria that are essentially quantitative and materialistic.

It is important first of all not to make judgements, not to consider a particular characteristic inferior or superior. Rather, it is a question of observing closely, for these alternative economic behaviour patterns are the cause of many failures as well as the key to unexpected successes. Today, an Africanist agronomist as well informed as Hugues Dupriez can state that growth in productivity will not be guaranteed by Western-style productivist agriculture. Perhaps it is not inevitable therefore, that the economic model currently dominant should spread across the entire planet. We shall return to this point later. Nor indeed, is it desirable that it should spread, for even in the West this model is far from having proved its ability to produce, over and above the GNP, the famous 'Gross National Happiness' that was dreamt of in May 1968. Furthermore, because of the way it forcibly establishes itself everywhere, this model has become an obstacle to the right to be different.

There is much food for thought in all the preceding, not only for economists, state planners and development bureaucrats, but also for the organizers of urban and rural grass-roots communities, and all those engaged in relations of solidarity with them. Without abandoning their socio-economic analyses, NGOs must intensify their sense of dialogue and be on their guard against any inopportune tendency to expect others to display reactions and behaviour patterns similar to those of their own Western culture.

Technology: taking a short cut

The enormous muddle that almost everywhere accompanies the introduction of foreign technology and machines is well known. Who has not come across 'ready-to-operate' factories or other 'turn-key' projects operating at less than half their capacity, or witnessed the tragi-comic spectacle of the tractor stranded somewhere in a village, rusted by tropical rains and already overgrown by weeds, parts of it having been rescued by the local blacksmith for some completely unrelated purpose?

Given that technological objects are crystallizations and manifestations of specific values, their rejection is clearly neither accidental nor haphazard. Such a rejection demonstrates the vitality of a culture for whom the object in question has no meaning, or not enough, or which feels its integrity threatened by it.

The participants of the symposium organized by the OAU at Monrovia appealed to business and research milieux and to teachers involved in vocational training to readapt traditional skills and knowledge in an effort to substitute for the transfer of foreign technology, an autonomous ability for research and the application of techniques truly designed to serve people. Collaboration and exchanges between countries of the South should be encouraged.

A special edition of *Ideas and Actions*, the bulletin published by the FAO's Freedom from Hunger Campaign, gives some examples of the sectors in which Third World peoples might call on their own traditions rather than accept the assault of Western mega-technology. For example: traditional medicine — in India there are 500,000 ayurvedic practitioners and 15,000 clinics; architecture — certain projects have shown the technical potential of traditional African architectonic customs; psychology — a kind of psychoanalysis has been in existence in Southern Asia since time immemorial. One could also mention pharmacopoeia — in the Philippines they make use of over 800 medicinal plants[31] — and many other examples.

When the Haitian, Georges Anglade, speaks of 'fruitful poverty', he wants to show that, over the centuries, different peoples have been able to perfect an assemblage of knowledge and tools which have assured their survival, despite the vicissitudes of their history.[32] It was in the acquisition of practical know-how spanning a period of three centuries that the people of Haiti were to find the roots and the road to freedom with dignity. He believes that the great advantage still at Haiti's disposal nowadays is that 80% of its population is rural and still retains remarkable practical abilities, notably their methods of commercial organization (*Madan Sara*), their transport systems (*Taptap*), their talent for turning to advantage the great variation in the gradients of their land to grow crops which are each individually appropriate to a particular altitude and soil composition, the various combinations of plants ensuring a regular flow of produce all year round. For Anglade, Haiti can revive itself by turning to account its people's own technical resources. But to do this, it must have the organizational and conceptual boldness to 'take a short cut' and, to a great extent, dispense with foreign technology, the costly financing it requires and the experts who accompany it. And it must be done quickly, for a civilization based on poverty is in the process of dying through degeneration into abject destitution. Anglade's assertion has been amply illustrated in a masterly fashion by the Canadian, Gerald Belkin, who has made video films of peasant agro-systems. Since the 1970s, his work has taken him from socialist villages in Tanzania to peasant groups in Haiti. His approach is rigorous: the project must have lengthy preparation, he and his team learn the local language and spend one to two years in at least two villages, living with the peasants, listening to them and speaking with them. During these encounters, video tapes of great richness are recorded which overturn many accepted ideas, notably that of the inferior standards of the agricultural methods of reputedly ignorant peasants. What emerges, on the contrary, is the competence these peasants have acquired, a remarkable knowledge of the environment, a rigorous attitude to work and the ability to appropriate improvements in technique when there are the means to do so.[33]

Some see the future in the form of a 'cultural cross-breeding'.[34] Destroying the myth of the primitiveness of traditional agricultural methods, Hugues Dupriez and Philippe De Leener stress the enormous interest of techniques, knowledge and work methods acquired over centuries and insist that people be allowed to promote their own ecoculture by means of a free and careful selection of those foreign techniques they consider useful to them.

> Farmers of Africa, remember this: very often we are told 'look at how European, American or Chinese growers do things; do as they do'. By all means let's look, but we should add this: 'look even more closely at what other farmers around you are doing, there is a lot to be learned in our own farms. Surely the most useful things for our progress will be within sight and reach. Should we, to improve village agriculture, listen to people far away who know neither the shape nor the quality and temperature of our lands? Can someone who comes from far away and just passes through give anything but words?' The words of visitors are like seeds. Who can say if they are good before sowing them in his field?[35]

Traditional, non-imported agricultural systems have worked for centuries and managed in the past to feed the populations concerned. Today, malnutrition and famine are spreading, especially in Black Africa. This is due to various factors, such as wars and political instability, repressive governments, the exploitation of the countryside by the towns and their dealers, the deterioration of the terms of trade and the international economic (dis)order, the irregularity of rainfall and in certain cases, demographic explosions. But another, equally decisive factor is agricultural research and training. These generally emphasize cash-crops and recommend monocultures for export (coffee, tea, cotton, hevea, etc.) while ignoring the farming systems established over the ages by local populations. By farming systems is meant here types of production which take into account climate, biological capital, soil and equipment and which assure productivity by means of specific combinations of soil and plant and by crop rotation and ingenious cyclical changes of location.[36] The training given to peasants usually takes into account only the plant in question, killing off everything that surrounds it. In the tropics, such a practice is disastrous. This is why the local peasants practise polyculture, where everything grows side by side in apparent disorder but which produces the organic matter the soil needs. In short, as a recent title states, peasants are 'efficient ignoramuses'. 'When we're weighing our words we call them uneducated, when we're in a hurry we call them ignorant. Those who have so much knowledge have no say in the matter'.[37] The situation is little better in the realm of cattle breeding. Thus, veterinary officers knowing neither the local language nor customs sagely concluded that a programme of artificial insemination of cattle belonging to Masai cattle breeders in Kenya could not be carried out without an army of technicians, the herders, according to the experts, not knowing exactly when their cows were on heat! Yet the Masai have been raising cattle for thousands of years. Obviously, their knowledge in the matter is great. But if no one is ready to listen to them . . .[38]

To the Western mind, poverty equals ignorance, one producing the other and vice versa. Moreover, as we have seen, 'developers' consider virtually all non-Western life-styles as tainted by 'poverty'. This belief is extremely widespread but is often a wrong, since Eurocentric, interpretation of social reality. Experts and general public alike constantly trot out insulting fallacies along the lines of 'the minute you turn your back, the peasants, through mistrust or fickleness, do the opposite of what you told them; you can't trust these people; they are ignorant because they don't have any education, they're illiterate; they're poor and dirty because they're lazy; they have no sense of responsibility and need guidance; we have to teach them and take culture and education to them!'[39] These elitist reactions stem from an essentially apolitical conception of development according to which poverty is to be tackled only by means of rural adult education programmes, functional literacy campaigns,[40] courses on hygiene and nutrition, classes in embroidery and pattern cutting and so on. In certain contexts, such activities can be useful when they derive from a concept of liberation. Otherwise, they allow a discreet veil to be drawn over the real causes of the problems, too politically sensitive to be tackled. Progressive NGOs no longer make such mistakes. They have dismantled the economic mechanisms that cause poverty. But have they examined the cultural dimension of the problems?

Let us listen for a moment to a fieldworker who is both heedful and respectful of the methods and techniques of the peasants of the African Sahel. This is Pierre Jacolin, an associate at the Senegalese centre, ENDA (Environment and Development). The text which follows is taken from one of his circular letters sent to his friends and to partners in NGOs. The latter possess vast numbers of first-hand accounts of this sort, full of perceptive observations and, frequently, cries of indignation. It would be a good thing if they had more opportunities to circulate such information among the 'experts' and the general public.

I well remember: it was in RCA,[41] at the end of the dry season, in 1982. In the fields, charred tree-trunks, shrivelled bushes, in short, devastated lands. Anxious, I ask: 'Is it like this every year?'

'Of course, every year, everything burns.'

'But if everything has been burning for centuries there should be nothing left!'

'Ah! but you see, in the past, in the villages, there were "fire masters". They told us what areas we could set fire to, and when to do it.'

'Land chiefs', 'fire masters'! Earth and fire, forest and fallow land, all had their 'masters'. And people submitted to them. The primordial elements were controlled: earth, fire, wind, trees, sowing of seeds, ploughing, livestock. . . . Now, 'everything burns', and the famous official 'agricultural campaigns' which start at the beginning of the rainy season have only one watchword: 'Produce!' (meaning of course, cotton, coffee, tea . . .) We have yet to hear that other order: 'Tend your soil!' . . . It has to be said without mincing words, the responsibility lies entirely with men. One of many witnesses (taken from *Sciences et Avenir*, No. 445 of March 1984, 'Deserts, the great threat', by Jacques Girardon): 'Drought is a catalyst rather than a cause,' says a Mauritanian senior civil servant who wishes to remain anonymous. 'If, in 1960, more attention had been paid to agricultural policies instead of believing that the economy would take off through the exportation of iron ore, we would not be in this mess today. But we had to sell iron, to build an army, maintain an administration, embassies, schools. . . . The sector which provides a living for 80% of the population was neglected. We copy economic models without knowing if we can handle them. Everywhere, you see money crystallized in the form of tractors, of machines of all sorts, abandoned and falling into disrepair. The Europeans who sold them to us (in exchange for iron ore) built concrete buildings for us. We entered into the world of machine, of fuel and fertilizers, yet we will never be able to produce all these things ourselves. What is more, agricultural machines are disastrous for our country where the layer of topsoil is so thin, so fragile that when it is worked too deep, it turns into dust and is carried off by the wind. We ought to have protected the environment. Think small! At the present moment, the logic of foreign financing means that the population continues to get poorer. When you say this, the governments think they are being attacked. In fact, they are up against a brick wall. In the Third World, as in the West, they are caught up in a system. Humanity is powerless, and the desert will continue to advance. The most frightening thing is that it could swallow up the River Senegal, and we could all starve to death!'

And yet, there is no cause for despair. The real Africa, that of the country and the huge suburbs surrounding the major towns, is teeming with local initiatives which are full of promise. Pierre Jacolin asks us to take the trouble to look for them, respect them and, if necessary, support them:

The task is enormous. But many initiatives have been taken by villages and peasant collectives to check the insidious 'leprosy' which is sterilizing their lands. At Yatenga, [Burkina-Faso], there has been a veritable mobilization of peasants, complete with their own organizations, to build irrigation dykes and micro-dams. In June 1984, the first rains had begun. On a visit there, I witnessed the results: where the water and soil had been retained, it was green. Millet was growing. Alongside, grey soil, stripped bare. In one village, near Thies, more than half the wells have dried up. The peasants have just formed a mutual-aid *tontine* [society] to dig their wells deeper. In another village, the water level of the river is getting lower and lower. The *seanes* [holes for drawing water] are now 5 or 6 metres deep. The villagers are organizing together to build themselves a dam. All along the River Senegal, the only resource is the water of the great river. Villages investigate matters and club together to buy themselves motor-driven pumps. They go to other, more experienced villages for information. . . .

Peasants sometimes ask for technical help, or information, or financial help. And it is true that some schemes do fail. But surely it is up to us, on the outside, to pay more attention to their concerns, to their ways of understanding their own soil and development. First of all, to listen and learn, before 'giving advice', as rural extension agents often say. 'Peasants are history's silent majority', someone observed. Not that they have nothing to say. But are they ever given the floor? Today, some of them are taking it. One such, who is in charge of a small rural training centre near Bambey [Senegal], explains: 'In the minds of most peasants, everything should be left to the state. And the state has instilled this idea into people: it does everything. We were never taught to take on our own responsibilities. . . .'

The danger of 'rural extension programmes' has perhaps been the desire to 'provide' too much. Obviously, peasants lack certain knowledge and techniques. But it is equally obvious that if the knowledge and techniques, the capacity for organization and innovation they *do* possess is not recognized and made to form the basis of development, it is futile to claim to be working towards real development. . . .

Even recently, I still hear well-meaning extension workers say that we must 'organize the peasants'! They have obviously not noticed the initiatives undertaken by many of these peasants to market their produce, procure food, organize a *tontine* for their wells. . . . The peasants are not fooled: the 'technical staff' of various ministries, the 'cadres' [what an ugly word! In French its literal meaning is 'frames'!], the *animateurs* (as though the peasants were 'inanimate'!): you should hear how the peasants talk about them. They have less need of 'cadres' than of 'companions', who would exchange experience and information with them, deliberate and analyse matters. They have an unerring knack of knowing whom they are dealing with: 'The goat isn't fooled by an empty water-bottle'!

So, I see the role of the foreign helper more and more as that of a companion heedful of what is happening in the local environment, careful to utilize its experience and methods of organization, making the most of its resources, respecting initiatives and innovations, bringing information, allowing the peasants themselves to come up with solutions, make decisions and organize themselves: 'Bring us information: we know our own soil. We'll soon see what suits us', said Denis to me on the subject of techniques of water and soil damming.

Accompany . . . be heedful . . . support without harming . . . be alongside and not in front. . . . It seems to me that is what 'aid to development' is primarily about. When groups of peasant men and women regain confidence in themselves, establish solidarity, exchange ideas, think things out, stand up and speak for themselves, no longer say: 'we are blind, you must lead us', organize together to confer with technical staff, build a dam, set up a market, refuse spoiled seeds, negotiate foreign aid, it seems to me that too is development. And not just machines, roads, cotton or diplomas. . . .

What conclusions can we reach from these observations on indigenous know-how? What is currently happening in certain regions of Africa, for example in Kivu (in West Zaire),[42] and in the plain of Mwera in Zimbabwe[43] illustrates perfectly our observations. Peasant communities in these places have managed to increase significantly their agricultural production and even to disseminate a considerable surplus of foodstuffs. This process takes place with the minimum of outside intervention. It is the work of the villagers themselves. But elsewhere, in other villages of the same regions, people suffer from hunger although formerly, during the colonial period, white planters obtained plentiful and extremely profitable crops there. These dramatic and aberrant situations demonstrate the limits of alien agricultural systems, both inappropriate and inappropriable. These systems and their accompanying techniques are inappropriate for at least three reasons. Generally speaking, they do not produce foodstuffs that are consumed locally, since they are geared towards exportation. They depend on a horde of machines and costly chemicals unavailable locally. They are mechanized and therefore generate few jobs, whereas local manpower is plentiful and capital is scarce.

Furthermore, the examples from Zaire and Zimbabwe demonstrate the vitality and the capacity for adaptation inherent in certain indigenous systems of farming. It is therefore possible, and sometimes necessary, to 'take a short cut', to reassess — and if necessary optimize — the abilities of the people. It has rightly been said that the solution to the food crisis afflicting so many countries depends on political and economic changes in the West. But that does not mean the solution will come from the massive introduction of Western techniques and products.

What has been said here about Africa is equally true elsewhere. Thus, although Asian farmers have convincingly demonstrated their skills, they too constitute a 'silent majority', looked down on by Western or Westernized development experts and agents.

Politics: stateless nations and nationless states

If different peoples have developed their own specific cultural characteristics in the economic and technological fields, the same applies to the legal and political arenas. Although profoundly influenced by the Western juridico-political system that dominates all states in the modern world, tradition remains a factor that still has to be taken into account. It is not as though state organization was unknown before the arrival of the Whites. The Zulus, the Khmer and the Incas all had strong states. Other groups lived in societies without states, or had types of intermediate organization (chieftaincies enjoying varying degrees of power). Most, however, had in common the safeguarding of public consensus, the balance of power and, if necessary, regional autonomy.[44] The authorities were 'multiple, specialized and interdependent' states Etienne Le Roy, a specialist in African law.[45] Nowadays, it has become obvious that most Africans hardly recognize themselves in the states their colonizers have bequeathed to them. Since the state sees itself as the driving force of development, the latter consequently finds itself profoundly handicapped. The frequency of *coups d'état* reveals not only the behind-the-scenes intrigues of neo-colonialism, but also the shallowness of the regimes' roots in society, the unsuitable nature of their methods of government and the very nature of their power.

In reality, the post-colonial 'state-idolatry' is equalled only by the profound absence of legitimacy of the authorities. An artificial entity, from the points of view of both its frontiers and its history, the African state, far from being the product of a long and spontaneous process of nation-building, exists in itself, and very often for itself and for the bourgeoisie which has taken control of it. The people are elsewhere and define themselves by a sub- or trans-state identity. The party system and the accompanying ideology, far from bringing people together and mobilizing them, exacerbates the repressive, alien nature of the state. National feeling is extremely weak. How many people nowadays think of themselves as Zairean, Ethiopian, Ugandan or Chadian? As an elderly Mossi man put it, 'To me, Mali just means tax'. Nothing more. A parasite-institution offering a ritual discourse on development in exchange for fiscal extraction and various other exactions carried out by an over-staffed bureaucracy. A case study carried out in Mali on the relationship between ethnicity and state reveals how paradoxical these terms have become nowadays. The state imposes centralization and homogenization, ethnic groups demand the right to their differences and autonomy.[46]

If Africa offers striking examples of the alien, inappropriate and often despoiling nature of the state, Amerindian peoples are also questioning the idea of states whose presence they have endured for over 450 years and which nowadays certain people reject. Asia seems better off in this respect, although it is shaken by numerous secessionist movements, sometimes ethnic in origin (for example the Karen in Burma), sometimes religious (the Sikhs in India, the Muslims in the Philippines) or yet again ethno-religious (the Tamils of Sri Lanka). The Indian state is a fragile construction. Gunnar Myrdal observed at the time that the principal national sentiment that Indian citizens had collectively experienced regarding the central state was civil disobedience.[47] A noted specialist in Hinduism even considers parliamentary democracy to be incompatible with the Hindu model of society.[48] Clearly, such an assessment must be treated with great caution as it may serve all kinds of nasty political goals. But, the problem will not be solved by simply ignoring it. As a matter of fact, Indian scholars and committed activists are thinking anew about state and politics in India, particularly in the wake of recent 'communist' violence. The debate is proving very challenging indeed.

As a research project in legal anthropology carried out in Casamance (Senegal) recently concluded, Africa ought to call upon its age-old experience to limit the role of the state both in its manifestations of authoritarianism and in its tendency to allow the exploitation of its nationals to take place under its auspices.[49] Failing such changes, there will be yet more direct confrontation, or spontaneous strategies of evasion, by-passing and diverting state institutions. There is, therefore, a pressing need for civil society to rally and assume the role from which it should never have abdicated. Le Roy maintains that the centralized ('jacobine'), 'unitarist' (reducing diversity to unity) model of the state is the major cause of the obstacles to development, and adds that policies of self-development are doomed to failure until this Leviathan-State is replaced by a model more respectful of local dynamics and overall pluralism, including legal pluralism.

The Zairean philosopher, Ntumba Tshiamalenga also maintains that Africa's political future lies in what he calls polycentricism.[50] Instead of opposing clanism as a source of parasitism and tribalism as worthless and a threat to modernity and the state, it would be better, according to him, to consider the possibility that the larger African cultural groupings might constitute appropriate focuses of political life and power. There is a pressing need to decentralize and deflate the state inherited from the colonizers. Let us cease therefore, he says, to deplore the multiplicity of tribal and ethnic groups, for it is precisely these ethnic groupings which will allow the existence and the vitality of decentralized political entities, which, in their turn, ought to be founded on the participation of smaller ethnic groups.

Another colonial contribution, no less inappropriate than the state, is law. Although traditional societies have produced a rich, flexible legal system, well adapted to circumstances and, what is more, much less hostile to change than has been admitted,[51] modern states have generally imposed a new legal system. This system, because it is state-oriented and imbued with foreign concepts, is inappropriate and incomprehensible to the great mass of society.[52] Fun has quite rightly been poked at this 'fantasy law'[53] whose ambition to change behaviour patterns and encourage development is illusory. The term 'fantasy law' dates from 1920 and refers to the civil code which the Dutch tried in vain to impose on the populations of Indonesia. Since then, there has been little improvement, although several African states have tried to integrate certain aspects of indigenous law into their modern legislation or into a unified judicial system.[54] In so doing, they have usually devitalized them for, rather than simply being a set of rules, indigenous law is a 'way of being', often irreducible to an article of law or a court decision in the Western sense.

Indigenous law, wrongly called 'traditional' (since it evolves) or 'customary' (since other sources of law than custom contribute to its vitality),[55] offers contemporary African populations a range of solutions very well suited to their needs. To this day, according to an experienced judge in Kinshasa, informal customary courts dispensing indigenous law pass ten times more judgements in Zaire than officially recognized courts dealing out 'modern' law.[56] A corpus of genuine folk law is thus being produced. It is fully endogenous, since it is the spontaneous creation of the masses in their struggle for life. It sometimes serves them as a refuge from external threats.[57]

What can we make of these observations on the state and law? First of all, let us establish the fact that the state apparatus and the legal system imported by colonization is characterized by centralization of power and — particularly when civil codes have been enacted, in the continental, Napoleonic tradition — by standardizing of customs. Independent states have generally clung to the imported legal tradition inherited from their former rulers. They often reinforced the centralizing, unifying tendencies bequeathed by their authoritarian forerunners. In countries endowed with a certain cultural homogeneity, centralization and standardization have, perhaps, some chance of functioning even if this is not necessarily desirable. One thinks of such countries as Pakistan, the Philippines, present day Rwanda, Morocco, Costa Rica, Argentina. . . .[58] In most countries, however, there is a plurality of cultures and consequently of indigenous legal systems. Furthermore, the decision-making process relies, in many non-European cultures, on consensus. It involves a slow, careful attempt to safeguard the collective harmony,[59] whereas the Western-style process of decision-making, by majority over minority, represents for them a sort of brutality, lastingly harmful to the social body. Western juridico-political culture, although omnipresent, therefore does not suit all the peoples of the world.

All of which leads one to believe that many states would be well advised to promote administrative decentralization and legal pluralism, thus recognizing and valorizing the cultural communities who inhabit their territories. The legal system, if it is truly to serve people, their liberties and their specificities, ought to be endogenous, relatively plural and — when no widely accepted indigenous legislative power exists — essentially 'customary' and judge-made. In any case, the legal systems of many Third World countries ought to depart from the Napoleonic model by which a given code freezes, devitalizes and standardizes customs, and imposes a state-oriented rationality.

As far as frontiers which date from the colonial period are concerned, they are capricious in Asia and America and downright absurd in Black Africa. States could at least allow existing cultural groupings inside and outside their territories the possibility of communicating and developing naturally without too many administrative obstacles. This would allow taking up again, in the case of Africa, the great federalist instincts of statesmen like Kwame Nkrumah who wished to oppose the Balkanization of their continent and to encourage unity in diversity by evolving towards the admittedly very delicate search for juridico-political systems which would be underpinned by a common culture and, consequently, towards a more real sense of nationhood.

As we have seen, the values, institutions and behaviour patterns, as well as the means and techniques of production of the various peoples of the South, are full of potential for creating alternative models of society. They have also helped in real terms to check, deflect or slow down the advent of the monocultural type of society which 'development' would have brought them. Judging by the state in which certain countries, such as Zaire, find themselves, one might well ask if we are not witnessing 'pseudo-development' and, in fact, the collapse of entire sections of Western-style modernity. We are witnessing, on the one hand, the deterioration of institutions of Western origin: the State, written law, public office, wage-earning and market economy, parliamentary democracy, technology in the areas of health and transport, commerce and industry, and so on. On the other hand, we can observe the vitality of the values and behaviour patterns based on elements of local culture. This state of affairs raises important questions. The Westernization of certain countries seems to have been, in some fields, a purely superficial veneer. Eurocentric blindness, along with the setting up of neo-colonial elites fashioned along Western lines has meant that we have often taken for deep-rooted and widespread a process which was in fact nothing but a superficial varnish.[60]

Some countries, instead of making progress, are regressing in the eyes of the 'developers'. Yet, what have been called obstacles to development might well represent an unconscious reaction to the anticipated dangers of uniformization and a deep-rooted resistance to alienation. Who knows? Such resistance is perhaps fed by the instinctive feeling that a society fundamentally based on power struggle and caught up in a technologicalization that imposes its own rules and rhythms on human beings, is ultimately doomed to self-destruction. Certain peoples seem to resort to non-cooperation in order to oppose alien development. Their attitude could be interpreted as a kind of civil disobedience, in opposition to the obligation to develop in the Western manner.

It is time to recognize and pay tribute to these silent, multi-faceted forms of resistance which various peoples oppose to the impositions and seductions that threaten their values. In some countries, the populations pretend to comply but, behind the scenes, there takes place a sort of subversion of the logic accompanying the imported object or institution. Etienne Le Roy aptly speaks of 'phagocytism', a term used in chemistry whereby one cell 'absorbs and destroys' another, and indeed one sometimes wonders who has actually absorbed whom. René Bureau also points out, in the two-way traffic between the original culture and the white institutions, all kinds of distortions, contaminations, desecrations and corruptions of the system imposed from outside.

Elsewhere, resistance has been less persistent but the setbacks inflicted on development nonetheless show a final burst of life when suffocation actually threatens. 'A lethargic state' Ahmed Miske has said. What if this is a, perhaps unconscious, form of resistance? In Haiti, the term *marronage* was used to describe the flight of slaves to places inaccessible to their masters, places where they took up again their African cultural practices, refusing domestication and any form of subjugation.[61] It is perhaps a vast operation of *marronage* that these peoples, anxious to conserve their own values, are currently undertaking.[62]

4. Indigenous Cultures as Sources of Social Struggle

Almost everywhere, the fundamental stability of societies has been shaken. Hitherto unknown living conditions (shanty-towns, widespread endemic famine, over-exploitation of peasants and workers, powerful military dictatorships) are amongst the consequences of this instability. To alleviate as quickly as possible the intolerable aspects of this misery that Western modernity has helped to bring about all over the world, should one not resort to remedies that have already proved their worth in the West? In particular, peasant and worker trade unionism, political action and the struggle for human rights. In other words: Western remedies for Western evils! To the outside observer, everything suggests that what is needed are the forms of struggle to which Western industrial capitalism has given birth. But will these types of struggle, developed by European workers in the course of their history, not simply exacerbate cultural alienation? We face here a real dilemma which only the people of the countries of the Southern hemisphere can resolve.

Non-conventional types of struggle

At all events, certain peoples seem not to conform to the types of struggle one expects. Their culture seems to generate 'non-conventional' socio-political struggles. Of course, the strictly 'Latin' part of South America (leaving aside the indigenous and African population for the moment) has given evidence of resistance in forms familiar in Europe. Trade unionism flourishes there, as does sophisticated political consciousness. But we are speaking about populations of predominantly European origin! This is why European and American NGOs working in Latin America find there a ready-made field of action. The solidarity they propose finds a ready response there. In contrast, their activities in Africa arouse less enthusiasm. Liberation movements (*cf. supra*) apart, Black Africa seems incapable of mass mobilization. Asian peoples too, display a sometimes incomprehensible resignation in the face of flagrant injustices. All of which leaves one puzzled. And yet, what if, beneath this apparent indifference, lay the seeds of struggles more in keeping with the spirit of the people? Has it ever occurred to Western NGOs and activists to offer solidarity and support to forms of struggle that differ from those which have developed in the West? Perhaps other forms of opposition to injustice, alternative ways of envisaging and seeking liberation must be allowed to emerge from the cultural depths of Africans, Asians and Amerindians.

Gandhi already proved this. The mobilization of an entire sub-continent against a mighty colonial power was achieved by calling on ancient Hindu traditions. Adapted to the needs of the moment, enriched by other contributions without being overwhelmed by them,[1] these traditions led to national liberation. Inherent in active non-violence is a remarkable power for action and change on an individual and collective level. In the West, it is regrettably still relatively unknown, apart from the struggles led by Martin Luther King. Cesar Chavez and certain great Latin Americans.[2] yet in Latin American grass-roots communities, the people experience it on a daily basis. They contribute to the non-violent, socio-political struggle a dimension never attained in Europe, founded on the Bible, profoundly spiritual and virtually inconceivable for the secularized activists of the rich world.[3] Again, in the Antipodes, in the capital of the Philippines, Marcos' tanks were stopped by an unarmed people, led by priests and nuns and, it must be admitted, by sections of the — relatively — more liberal bourgeoisie (which later turned its back on the demands of the people). The militants of the traditional left could hardly believe their eyes!

In Africa, the behaviour of the workers in the face of exploitation in the factory or in the large plantations is often puzzling for the activist concerned about effective resistance. One anthropologist who has tried to decipher this behaviour believes that it falls into three phases. First, there is a slackening-off phase. The worker counters the rhythm and discipline which are imposed on him, with inertia or slowness. In the second phase, there is partial delinking from the modern economy to which the unit of production in question belongs. The worker keeps one foot in this camp, the other being firmly planted in the traditional milieu, where family and clan solidarity reign. Finally, if the price to pay for the coveted salary is too high, there is total withdrawal and a return to the original community. It all takes place as though capitalism is accepted only in so far as it offers certain products and services. Its 'philosophy' and ethic, based on thrift and the struggle for personal enrichment, still seem basically foreign to the indigenous worker. These African workers accept Western-style modern economy and adapt to it only to the extent that it serves their own purposes. But, if the cost becomes too high, they pull out of it, at least where possible. Such possibilities are apparently widespread, not only in the countryside where the land can provide for their needs but also in urban areas, as shown by the 'miracle' of the survival of the inhabitants of large towns like Dakar, Kinshasa, Nairobi, Douala, and so on.

If one looks in Western and Central Africa for examples of unrest and subversion leading to a people's revolution, one will be disappointed.

Jean-Marc Ela is of the opinion that laughter, meaningful silences, humour and the African's art of ridiculing political personalities are forms of struggle that currently show there is neither unawareness nor resignation. To this must be added the power of secrecy. Many Africans operate under cover of secret societies, even in politics. They carry on the struggle using every aspect of their culture. This is true of various Third World countries.

Women, whose essential role in social and economic life — particularly in matters of food production — is only now being recognized by the authorities, are capable of resisting exploitation with a fierce, formidable strength. When large government projects threaten local interests and dangerously disturb the ecological balance, it is often the women who react. They do so by 'alternative' means. They refuse to leave their farms when it is planned to submerge them beneath a reservoir for some hydro-electric dam. In India, the well-known and highly successful Chipko movement aims to stop the merciless exploitation of forests by companies whose only concern is to increase their immediate profits. Women resort to hugging ('chipko') the trees about to be bulldozed, just as they would hug their babies if they were under immediate threat. In Africa, women will often withdraw their food products from the market. And when Bokassa had his soldiers kill children, women publicly took off their clothes in front of the 'emperor' and laid curses on their own fertile bellies. It was their expression of revolt and their way of fighting back. It had its effect on the Central African head of state, more perhaps than any demonstration conforming to Western ideas. As Vachon has written, such resistance often remains invisible to the Western progressive, because it does not always employ 'the direct, belligerent, visible approach of denunciation, organization and declaration of rights to which the Westerner is accustomed'.[4]

Hidden in all of this is a lesson for those NGOs who claim solidarity with the Third World. They must become more aware of their Eurocentricism and resolutely abandon their monocultural preconceptions in order to move towards a more attentive and respectful consideration of other peoples and *their* perception of suffering, of social struggle, of liberty, in short, of the meaning of life.

Religion: opium or liberation

What has just been put forward on the subject of indigenous cultures as sources of alternative forms of struggle is all the more valid for spirituality, which is both their noblest and most enduring expression.

When sociologists of religion analyse the social functions of Hinduism, and to a lesser extent of Buddhism, they stress their conservative, or at the very least equivocal natures.[5] According to them, other forces will be needed to trigger off the social struggle against exploitation and domination. To challenge unjust structures and hasten radical social change, workers and poor peasants are expected to mobilize as an exploited class on the basis of secular issues. But who are these peasants and workers, if not men and women permeated by the surrounding culture and thus by religion? As the Iranian revolution seems to indicate, neither proletarianization nor economic growth caused by introducing the capitalist mode of production necessarily lead to a renunciation of religion. On the contrary, religion came to occupy a central place in the struggle against the Shah's dictatorship and in the development of the no less bloody republic of Ayatollah Khomeini: a central, even overwhelming place, leading to the worst excesses and to a reactionary and morbid cultural and political isolation. But we must analyse carefully the profound significance of the Islamic revolution in Iran, looking beyond its sensational, shocking aspects to establish the driving force behind such massive mobilization. Should we not see in this the refusal or, better still, the wholesale rejection by an entire people of the Westernization and secularization introduced, not to say imposed, by the preceding regime? Whether one likes it or not, the fact remains: religion contributed greatly to upsetting and bringing to an end one of the oldest, most powerful and richest states in the area, an ally of the United States, supported and armed to the teeth by the latter, charged with standing guard over its imperialist power in that part of Asia. Instead of seeing in religions only reactionary ideologies — and never forgetting one must denounce and combat their excesses wherever they arise — we must also examine their capacity for mobilization and struggle.

The Iranian example apart, one can see that almost everywhere in the Third World, be it Islamic, Christian, Animist, Buddhist or Hindu, market economy has failed to bring about a decline in spirituality. There has certainly been an increase in secularization in many countries, but detailed studies are necessary to determine who exactly is touched by this and to what extent. One would very likely discover that it is mainly intellectuals who have turned to atheism, whether it be the atheism produced by the indifference of practical materialism (capitalism) or that which imposes itself as a result of theoretical materialism (Marxism). There is also a need to examine the role of religion in the lives of citizens of officially socialist states. To take only one example, it is quite obvious that the Amhara and the Tigreans of Ethiopia will not readily give up Orthodoxy in favour of what they contemptuously refer to as the 'new Holy Trinity', namely Marx, Lenin and Engels, whose portraits are everywhere on show for the veneration of the masses. In Europe itself, the case of Poland demonstrates the enduring quality of religious feeling and its capacity for mobilizing the people against oppression.

There is, therefore, a reasonable basis for examining the way religions can serve as driving forces for peoples' struggle for more justice and dignity.

The experience in Latin America offers an example of this. There, religion thrives and plays an important role in the hard, essential social struggle. Catholicism had long been associated there with the establishment, playing the role Marx attributes to religion. But, during the last few decades, the people have 'reappropriated' the Bible and drawn from it an interpretation which is liberating both on the personal and on the social, political and economic levels. The actions of basic Christian communities combined with exegetic research has given birth to the theology of liberation and the development of a Church that feels called upon by the God of Moses and the Exodus to 'bring forth my people held in bondage'.[6] Today, the contribution of Christians engaged in social struggles has, from Chile to Nicaragua, assumed a crucial importance. A man like Fidel Castro has become well aware of this.

Contrary to what a section of the general public still thinks about Latin

America, violent struggles such as those of yesterday's Nicaragua and today's El Salvador and the extremist and largely non-popular guerrilla of the 'Shining Path' in Peru have become rare there, whereas struggles inspired by evangelical non-violence are increasing. There are now many examples of peoples' conquests or at least of successful resistance action inspired by the non-violent struggle of the grass-roots Christian communities. One of the struggles that nowadays serves as an example in Brazil was that of Alagamar, in the north-east of the country. In this remote municipality 700 families lived in peace on land vaguely rented from some distant landlord. When the latter died, his heirs sold his property and the buyers decided to undertake large-scale farming of sugar-cane and livestock. This meant putting an end to food crops, getting rid of the majority of the peasants while retaining a few as agricultural workers. Some of these measures were taken in violation of conditions laid down by law but with the tacit blessing of the authorities. Several peasant families accepted a paltry compensation and left, no doubt to swell the ranks of the shanty towns of Recife, the huge capital of Pernambuco State. But the majority refused point blank to be ousted and clung to what they saw as virtually ancestral land. The owner's reaction was violent: dwellings burned down, crops destroyed, attacks by thugs armed with rifles and machetes, enjoying complete immunity. But the peasants held on, without a single act of violence on their part. At present, they are still there, having finally won their case after seven years of extremely harsh confrontation. Accompanied by their Bishop, Dom José Maria Pires, they observed with a calm determination what they call 'the five commandments of non-violent struggle', namely 'never kill, do not injure, always stay united, remain alert at all times, and disobey the commands of the oppressor'. The third 'commandment' concerns the need for solidarity and the necessity to meet regularly despite all the obstacles put in their path by the enemy. The fourth rule is a call for organization and inventiveness. Thus, instead of allowing themselves to be intimidated, the peasants are now extending their farming, setting up communal fields, installing flour mills and restoring an abandoned house. This is what Dom José Maria has to say on the subject:

> Non-violence that is merely defensive, which takes the blows without translating them into actions that are firm and courageous while being imbued with love and understanding, is an ineffective non-violence. It does not help to liberate from oppression, it does not contribute to the conversion of the oppressor. Non-violence is a sword, like that of Gideon (Judges 7: 14), of Christ (Mth. 10: 34), of the Holy Ghost (Eph. 6: 17). At Alagamar, the Non-Violent Battle was intelligent and inventive, as the people can be when given the opportunity. They do not allow the enemy to take them by surprise or fool them: they are always alert.[7]

That is the kind of struggle that is being fought nowadays. Are Western progressives ready to admit that it has become a widespread type of popular action, and that in confrontation love can be an effective strength, 'the strength of the weak', as they say in Brazil? Who will dare to believe in these fools of God and give credit and solidarity when they proclaim:

> Let us renounce the weapons of the oppressor, his lies, demagogic propaganda, assaults on the rights of others, discrimination, vengeance and hatred. Let us take up the weapons of Christ, the weapons of truth and justice, of faith, the gospel of peace and the sword of the Holy Ghost which constitutes the Word of God. Let us love our enemies and pray for our persecutors. The practice of justice, of material disinterestedness, of fasting and prayer, can transform hearts of stone into hearts of flesh and blood. Let us rip out the oppressor within each of us and we will convert the oppressors within church and society. For evangelical non-violence to triumph, we need rigorous self-discipline and a critical analysis of our class society. It is those who are ready to risk their lives in bearing witness to the Beatitudes who will become the true architects of history.[8]

The spirituality of liberation and evangelical non-violence are becoming an integral part of the culture of the Brazilian people. Obviously, religion is still manipulated for other ends in Latin America (particularly by the new fundamentalist sects of North American origin) but it also constitutes a force to be reckoned with, a force for resistance and struggle.

Can the case be extended to cover Asia? The majority of Oriental spiritualities are probably more based on being than doing, and therefore seem less susceptible to exhortations encouraging socio-political action. Be that as it may, might not Asia's oppressed masses one day discover the prophetic spirit of protest buried in the heart of their religious traditions which have often been confiscated by the authorities in power? Buddhism has already given several examples, as can be seen from the role played decades ago by monks in the independence movement of Ceylon, their opposition to American intervention in Vietnam (the 'third force'), and their present actions of solidarity with the Thai peasantry. During the Vietnam war, reverend Thich Nhat Hanh, who was director of a Saigon training school for social workers founded on the principles of compassion and non-violence, wrote a 'manual on meditation for the use of young activists', thus putting the very essence of Buddhist spirituality at the service of social and political action.[9]

Within the complex mix of religions, spiritualities and rules of conduct which we call Hinduism, there also exist possibilities for reaffirmation. As will become clear from the chapter devoted to Hinduism (Part Four, Chapter 14), Vedanta philosophy, aristocratic in origin, seems relatively less amenable to a process of popular reappropriation. Its modern devotees have, however, undertaken some interesting reinterpretations of the Bhagavad Gita, one of the holy books of India. The Gita deals specifically with action and serves as a reference for *karma-yoga* (the yoga of action), whose contribution to the ethics of social struggle could be important due to its insistence on the necessity of remaining 'detached from the fruits of one's action'.[10] It is a salutary warning against the temptations of power and the prestige which can result from political action! But it is mainly within the less gnostic and more mystical branches of the Hindu religious universe that we may have to look for the seeds of a renewal on the social level, particularly in the *Bhakti* movements. According to *Bhakti* tradition, God has shown His love for people, who are called on in their turn to show solidarity amongst themselves. Mention must also be made of the groups of radical young Gandhians belonging to the *Vahini* movement, as well as the anti-Brahminic Dravidian movements of Tamil Nadu striving for the abolition of the negative aspects of the caste system. And finally, it should be said that in India the great social leaders have generally been mystics and saints, either Islamic or Hindu. Gandhi is the most famous example of these. For him, religious faith necessarily led to social and political commitment. As a final word on India, mention must also be made of the Messianic movements whose origins lie in the pre-Vedic indigenous religions practised by the tribal populations.

In the East, the term liberation has different connotations than in Europe or Latin America. Asia is the cradle of all the major written religions. One would hardly expect its conception of liberation to be secular or basically socio-economic. For both Hinduism and Buddhism, liberation is achieved through a primarily spiritual, inner experience. It is this that mystics all over the world have experienced and it radically relativizes the external world and the present time. Too often one forgets that this mystic experience can also be a protest when it rebels against anything that takes itself too seriously, makes itself the centre of the world, or tries to take the place of God. It distances itself then, by wisdom and by humour, from everything that tries to pass itself off as having absolute value: the charismatic and dictatorial head of state, the consumer society, the race for profit, racial and cultural prejudices and all the illusions engendered by the absolutization of worldly values. Eastern spirituality calls — at least potentially — for a total liberation, as much on the psychological as the social level. The message of Eastern spirituality is the following: it is not only exploitation, domination and material poverty that ought to become objects of the struggle for liberation. There is another poverty, at least as serious: that which is engendered by self-interest and egocentricism. In the East this poverty is called *Maya*, illusion, and becoming aware of it represents the starting point of its spiritual journey.

Asian Christians have understood this message and point out the dangers to anyone, Asian or Western, attempting to apply in the East a ready-made, Latin American style theology of liberation. To them, such a theology, by virtue of its preconceptions and methodology, is typically Western.[11] Socially committed Asian theologians readily admit that the Latin American theology of liberation is better equipped to answer the needs of the Third World than theologies worked out in Western universities for the benefit of the West's own rich, secularized societies. Western theological and philosophical concerns are quite alien to the real preoccupations of the Third World, and logical deductions of an academic order leave them cold. So, Asian Christians readily acknowledge that the Latin American theology of liberation of Gustavo Gutierrez, Enrique Dussel and the Boff brothers, helped them to shake off a theology which often seemed to them lacking in incisiveness, as well as a disincarnate, privatizing spirituality bequeathed by Europe, which local popular religiosity often reinforced. But they propose the creation of a truly Asian theology and spirituality of liberation, which would be concerned with personal fulfilment as much as social transformation.[12] Such a theology will be, like that of Latin America (and like ancient patristic theology), experimental, a product of the 'people of God', that is the mass of believers, in their specific context of social struggle. Non-Western, it will be neither abstract nor 'scientific', nor, however, will it only be the straightforward 'product', as they say in Latin America, of a 'social praxis' (that is, the life of the oppressed and their struggle against poverty and oppression). It will also find its inspiration above all in the spiritual asceticism of the individual, for the oriental tradition of renunciation cannot be ignored. Certainly it will no longer be a question of merely explaining the world, but of transforming it. In this respect, it is in complete agreement with European and Latin American political theologies. But Asian theology, says one of its protagonists, will be born of the totality of human experience: holistic human experience (personal and communal, mystical and social) will replace the social praxis as the hermeneutic starting point for the theology of liberation in Asia. It is interesting to note that while differences clearly exist between intellectuals (theologians of Asia and America), the grass-roots of these two continents apparently see eye to eye. Thus we see Latin Americans spontaneously living out the spiritual asceticism to which we have just referred. We should bear in mind the example of Alagamar and the faculty for prayer, for fasting and the gift of self which underpinned it.

In Africa, indigenous religions show a remarkable vitality and have proved themselves capable of resisting external influences.[13] Some people even see accusations of sorcery as a 'progressive option', in as much as they are curbs on inequality. Indeed, such accusations have a regulating effect, their aim being to keep social disparities in check. The accused will be a member of the community who, through ambition, is destroying its harmony by creating a social rift.[14]

Jean-Marc Ela points out that, ever since the slave trade, Blacks have been turning to the gods of combat, of withdrawal and defiance. He believes that instead of splitting hairs over the confrontation of cultures, African intellectuals and theologians would do better to revalorize the 'culture of confrontation' which lies buried in the heart of African religious feeling.

African religions followed the slaves to the Americas. If the Brazilian *candomble* and *umbanda* scarcely seem to contain a message of liberation,[15] the same cannot be said of the Haitian Voodoo. Admittedly, for many years there, 'the imaginary was under control'.[16] Traditional culture, of which Voodoo is part, was exploited there for the benefit of the *noirisme* (blackness) policy of François 'Papa Doc' Duvalier. But it also contains the seeds of liberty, of the vital energies, admittedly long dormant, but capable of being revived. It was Boukman, a Voodoo priest, who was to set in motion the 1791 struggle for the independence of the first negro republic in the world. The revolutionaries came from the slave masses who had lost none of their African traditions. Voodoo certainly played a role in this great rebellion.[17] It also played a considerable, but somewhat occult, role in the overthrowing of Jean-Claude 'Baby Doc' Duvalier in February 1986. And the Voodoo sector of the population took part in the debates on the new Haitian Constitution. In particular, Voodoo formulated unforeseen demands concerning the respect of nature, forestation, the struggle against erosion, pig breeding, among others. Obviously, its present role is not without dangerous ambiguities, but this is true of any religious movement.

Ecumenical meetings of theologians from different countries of the Third World are held regularly. They underline the importance of popular religious feeling in the process of social liberation.[18] But each continent has its own specific approach. If Latin America expresses itself in essentially social and political terms of liberation, Africa stresses the need for a mental decolonialization of the churches and the development of theology and liturgies rooted in traditional values and respectful of 'Animist' cosmologies. Asian theologians on the other hand, propose, as we have seen, a wider understanding of the concept of liberation, and take pains to 'inculturate' Christianity by means of intensive exchanges with the believers of other local religions. Thus, one may read in the final declaration of the Congress of Third World Theologians held in New Delhi:

> Given that the great majority of the peoples of the Third World practice other religious faiths, the sudden ascent of the Third World is that of a world that is not Christian. It has expressed itself throughout history in a voice that is all its own, demanding justice and equality, reaffirming its religions and secular cultures and questioning a Christian interpretation of the world that is too Eurocentric and narrow. No revolution in the Third World can be effective or lasting unless it takes into account and incorporates the religious experience of the people.

5. Development: A Trojan Horse?

The foregoing remarks on culture require some further comment on its complex, hybrid, changing nature.

Let us begin with the currently dominant culture, that of the countries of the North. In the first place, this culture varies according to the different countries and continents. It is influenced by the philosophic and political systems that are currently in favour and by prevailing economic and technological conditions. What is more, Western culture has evolved throughout the ages. It was regularly intersected by diverse, even contradictory, currents. Today, the majority of Westerners are facing the 'clash of civilizations' and may even partake of several forms of rationality.[1] Nowadays, this cultural pluralism opens the way for the coexistence of heterogeneous cultural elements; thus one finds acupuncture, Chinese by tradition, taught in Western medical schools. The West is currently being shaken to its very foundations by formidable doubts raised by the question of 'progress'. People in the West remember how, according to the classical myth, Prometheus ended up enchained by the gods, his liver devoured by a bird of prey, for having stolen from them the sacred fire of knowledge and technology. They wonder about the future and worry that we might have entered the Age of the Vulture,[2] the age of stress, pollution and the nuclear threat. The age also of a certain despair, symbolized by the punk slogan which covers the walls of the cities of the North: 'No future!' In the West, material progress no longer enjoys the generalized and virtually unconditional approval still accorded it by immediately preceding generations. Even science, despite its pretensions to universality, no longer has the arrogance and intolerance which characterized the scientism of the nineteenth century and went hand in hand with imperialism. Pushed to its ultimate limits, scientific research has resulted in the staggering discovery of new paradigms and the admission of the pluralism of systems of rationality and references.[3]

The basic character of the current questioning could lead to a new life-style in industrialized societies and to a sort of subversion of established values. We shall return to this in a subsequent chapter.

If no uniform, unalterable, undisputed culture exists in the West, the same may be said of Third World countries. In reality, there is no such thing as culture in the pure sense, developing in isolation from socio-economic factors, foreign influences, from constantly renewed challenges. Rather, there are specific peoples living in quite concrete conditions and tossed by diverse cultural elements, the fruits of numerous borrowing, contradictory evolutions, complex cross-breeding. Long before the West invaded their world, the various cultural communities of the Third World had mutually influenced each other.

Acculturation – inculturation

Two neologisms are used nowadays to describe the mutual influences cultures have on each other. These are acculturation and inculturation. It may be useful to define their meanings.[4] The reciprocal influences between Oriental cultures and religions offer a good illustration of what these terms mean. There is said to be acculturation when a culture of foreign origin profoundly influences an indigenous culture. Thus Buddhism, Indian in origin, has become widespread in Southern and South-Eastern Asia (Ceylon, Burma, Thailand, Cambodia, for example). These countries were converted. Their cultures became profoundly impregnated by Buddhism and, indirectly, by Indian culture. Therefore, acculturation had taken place. This may sometimes be spontaneous and desired; at other times it is imposed more or less deliberately. It then brings about alienation, a greater or lesser cultural renunciation. Conversely, there is said to be inculturation when an indigenous culture profoundly influences a culture of foreign origin, to the point where the latter is transformed. Thus, Buddhism has not essentially 'Indianized' China; instead it has been modified by Chinese culture. *Pali*, the canonical language of Buddhism, has died out in favour of Chinese; other disciplines (Ch'an, which became Zen) and new religious concepts have been developed and the end result was to give Chinese Buddhism a character that is quite unique and so influential that it is this form of Buddhism which was adopted outside China, notably in Japan and Korea.

The Western cultural imperialism dealt with in the present book has brought about a massive process of acculturation of non-white peoples to the West, but this goes hand in hand with certain manifestations of inculturation, of which modern Japan and Korea are perhaps the most striking example.

Acculturation is accompanied by manifestations of inculturation and vice versa, with the result that, throughout their histories, the entire world's cultural communities have undergone mutual influences of varying intensity, desired to a greater or lesser degree, and this long before the West invaded their world. The remarks made above on Buddhism in the East could well apply to Islam in Black Africa, where even today it still provokes an intense cultural and spiritual melting-pot.

As for Christianity, it has spread everywhere and the different ways in which it can influence believers deserves mention here. In its early days, Christianity, too, allowed itself to be 'incultured'. Is not this what the apostle Paul wanted to encourage when he enjoined people to be Jewish with Jews and Greek with Greeks? Even the first missionaries of modern times, such as Matteo Ricci and de Nobili, were careful to allow the Christian faith to be 'incultured' by the people amongst whom they lived and whose rich culture they were discovering with admiration. They had remarkable success in establishing and adapting a dialogue, the former in China, the latter in India. After these precursors, and largely due to colonializing triumphalism, missionaries became more and more the tools of acculturation. The results were sometimes appalling.[5] Nevertheless, decolonization opened new perspectives. It also led to the increasing independence of the Churches of the Third World. As a result of the appeals of the Second Vatican Council,[6] and the World Council of Churches, indigenous Christians and foreign missionaries no longer see Christianity as a fully grown tree to be transplanted from Rome, Geneva or elsewhere, but a seed to be scattered over the ground. The different qualities of soil will produce plants adapted to the area and bear fruits which will be no less delicious for being hitherto unknown. The future of Christianity amongst the peoples of the world will greatly depend on their ability to inculturate Christian faith deeply and free themselves from the monocultural Western yoke, yet without falling into stifling particularisms. This process is well under way in some communities on the Asian continent but much remains to be done. Inculturation is particularly urgent, important and difficult in Black Africa. Here and there, it has already produced admirable results, despite the obstacles and alarms raised by those who still confuse Christianity with Western culture, apparently forgetting that Jesus was not a European, and reducing the Christian revelation to one race's perception of it.[7]

Today, there are already almost as many Christians in the Third World as in the Northern hemisphere. The ever-increasing process of inculturation will, providing the crux of revelation remains intact, allow an unprecedented diversification and enrichment of the Christian faith, its theology, liturgy, spirituality and, ultimately, the forms of commitment and the models of society resulting from this process. Through their failure to rid themselves of their Eurocentric messianism, Western churches have almost reduced Christianity to a parochial religion, the product of a given culture. Only inculturation in different regions will make of it a truly universal religion.

Today, all cultural communities — with a few rare exceptions — are affected, to varying degrees, by Western modernity. Their reaction to it ranges from eager welcome to violent rejection. Even within each community, attitudes may vary. Manifestly modernist elites may try to safeguard some aspect of tradition whilst traditional circles accept without apparent difficulty some foreign element or gadget. The processes of acculturation–inculturation have become extremely distressing. Today, millions of human beings feel torn between two different, often contradictory, cultural universes. It is noticeable that while some appear to live out this coexistence harmoniously in their innermost selves, others experience quasi-schizoid difficulties regarding it. At all events, countless human communities nowadays possess a hybrid culture. It is good that intercultural contacts are increasing. The problem would, on the contrary, be that Western culture imposed itself to the exclusion of all other contributions, or was adopted blindly. The current strain in cultural exchanges curbs peoples' vitality and threatens to lead to the progressive stifling of a standardized humanity. It is for this reason that we must militate for the right to be different.

Cultural resistance

At times by force, at times by seduction, Westernization is rapidly advancing into the remotest corners of the world. And 'development' has been well and truly introduced, like some modern Trojan Horse, into foreign territory. Of course, there is Western knowledge and know-how whose interest is undeniable and whose attraction is justified. Unfortunately, their introduction is usually accompanied by a social and economic process which is often destructive. Almost everywhere in the Third World, one can see signs of social destructuration which must raise grave doubts about the benefits of intercultural melting-pots. Such melting-pots are productive only where there is genuine interaction and not merely unilateral imposition. The balance of power, particularly economic, currently works in favour of cultural domination by one partner, not in favour of mutual fertilization based on relative equality. Thus, from the Andes mountains to the plains of the Sahel, from Indonesia to Guatemala, we are currently witnessing the most distressing scenes. By means of a complex game of collusion, conducted by transnational companies, governments and local investors, peasants are forced off their land, allowing it to be absorbed into agro-industrial enterprises, and find themselves reduced to selling their labour in exchange for beggarly wages. Rural communities are disarticulated, their members caught up in the modern machinery of economic exploitation. Elsewhere, it is the enormous power of seduction exercised by Western consumer society that works such havoc. Ivan Illich is quite right when he speaks of an 'astoundingly alienating culture'. Let us take as an example those coffee-bars and cheap eating places, once convivial meeting-places, now transformed into 'video-bars' where the customers are plunged in darkness, their eyes riveted to the small screen. What is more, the screen in question offers films that rival each other in grossness, in which scenes of violence alternate with scenes of a Hollywood-style material affluence which give a completely false idea of the Western world.

Everywhere, authentic indigenous cultures are under threat. Thus the Rio de Janeiro carnival now survives only as something seen in private clubs and watched from grandstands, where people pay for the right to look at something in which they themselves were once involved. Music, dance, fantasy, have all been reduced to the status of commodities. Even if their social function was dubious, they did express and consolidate the exuberant life-force of the Brazilian people who now find themselves offered only American pop music in return.

There is no doubt that so much aggression and fascination leave their mark everywhere.

Some people conclude from all this that the Westernization of the world is inevitable. Whether we want it or not, humanity is on the road to standardization. It is seen as an irreversible process. For some, this is cause for congratulation. These are the heralds of the messianic triumphalism of Western capitalism and socialism, the obligatory models for our planet. Others, on the contrary, view the process with resignation for they have witnessed the damage it causes. They are aware of the suffering it brings but believe this to be inevitable. They are caught in a kind of fatalism, according to which the world is irrevocably on the road to Westernization.

The first thought that springs to mind in this connection is that one must not confuse modernization with Westernization. There are, perhaps, *alternative forms of modernity*. If the West has indeed been the cradle of considerable progress, it nonetheless does not have the monopoly on it. Consequently, the desire which various peoples have to 'develop', and the need some feel for rapid progress in order to free themselves from destitution, need not lead to mimicry.

In any case, is not the so-called irreversibility of Westernization contradicted by the facts? A closer look shows that, in the long run, different peoples have managed, one way or another, to resist the Western steam-roller. What has been said in the preceding pages on the collapse of Western-style development and the enduring quality of indigenous cultures offers some examples of this. There has been resistance to 'deculturation' in various forms and to varying degrees. But the most tenacious resistance to alienation might well be the least visible, which would explain the fatalism of those who have allowed themselves to be taken in by external appearances. In fact, acculturation takes place on three different levels, that of external forms, that of institutions and, lastly, that of value systems.

Thus, one community may retain the most visible forms of its culture, for example in matters of housing, food and clothing. In which case, it is generally agreed it has not (yet) been fundamentally Westernized. Another people may have abandoned the external forms of its traditional culture while retaining, to a greater or lesser extent, its own structures. In which case, an observer will discover, in a society of Western appearance, indigenous institutions on the political level (for example, a chieftaincy) or in the area of social organization (in particular, the family or clan structure or some form of collaboration which has remained alive, such as the *tontine* in Africa). Other cultural communities have lost both their external forms and their own modes of socio-political organization, but continue to be nourished by the values that underpin them. In this respect, there is no doubt that religions play a particularly important role. This is due to the fact that religions (even when they have been obliged — as was the case with Animism in Africa — to go underground to be out of sight of the colonial power) represent 'the locus of the greatest coherence' of the societies in question.[8] For most cultures in Third World countries, religion underlies every aspect of life: family, law, politics, land ownership, agriculture, technology, food, and so on. These elements are not autonomous but complement each other. Thus, millet- or rice-growing is as much an act of worship as an operation of production. As a veritable social cement, religions have a basic function: that of bestowing on societies an internal coherence. This is why they are also the source of the greatest resistance to external aggression, which is a sign of health, even if, from the 'developer's' point of view it represents an obstacle. In the colonial era, traditional religious leaders, referred to by the colonists as sorcerers, had to go underground to avoid repression and retain their function. This is why such religions have become less and less visible, which does not mean they have ceased to exist. Today, we know how very much alive are the religions of the Bolivian Aymara who were thought to be Christian, of Haitian Voodoo devotees, of African 'Animists', of the Korean followers of a shamanist mudang-priestess. . . . And this despite the fact that more 'respectable' religions and the established political authorities have done their best to eradicate them.

Behind the façade of Westernization, the traditional value system often remains intact and continues to determine certain behaviour. As Professors Latouche (Lille) and Zawal (Rabat) have claimed, capitalism may well cause numerous disruptions, but frequently only penetrates in the form of consumption and not as a 'metaphysic' of production and exploitation. They even believe it can be claimed that it is capitalism that sometimes finds itself at the 'periphery', having only a superficial contact with the society in question.[9]

In fact, regular contact with Third World communities, experienced in conditions of mutual confidence, reveals to those who are willing to listen, that Westernization is not as complete as it appeared at first sight.

When all is said and done, resignation is perhaps as questionable as triumphalism in matters of Westernization. Human nature, luckily, is extremely complex and human beings have more than one trick up their sleeves.

Part Two:
Underdevelopment and Overdevelopment

6. The Withering Away of People's Identity

> A man with no memory or past is like a pilot without a compass.
>
> Oscar Bimwenyi Kweshi

As we have seen, it is the most internalized features — systems of representation, ancestral myths, archetypes, forms of spirituality, religious attitudes, values — which offer the most enduring resistance to cultural disintegration. When this base *is* affected, however, the worst is to be expected, for there is then a 'withering away', an atrophying of consciousness itself[1] and, unless the latter can recover, the process may well become irreversible.

The tragic nature of such a process must be stressed. When a people is stripped of its identity, it is no longer capable of self-determination. Society, in such a case, disintegrates and is no longer able to function as a society. Such is the ultimate outcome of 'underdevelopment', which Vincent Cosmao so aptly describes as 'an accident caused by one society being in contact with another which is in a dominant position'. Underdevelopment is, therefore, the result, rather than the starting point of Third World peoples' recent history. The real tragedy of 'underdevelopment' is that of the gradual destruction of consciousness, by forcing people into dependency. The resulting disintegration or destructuration of society may go as far as an internalized negation of one's self and thus of one's real vitality.

> Much more than the technical, economic, social or political aspects, the real tragedy of underdevelopment is cultural and spiritual, in the sense that there is always hope as long as the collective consciousness still exists, even if only potentially, as long as the embers still glow, as long as, beneath the ashes of passivity, or resignation and fatalism, there smoulders a spark of life which a single breath can revive.[2]

Cosmao goes on to conclude that, more than the sickness, it is the people affected by it who must be taken into consideration for, ultimately, only they can cure themselves if they want to live.

Fortunately, the sickness does not attack everyone with the same virulence. As in the fable, not everyone dies, but everyone — or almost — is affected. We have said enough about the current process of deculturation. Let us now look at the forms of solidarity that can be offered to the different peoples of the world whose condition conforms to the preceding diagnosis and who agree with it. And let us recognize straight away that we must distinguish, in each case, between those whom the sickness has already seriously affected and those who have, till now, more or less succeeded in controlling it.

Development, a term to be discarded?

The aim in matters of international co-operation for development is that everyone should have not only the *right* to live, but also *reasons* to live. Every human group must be able to draw these reasons from its own ethos. Each society's material life must, at the risk of fatal disasters, be founded on the basis of its own indigenous culture.

It is not a question of rejecting modernity *a priori* nor of returning to the past, accrediting it with unconditional value just as one had once done with Western-style progress. Rather, what is necessary is that one should become aware of the disasters incurred and of their causes. What is necessary is that the cultural communities who need it work towards new, *sui generis* conceptions of modernity. It is they who must reconstruct their societies, who must reconcile past and present.

What is needed, according to Cosmao again, is not a nostalgic, sterile return to sources, but to have 'recourse to sources' in order to unleash repressed, withheld energy.[3] By re-rooting itself in its collective memory, a people which has been dispossessed of itself can then try to reconstruct its identity and find the necessary assurance to fight urgent battles and make new starts.

Far from being some kind of folk revival, it is a question of sinking to the bottom in order to rise again and, if necessary, evolve and change. For change is often the price cultural communities must pay to remain what they are, so much is the external world present, constantly threatening to disrupt secular harmony and contaminate the innermost values. This 'recourse to sources' is no Rousseauesque dream but a burst of life to regenerate oneself. As Aurobindo, the great sage who combined tradition and modernity, said: 'We must hold the past sacred, but the future even more so'.

Must we abandon development, put an end to the programmes and projects which try to promote it, stop the work of NGOs working with the Third World? To reply to these questions we must first reach an understanding of the term 'development'.

Development is a highly charged term. It grew out of a conception that, though dynamic and positive, was founded on the paradigms of one single culture, Western culture. Now, this culture is characterized by a specific mentality (anthropocentric, evolutionist, rationalist) and is determined by a clearly defined socio-political model (pan-economism, consumerism, the sovereignty of the nation-state, technocratism). In practice, the term 'development' is often simply a euphemism for Westernization. Furthermore, the term lacks precision, so that nowadays we find it paired off with all sorts of qualifying adjectives: 'human', 'integral', 'self-reliant', 'alternative', 'endogenous', 'upward'. . . . . Attempts have been made to rid it of its anthropocentric connotations by speaking of 'ecological development'; of its heavy bureaucratic, productivist past by searching for 'strategies for alternative development'; of its Eurocentrism by trying to mobilize the indigenous culture as a 'tool for development'.

Today, some people attempt to substitute for the term 'development' other symbols representing what is good, what is desirable, the realizing of human potential, personal and collective. At the workshop on intercultural co-operation held at Marlagne (Namur, Belgium),[4] the participants devoted one full session to the search for 'homeomorphous equivalents' to the term 'development'. The expression comes from Raimundo Pannikkar and stems from his attempts to understand, from the standpoint of a given culture, ideas formulated by another.[5] What is meant by such 'equivalents' is not analogies but functional equivalence in different cultural systems. Among the suggestions voiced during the aforementioned session, let us retain, to replace the term development, the expression 'a good life'.[6] Achieving the necessary conditions to lead a 'good life' may be a less Eurocentric and more universal exercise than promoting 'development'. Be that as it may, the choice of terminology matters little. The real interest of such research is to radically 'relativize' the concept of development. It must be understood that development is not the only reference for what is desirable. Since there are many cultures, there are also many ways of envisaging life, happiness and unhappiness. Many ways, also, of perceiving progress.

Already progressive organizations in various countries avoid the term 'development' because it carries the ideology of 'catching-up' modernization based on Western capitalism. They speak more readily of liberation, in the economic and political sense. The cultural problematics are yet another reason to avoid usage of the word 'development' which is altogether too ambiguous. In the Third World, men and women engaged in what were hitherto called development projects have understood this. They use other terms. Working in the shanty-towns of Port-au-Prince, one nun prefers to speak of 'redressing'. In the Sri Lanka countryside, a peasant movement calls itself *Gam Pubuduwa*, 'Awakening of the village'. In Brazil, the Indians speak, not of 'development' but of 'survival'.[7] This term is no exaggeration when one remembers that the indigenous population of the American continent has been, since the invasion of the white man, the object of a double aggression, involving both ethnocide (the assassination of a culture) and genocide (the assassination of a people). Lately, the Tapirape, an Indian nation living in central Brazil, has lived through the experience of progressive annihilation and a lingering death, followed by an astonishing resurrection. They were down to less than fifty people and their women were no longer bearing children. Their whole being had ceased to believe in life. Then a handful of nuns appeared amongst them. Their altruistic, sisterly presence allowed the Tapirape to regain their taste for life and take up the numerous challenges thrown down by the 'civilized' world outside. Today, there are 300 Tapirape. They have not achieved 'development'. For them, this would mean integration with the world of the whites, an integration they had opposed by allowing themselves to die out. Rather, they have assured their survival and their capacity to lead a 'good life' as they understand it.

In Black Africa, research has shown that the word 'development' is totally untranslatable in many local languages. For certain ethnic groups, it evokes perjorative notions such as 'chaos' or 'regression'.

Discarding the term 'development' does not mean the rejection of all ideas of solidarity. Yet certain discussions on culture threaten to lead to just that. To dissociate oneself from the Third World from fear of contaminating its indigenous cultures even more would be tantamount to burying one's head in the sand. The political, economic and cultural imperialism of the major blocs continue to ravage the countries of the South and will cause even more damage there if we do not struggle, *both here and over there*, to prevent it.

7. Alienation Amidst Plenty

Because thou sayest, I am rich and increased with goods, and have need of nothing; and knowest not that thou art wretched, and miserable, and poor, and blind, and naked.

Revelations: 3:17 (King James Version)

It is not for a Western author to look further into the description of cultural impoverishment in the countries of the Third World. Such an undertaking would be of little use, for it is up to the men and women who belong to each cultural community to assess the damage and take whatever measures they consider necessary. What is more, it would be in rather poor taste. Indeed, there is something insulting and narrow-minded in speaking only of 'the problems of the Third World' as if humanity's evils were confined to the tropics and to people of colour; as if the West, in contrast, was sheltered from all the misery and depravity that thrives overseas. I am sometimes asked if it is not depressing to make frequent journeys to 'poor countries', to be confronted regularly by human suffering there. My reply is instinctive: it is no. There is also a vitality there, a taste for life, human qualities and a sense of the sacred that leave a lasting impression of hope. On the contrary, it is when I land in one of those asepticized airports in Europe or North America that I am over-whelmed by sadness. Everything there is perfectly organized but the people look despondent and seem nervous. Are they happy, these Westerners whom everyone envies so? Several friends from overseas have told me bluntly: 'We are underdeveloped economically, but you in the West are underdeveloped on the human level'.[1] They are shocked that we can do our shopping without exchanging those few words that give the human touch to the act of buying and selling. Whether sitting in a university classroom, a doctor's waiting room, a church, or in an underground carriage, Third World visitors are surprised by the harshness of the conversations, the anonymity of the contacts, the utilitarian purpose to which so many actions are reduced. Though the West may fascinate with its science, technology and organization, it also saddens them. And the nostalgia of a more joyful, convivial way of life stirs in them.

And what if the West, like the Third World but in its own way, was also plunged in a cultural crisis? It is certainly, as everyone agrees, in a crisis situation. Let us outline the general features of this crisis, not through any desire to wallow in misery but because it is important to make a dispassionate affirmation of what is wrong. There are at least four reasons for this.

Firstly, it bears repeating, because it is unfair to describe the problems of the Third World, including its cultural problems, without referring to their equivalents in the West. We must rid ourselves once and for all of the arrogant, mistaken notion that the Third World has the problems, and the West the answers.

Secondly, we must publicly describe and analyse what is wrong in the West for it still serves as the envied model and universal goal of hundreds of millions of human beings. So many Third World inhabitants are attracted by the positive aspects of the West, but also fascinated and deceived by the advertizing and ideological propaganda of both the East and the West, whose torch is often taken up by local elites. This persistent, servile admiration must be replaced by an explicit inventory of what is useful and good and the rejection of what is harmful.

Thirdly, it is crucial for the sake of the rest of the world that the West change course. And for that we must describe, denounce and analyse. The Northern hemisphere imposes on the rest of the planet — if necessary by means of interposing a local bourgeoisie — economic exploitation and political domination. Obviously, the West invented neither exploitation nor oppression. Both existed before its invasion of the countries of the South. But it has given them a global dimension and, today, they contribute to the production of widespread famine, poverty, violations of human rights and cultural alienation. The Western model is omnipresent. And potentially deadly. One has only to think of the arms race, the nuclear threat and the dangers to the ecology. Our Third World partners tirelessly remind us: 'The origins of our misfortunes lie largely with you. To combat hunger, injustice and ecological imbalance, the West must change. A halt must be brought to political and economic imperialism provoked by states or by multinational companies, as it is this imperialism that forces us into a poverty-stricken dependence.'

Finally, the Western crisis must be described in order to ascertain whether its origins may not lie in the cultural, spiritual alienation which is the subject of this book and of which Westerners themselves are as much the victims as the promotors. Clearly, the monocultural model denounced in the preceding chapters has its origins in the West. But is this model really the expression of the entire culture of the peoples of Europe and North America? Are these people not victims of a tremendous overemphasis of only certain aspects of the Western spirit? Is what we are experiencing today, in the North (both capitalist and socialist), the fruit of the entirety of the cultural and spiritual values of white people? If it is not, if the West is also being suffocated by an alienating economic and technological system, there are grounds for demanding for it as well as for the Third World the right to be different *vis-à-vis* the dominant cultural mould.

Crisis within crisis

What exactly is the crisis that afflicts the countries of the West? Its more superficial aspects are well known.

Their economies no longer create jobs and can offer vast numbers of young people only a grim future of marginalization to the periphery of 'productive' society. The recent introduction of computer technology, automation and the use of robots will unquestionably disrupt the job market even more, and the very nature of work itself. The populations of Europe are growing older and its societies are at a loss as to what is to be done with so many elderly people whom the prevailing economic rationality no longer recognizes as useful members of society. Today, the structural inequalities are further complicated by the 'new poverty' resulting from the economic crisis. The West increasingly squanders irreplaceable material resources which it must then seek in other parts of the world. At times, this need produces dependence and vulnerability, at others it results in all kinds of imperialist interventions. Its soil is saturated with chemicals, its seas and rivers polluted by all sorts of waste material. The air contains toxic fumes and acid rain. These pollution problems could one day culminate in a nuclear catastrophe, civil or military. As Paul-Marc Henri of the French UNESCO Commission has put it, it is as though the West has been invaded, occupied, using these terms as one does in speaking of a country under foreign domination. Physical space is more and more restricted. The countryside is built up and Europe has become one immense block of concrete. Freedom is out of reach, beyond the congested motorways, or illusory, on noisy, fouled beaches. Even more serious is the fact that mental space has also been invaded. It is submitted to a constant barrage of information by the omnipresent television, radio and press. In the future, this information overload will be drastically increased by data processing. The systematic bombardment of information makes famine and oppression seem common-place, each catastrophe driving out the memory of the previous one. This surfeit of information leads to our being underinformed and what Edgar Morin has called informational destitution. Mass-media 'culture' is spreading coninuously, with its often debased values, its mercenary logic and its way of reducing human life to the spectacular and, if possible, sensational and tragic. The unconscious is assailed by violence, coarseness and trivia. State bureaucracy occupies a constantly expanding space in the peoples' lives, increasingly depriving them of both the means and the desire to take charge of their own and their society's destinies in a responsible, creative manner. As a Brazilian friend visiting Europe pointed out, a man lying in the street is no longer a brother, but a social case, and as such is the state's responsibility. Having devoted itself quite rightly to the protection and well-being of the individual, the Welfare State has at the same time extended its jurisdiction into most realms of life. Techno-bureaucratic developments allow it, as well as foreseeing and regulating, to control, arbitrate and repress deviance or originality. This jeopardizes the right to be different. Thus, a paternalistic state develops, if not always totalitarian then certainly totalizing, in other words extending to and controlling all dimensions of human existence.[2] The solution to this stifling bureaucratization, however, is not to be confused with individualistic neo-liberalism. Fashionable slogans about 'rolling back the frontiers of the state' are often synonymous with a crude return to *laissez-faire* capitalism. Freedom and creativity are then reduced — to the level of economic entrepreneurship! For many citizens, this means the freedom to be marginalized! Reducing freedom to the economic level is a typical phenomenon of Western materialism. It is a perfect illustration of our cultural crisis!

Thus, in this slightly simplified overview of the superficial aspects of the Western crisis, we find the same three factors of deculturation that caught our attention in the Third World: economy, technology and the state! All three increasingly cease to be in people's service and respond to a logic that eludes them. There is, therefore, in the countries of the North, both capitalist and socialist, and apart from the generally recognized phenomena of crisis, a culture crisis. The West is suffering from *malaise*, as is proven by the suicide rate among the young, violence, tranquillizer and drug abuse, the rush to psychiatrists. It is as though the West was suffocating in its own affluence. In Eastern Europe, the regimes in power seem bound up in obdurate bureaucracy. In the West, the ugly heads of racism and fascism rear. Through lack of any profound sense of identity, people in the West are ready to kill others for ridiculous, confused reasons, as can be seen from the Falklands War or the tragedy that took place in the football stadium in Brussels where over-excited supporters brought about the massacre of almost forty 'enemies'. This highly symbolic tragedy reflects the despair of Europe's young people, pushed to their limits by chronic unemployment, the exacerbation of the feelings aroused by the obsession to win and the race for affluence and by senseless chauvinism. Alas, the same Europeans who are quick to denounce the transgressions of the Third World saw in the 'Heysel tragedy' only the excesses of a few drunken hooligans and the inadequacy of the police.

Positivist futurologists, scientists, management specialists and politicians dangle before us the enviable future that new technology will bring about. Up until now, the West has, indeed, brilliantly succeeded in solving certain quantitative problems, in supplying answers to the question of 'how' things are to be done. But will the West be able to say 'why' they are done, and take full advantage of its remarkable discoveries in order to guarantee in qualitative terms a way of life that is humanly satisfying? New technology such as micro-electronics and biotechnology are admirable fruits of the most advanced scientific thought. They could be instrumental in solving certain aspects of the current crisis but could equally make them worse, particularly from the social point of view. In fact, the West has become a sorcerer's apprentice. The consequences of its mistakes and desires will henceforth be fatal, for it is no longer master of its own creations. The nuclear holocaust has entered the realms of the possible.

If all the knowledge of the economists and the ingenuity of the scientists seem unable to guarantee the West any lasting immunity against the *malaise* which afflicts it, social and political mobilization offered a ray of hope at the beginning of the present decade. When France voted socialist in 1981, Europeans and many people in the Third World looked on, curious but optimistic. The French were about to pay up, to share things out and therefore experience a certain austerity, in an economy geared for human beings. More equitable relationships would be established among them and between France and the countries of the South. Humanist socialism would offer a solution to the crisis. But far from achieving a more fraternal society, what happened was flight of capital, a widespread perpetuation of established rights; and a tightening of the grip on property and power by those who, for a brief moment, felt these assets slipping from their grasp. In the final analysis, there was scarcely any change in the established social and economic order. Of course some improvements did take place, but the great dream remained unfulfilled. It took a back seat to the increasingly profitable export of sophisticated weapons all over the world, to a policy of nuclear 'defence' in keeping with Reagan's and to the ridiculous but scandalous attack on the 'Greenpeace' boat.

There is considerable room for doubt that the solution to the crisis will be supplied solely by scientists, economists or politicians. For its fundamental causes lie outside the scope of the analyses and solutions they have to offer. A society that offers neither jobs nor reasons to live, that literally dispenses with human beings — whether by means of robots or missiles — that designs factories with no regard for their social functions, that reduces everything to profit, acquisition and power is a sick society: sick in the very definition of its values, sick to the depths of its cultural being.

The West has become culturally underdeveloped because it, too, is the victim of the idea of progress and the model of development which it has transmitted to the Third World and which it imposes on itself. People in the West suffer from the 'withering of consciousness' mentioned earlier. And what was said about the disintegration of indigenous cultures in the Third World applies equally to the West. Increasingly detached from their fundamental cultural identity, Westerners, too, find self-determination difficult to achieve. This is the meaning of the current crisis whose economic, ecological, political and social features are only the visible part of the iceberg, emerging from the deep, icy waters of cultural and spiritual alienation. It is an alienation amidst plenty at least as dehumanizing as alienation in poverty.[3]

Today, the West is under threat from its own pan-economic model, which reduces everything to its market value. Such a reduction, combined with an obsession with productivity, consumerism and competitiveness sow unhappiness and confusion. Paradoxically, this occurs while the quest for happiness, greatly aided by advertising, is increasingly advocated. 'Happiness' has become the object of a veritable ideology and it is striking that the West can talk of nothing else, whereas the question of happiness rarely arises in societies of the Third World. Consumer society relegates the desire for happiness to the level of a 'slap-up meal' instead of recognizing in it the echo of a great Desire which lies in the soul's very depths. This desire is like a gaping void, an intense longing that beckons inwards, that yearns to be deeply centred. It constitutes the vital force of human beings. The West has tried to fill this void, to ignore inadequacy, emptiness, pain and death. In its morbid hunger, it has tried to satisfy not this great Desire but a multitude of superficial pleasures. It has done so by an often desperate search, clutching at objects. Waiting has become unbearable: we must have everything immediately! Plenitude, the West has declared, means having plenty.[4] The advertisements that cover the walls of our towns shout it loud enough. Who has not been overwhelmed by those bronzed women, unnaturally beautiful, who brandish such-and-such a deodorant or sip such-and-such an aperitif, suggesting with a calculated sensuality that, thanks to these products, they live 'fuller' lives, find love and 'fulfil' themselves?

Western modernity is in pursuit of a 'false infinite', that is to say a quantitative in-finite according to which one constantly produces, consumes and 'progresses' more and more. Today, the consequences of this Faustian undertaking are devastating. As Raimundo Pannikkar has said, Western modernity produces a substitute for transcendence.

A cultural winter

The crisis in the West is a serious matter for all its victims. But does it not, at the same time, offer them a ray of hope? It may well herald the collapse of a model that is choking to death. This model cannot last, either for Westerners themselves or for the majority of human beings, those of the Third World, who are reduced to poverty by the West's affluence. Just as a personal crisis can be an opportunity for growth in the individual, the current collective crisis may be the harbinger of profound changes. According to Ilya Prigogine, Nobel prizewinner in chemistry and professor at the Free University of Brussels, we have now reached a turning point in our understanding not only of physics and biochemistry but also of social relationships.[5] The role of our current stress will be to impel us towards a higher order. In the chinks of the edifice that is starting to totter, new values are emerging, offering hope. They have been with us for some time. There was the hippie movement with its rejection of bourgeois security; Marcuse and the protest against alienating prosperity; May 1968, the libertarian movement and the realization of the need for a cultural revolution and self-reliant socialism; the womens' liberation movement and the demystification of male strength and power; ecological sensibility and the awareness that our planet is like a imperilled ship, whose crew must unite at all cost to save it; the green parties (political ecology) which try to restore to the citizen creative space, a sense of personal responsibility and conviviality; transpersonal humanist psychology and 'New Age' groups which aim to release the individual's potential and bring about self-fulfilment; the peace movement which challenges the lethal logic of superpowers, and the non-violent movement that, following in the footsteps of Gandhi and Martin Luther King, is resorting to forms of struggle whose methods are in accordance with their aims; spiritual renewal attained through contact with Taizé (France), the Iona community in Scotland, charismatic communities and politically committed grass-roots communities, Orthodoxy, with its mystical yet very earthy theology; yoga, Zen meditation and new forms of cosmocentric, spiritual awareness; and finally, the discovery that the exploited peoples of the South are entitled to the political and economic solidarity of the inhabitants of the North and are the bearers of precious values capable of regenerating them. The seeds of cultural mutations are in the air. The brief but effective surprise appearance on the political scene of French university and high-school students in December 1986 confirms this. Their movement had a cultural dimension. Sociologist Edgar Morin sees in it a 'rather moving historic phenomenon': young people regenerating their own identity and refusing to be lost in the anonymity of a civilization producing hierarchy and homogeneity based on criteria that ring false.[6]

The Age of the Vulture which brings to an end the Promethean era might, it is suggested, make way for the Age of Aquarius and new paradigms[7] which could lead our knowledge and behaviour towards a Copernican revolution. These paradigms are not merely additional knowledge but new ways of perceiving reality. Amongst them is the holistic perception of life, whereby everything is interconnected, involving energy fields that are at the same time complementary and opposed.[8] The most advanced scientific knowledge in biochemistry and physics is in blatant contradiction with the rationalist, materialist scientism that has trammelled our century. Basic physics is increasingly broadening into metaphysics and the societal behaviour patterns of human beings could well be affected by this.

The prevailing scepticism scarcely helps to spread the hope contained in such a vision of the future. But in fact, pessimism and scepticism are part of the Western cultural crisis, whereas hope is the strong point of many of the peoples of the Third World. This is what Clodovis Boff, Brazilian theologian of liberation, has given as his main impression of Europe. But, unwilling to give in to pessimism himself, he speaks of a European 'cultural winter', implying by this metaphor that the 'decadence' is more apparent than real. When a tree seems dead in winter, its roots are still alive, and spring is on the way.[9]

Hildegarde Goss-Mayr and Joe Holland are both products of the movements mentioned above.[10] Committed players in the drama of cultural and socio-political change now being enacted in the West, they are agreed in attributing a double cause to our crisis: on the one hand the existence of social structures and economic enterprises whose ultimate aims are not in the service of human beings and their fulfilment in society, and which culminate in injustice, both here and abroad; on the other hand the prevailing materialist rationalism which has confused standard of living with quality of life, has limited mind to mere intelligence and reduced the sacred to a few obsolete devotions. These two causes, injustice and rationalism, cry out for commitment to justice on the one hand and the sense of transcendence on the other.

They are closely linked, and determine each other. That is why there can be no solution to the crisis if we merely change structures without effecting the sort of personal conversion that allows collective changes of mentality and behaviour. The West truly has need of a profound cultural transformation.

8. Third World Aid to the West

People are not just problems to be resolved but also mysteries to be explored, not vacuums to be filled but riches to discover.

Robert Vachon

Like the Third World, the West is suffering from cultural uprooting. To a large degree, the individual in the West has lost touch with his innermost cultural and spiritual being. He is in exile from himself and all that is most profound in him. The great Promethean adventure, embarked on at least five centuries before the birth of Christ but intensified during the last 300 years, has made him stand aloof from all that surrounds him: his own body, matter, nature, society. From relational beings, many Westerners have become creatures of domination and competitiveness. From being cosmocentric they have become egocentric.[1] I am not interested here in systematically criticizing everything Western or, to use an ugly play on words, to blacken everything white. The West contains much of great value and non-Western cultures are far from being totally admirable on all points. It is precisely in order to regenerate these Western values that a critical examination of its modern culture is imperative. The Northern hemisphere now finds itself prompted to this self-criticism by the questions posed to it by other cultures, and by the possibilities of change they suggest. As it happens, these changes fit in remarkably well with the most profound teachings of its own spiritual heritage. Here are a few examples.

The present-day white person has an almost masochistic relationship of domination towards the body and treats it like an object rather than inhabiting it as an integral part of the self, the temple of innermost being.[2] There are many Third World peoples who can help him or her to regain contact with their body. One has only to think of Indian or Irano-Egyptian yogas and their conception of physical and psychic harmony. African dance is another appropriate example of this. The current *malaise*, along with many other illnesses (referred to as psychosomatic, by the way) has its origins in a somewhat unhealthy attitude, at times guilt-ridden, at times utilitarian, towards the body. The wisdom of the peoples of India or of Buddhist countries invites the Westerner to a more sensitive, joyful, and also more sacred relationship with his or her own body and that of others. In particular, it encourages them to become aware of the fundamental importance of correct breathing for physical, psychical and spiritual well-being.

As far as matter is concerned, the Westerner has achieved fantastic successes, but the most advanced researches have led to the most terrifying means of destruction. Nature, controlled, pillaged and defiled, today is taking its revenge. Careful attention paid to the various religions and forms of spirituality contained in the Third World would help the Westerner overcome this relationship of aggressive control towards matter and nature in general. The notion of vital forces nourishing nature which characterizes African or Amerindian cosmologies, could awaken a truer conception, more respectful of and more in harmony with the environment. This is also true of Chinese Taoism which has an almost amatory understanding of matter and the subtle but powerful forces that structure it. What is more, these conceptions fit in with current scientific discoveries: that particles seem to be imbued with intelligence, driven by a vibratory energy that could well be spiritual. The cosmos is not some great mechanical clockwork but our natural habitat with which we must live in harmonious partnership.

In relations with others, Westerners have learned to be competitive. How much they could learn from the hospitality practised in Islamic countries, or among the Indians of the American continent! The Western traveller is constantly struck by the sense of conviviality that seems to activate Third World villages. NGO project officers and passing journalists are astonished by the feelings of solidarity that activate the peoples of the South in their social struggles that are harsh while still retaining a sense of celebration, human tenderness and, ultimately, the desire for social harmony.[3]

A respectful, considerate dialogue with the cultures and various forms of spirituality of Third World peoples offers a way for the West to resolve its crisis. The Third World is at its door, inviting it to rediscover the human body, nature and society as sacred shrines inhabited by the Spirit. The wisdom of other peoples reinforces what its own poets and mystics are constantly telling it: 'Look inward. Man mistakes his own identity when he limits himself to his tiny physical and temporal self. He also mistakes his faculties when he limits himself to his intellect.' The whole of Asia, from the orthodox Middle East to Buddhist Japan tell him: 'You have within you something essential that transcends you. Live by that!' In their own ways, Africans and Amerindians echo this.

The re-rooting of the West in its own culture will take place by spiritual means. It is in this sense that, to resolve the crisis, Joe Holland calls for an embodied spirituality, a creation-centred spirituality embodied in the self, in nature and in society. It is perhaps by calling on such spirituality that the West can find the strength and inspiration necessary to overcome its crisis. The experience of transcendence, far from disembodying their spirituality, ought to lead Westerners to embody it more profoundly. It is, in any case, exactly what their own Judeo-Christian religious heritage offers them. This is what Christmas is all about for instance. A spirituality incarnated in the human body, in matter and society, all of which are experienced as mediators and vehicles of grace and mystery, finds in the Christian revelation a powerful inspiration and confirmation. The divine is at once transcendence *and* immanence. It is nearer to me than myself. Being incarnated, it inhabits me and the world of my fellow beings. It calls me, along with the cosmos and all human beings to a process of transformation towards deification.

Of course, it is not only believers who are capable of this re-rooting. For Edgar Morin, agnostic sociologist, atheists must discover in their own way a liberating belief that will lead them to discover the irrational foundation of reason and 'come to terms with myths and their reality'.[4] They too must outstrip the rationalist and positivist attitude towards the body, nature and social life.

There is in Western cultural and spiritual tradition an enormous vital force, capable of mobilizing Westerners to emerge from the present impasse. Dialogue with the peoples of the Third World offers them the providential possibility of rediscovering their own richness and of undertaking the necessary re-rooting by means of an embodied spirituality. The cultural winter might then be able to adorn itself with the first glimmerings of spring.

Indeed, genuine intercultural dialogue involves mutual fertilization and reciprocal enrichment. But, if intercultural dialogue between the peoples of the North and the South needs to be intensified, it must not lead to some vague, shallow, haphazardly established eclecticism. On the contrary, such a dialogue must lead to the discovery and affirmation of who we are in the deepest sense. The West is too concerned with the exterior of things, their functional, utilitarian, juridical and organizational aspects. The Third World can turn all this to profit, whilst Western perception would be improved and enriched by the interior vision, the intuitive, symbolic intelligence and the sense of both joy and sobriety which activates the peoples of the South. The West resolutely embeds itself in history for which it claims to be responsible and co-creator, whereas the peoples of the South possess a great sense of gratuitousness and detachment. What lessons might not be drawn from this by both parties in a dialogue of equals! This is how that old European sage, Zen Master, Karlfried Graf von Durckheim put it:[5]

I would say the terms 'Orient–Occident' must not be taken in a geographical sense. The best example of this is that of man and woman. The human being is not only man or woman. She contains him, he contains her, and to the extent that man does not develop the feminine in him and vice versa, he becomes not a man but a robot! If the West wishes to remain human, it must take seriously the Oriental element within it, and the East can only survive by integrating something of that particularly masculine Western strength.

One can therefore say that the interest we Westerners are currently showing in the Orient stems from the fact that the Oriental within each of us is stirring into life and saying to us: 'Listen, my friend, if you do not accept me you will die, suffocated in the concrete tower blocks you construct with your rationality!'

An embodied spirituality for activists

According to Hildegarde Goss-Mayr and Joe Holland, materialistic rationalism and unjust social structures are the main causes of the crisis in the West. Consequently, these writers call for a sense of transcendence and for active commitment towards a more fraternal society. This double imperative, as has already been suggested, will come about through an embodied spirituality. But politically committed activists are indifferent, reticent or downright hostile towards anything that smacks of spirituality. Many have turned sharply away from it, having too often found religion to be in league with, or at least indifferent to, the very injustices they are fighting. The modern left was initially secular then, influenced by Marxism, rationalist and materialist. It is a victim of the state of mind inherited from the Enlightenment and the Industrial Revolution. It suffers from cultural debility. Being itself one of the consequences of Western modernity, the left is caught up in the prevailing cultural and spiritual crisis and thus finds great difficulty in offering any real alternative. (That it is well aware of this can be seen from the recent opening of its doors to various movements: feminist, ecological, ethnic, regionalist and also, finally, to certain religious movements.)

Believers who respond to the keen sense of justice and social commitment shown by secular left-wing activists have adopted their ideas and struggles on their own account. The problem, however, is that they have often adopted at the same time a large part of the philosophic conceptions of their atheist fellow travellers. Some no longer can, or dare to, fully express the spiritual basis of their activities. Amongst politically committed Christians, anything seen as 'mystical' is treated with extreme discretion, bordering on suspicion. The entire left suffers because of this. Obviously, this attitude is partly due to a healthy annoyance inspired by token, sanctimonious piety. The problem does not lie in the rejection of individualistic, demobilizing forms of religiosity, but in the fact that they have not always been replaced by the taste for a practice of stronger, better-suited forms of spirituality. The dominant ideologies weigh heavily on Western spiritual re-rooting.

Luckily, the Western left can be helped in accomplishing this necessary spiritual re-rooting when it listens to the peoples of the South. The basic Christian communities of Latin America live this experience on a daily basis and draw from it their extraordinary strength of resistance and creative energy. The dualism introduced in the West between the temporal and the spiritual is unknown to them. Life there is not cut up into pieces: struggle and contemplation are closely linked. This is testified to by thousands of peasant and worker groups as well as such men of prayer as the Brazilian Dom Helder Camara, both an activist and a contemplative, and Monsignor Romero, Bishop of El Salvador, who was shot dead before the altar by a squad of extreme right-wing assassins for having stood up for the people.[6] Grass-roots communities in the Cameroons, Zaire, South Africa, the Philippines, for example, offer their own examples of deeply-rooted spirituality, as well as progressive Christians who are not shy in celebrating their faith.

But if the example of these embodied spiritualities of the Third World can lead to a regeneration of the sense of transcendence on the part of Westerners, the latter can also draw on the most advanced conquests of their own science for reasons to transcend a stifling secularism[7] and rediscover the sacredness of life. This is strikingly expressed by Jim Douglas, the American militant pacifist.[8] He refers to Einstein's famous equation according to which mass and energy are of similar nature and mutually influence each other. $E = mc^2$ indicates that mass and energy are two facets of the same reality. Therefore, energy acts on matter. If one accepts this principle, and if one believes that contemplation (be it Zen meditation or Carmelite prayer) produces a form of energy, it is not unreasonable to conclude that this energy actually and effectively acts on the world, on people and events. Meditation and contemplation, when inspired by the power of love, produce undreamt of vibratory energy. This is unthinkable in the mechanistic materialism that still influences us, but is vouched for by all religious traditions (and the miraculous events they describe). We come back here to the idea of a profound interdependence between all beings and between them and the whole cosmos. Since time immemorial, non-dualist philosophers, from Cankara to Meister Eckhart, have had an intuition of this idea. In Christian terms, this ultimate solidarity in 'the mystic body of Christ' is called 'communion of saints'. Certain of Jung's writings as well as recent experiments in parapsychology follow a similar direction, together with what in modern secular terminology is called 'the power of positive thinking'. The most up-to-date scientific knowledge, used till now for ends that are usually materialist or even destructive, thus make the most ancient mystical intuitions both plausible and credible. They are an incentive to progressive people to speculate about the true scope of meditation and allow believers to shed new light on prayer. The latter should not be considered only as a means of personal or communal replenishment — though this is clearly essential, particularly for militants caught up in the turmoil of activism. Meditation and contemplation may also represent real, concrete acts of solidarity through the 'energy' they produce around them and in the world at large, Gandhi too used to claim there must exist an as yet inconceivable law governing the transformation of the world by means of spiritual forces. For him, a single individual or a small community could liberate an enormous spiritual energy, capable of changing society and the world. The Brazilian peasants of Alagamar were well aware of the part their asceticism played in the outcome of their struggle. In the quotation cited in the preceding chapter, they relied on material detachment, prayer and fasting, thus allowing themselves to become 'architects of history'. All over the world, grass-roots communities are becoming aware of this and beginning to understand that contemplatives, even in seclusion or cloistered, play an important role in world affairs. We will find this idea echoed in a later chapter devoted to Hinduism and development.

This being the case, believers no longer cede to the right the virtual monopoly of religion. As Joe Holland stresses, they will no longer allow the neo-conservatives of the American 'silent majority' nor the European funda-mentalists to present themselves as the official defenders of the Christian

West.[9] Just like the left, the right is the victim of Western spiritual and cultural impoverishment. A certain section of the right justly denounces the secularization of the Western world, but it does not see — or does not want to — that this is a product of industrial capitalism. The left has understood the injustices and aberrations of systems founded on the acquisition of profit, but without seeing — or unwilling to admit — that this is the result of materialistic rationalism. This blindness on both sides regarding the ideological spectre has led to the present impasse. The social vision of the left and the spiritual and moral preoccupations of the right are equally inadequate and distorted/ truncated. They are part of the crisis of Western modernity and must be superseded.

NGOs: struggle and contemplation

Christian NGOs in solidarity with the Third World have their own specific role to play in this undertaking. Charged during Lent with the task of sensitizing their countries' Christian communities to the need for international solidarity, they have in the notion of the 'Lenten Campaign' a powerful educational tool as long as it is not confined to the raising of funds or a call that limits itself to militant activism.

Christian tradition has always associated Lent with prayer and fasting. Many Christians who have lost touch with the deeper significance of fasting have relegated it to the level of an obsolete practice. Some have come to believe that only socio-political commitment matters. Most have replaced fasting with a financial donation. The success of the 'Lenten campaigns' launched by NGOs involved with the Third World, in collaboration with Catholic and Protestant churches, was based on this. And yet, does not fasting represent for the over-fed West an opportunity to experience both emptiness — that only the Essential can fill — and solidarity (if only temporarily) with the peoples of the Third World who suffer hunger?[10] Let us not forget that in the early church the time and money freed by the fast was actually shared out. Money has all the more significance when it is the fruit of fasting experienced as asceticism based on solidarity. The funding of projects made possible by this money cannot be reduced, in this case, to a simple exercise in accounting. As for the time gained when a meal is missed or cut short, it can be put to good use, either in militant action or in prayer. If one admits that the latter is a concrete act of solidarity, one is forced to conclude that Christian funding agencies might, without in any way diminishing their socio-political activism, go further in encouraging believers sensitive to the Third World to intensify their practice of prayer. Why not substitute for the feeling of being 'fed up to the back teeth' that people experience regarding boring religious duties, tainted with verbosity and introspection, the receptiveness and accessibility that inner silence encourages?

What has just been said regarding Christian NGOs applies equally to secular groups. They could introduce their followers to the meditation techniques of the East.

It will be objected that educating people towards a greater sense of interiority lies outside the province of NGOs working with the Third World. Yet this is far from certain. Contemplation is necessary for everyone, including activists. It is, I repeat, a concrete operational way of 'helping the Third World' and of influencing reality. Furthermore, anyone setting out on this path opens themself to their essential Being, and discovers a love and a strength that transcends them and can inspire them to redouble their efforts for a more just, humane world. NGOs are privileged to be in contact with cultural communities where extremely rich forms of contemplation exist. They could act as relay stations, spreading in the West the meditation techniques and various forms of contemplation practised in such communities. There are many Westerners for whom the discovery of Eastern religions was the road to a deepening of self that led them ultimately to live out with a hitherto unsuspected intensity their own Western spirituality, which they had allowed to atrophy.[11] By concretely helping their public to deepen their spirituality, Christian NGOs would also help combat the causes of the Western crisis, since the following aspects of prayer can offer particularly appropriate solutions to current Western poverty. Thus, the act of adoration is an interior predisposition by means of which human beings can free themselves from egocentrism to become aware of their profoundly relational and 'cosmotheandric' nature (the dimension that is at once cosmic, divine and human). The act of praise is a celebration by means of which one casts off the stress of demands to experience the joy of altruism and wonderment. Repentance is the awareness of the personal and collective limitations that prevent the coming of a world that would measure up to its creator, such limitation being largely due to a lack of embodied spirituality towards oneself, nature and society. Supplication is an act of solidarity that helps to propel the world on its path towards divinization.

Those who militate for a more just society are called upon to meditate as well. Mystical experience and prophetic action are both integral parts of biblical tradition. Non-Christians like Gandhi perfectly understood their complementary character. They are the daily bread of many poor communities in the Third World. NGOs are well placed to be witnesses to this and to encourage people to gain inspiration from it. Surely making the public more aware of the Third World would also mean inviting it to practise fasting and contemplation? If this point was generally accepted, Christian NGOs would have to offer their public adequate teaching facilities and introductory training sessions.[12] This would lead on to an introduction to the practical uses of certain 'tools': how to meditate, pointing out the immediate connection between action and contemplation, in other words, the political dimension of contemplation; and how to fast, showing how it can operate a profound personal and social transformation by means of the new hierarchy of needs it establishes, and stressing the deeper meaning of the money and time it makes available.

9. Intercultural Solidarity

Give yourself, let your hands open like eyes.

Paul Eluard

In the preliminary report compiled by a consortium of Western NGOs[1] on agricultural problems in Latin America, one South American researcher wrote the following reflections:

> How long will the West continue to believe itself involved in an act of charity towards the Third World? First, it was to 'civilize' it and the Third World was despoiled of its precious metals and its sovereignty, then it was to 'develop' it and the Third World was dispossessed of its raw materials, then to 'modernize' it and the Third World was drained of its financial reserves whilst the North got rid of its industrial surplus and got back three dollars for every dollar lent, and now it is to 'feed' it. What price will have to be paid this time for Western charity? Those in the majority in the Third World, the peasants, are already suffering the consequences. Enough of the hypocrisy! The countries of the South ask only for their freedom and respect for their sovereignty. The process of decolonization is not yet complete. Under such conditions, how can the North speak of co-operation, of aid . . . ?
>
> The peasants of the South are not asking for help or for financial charity, any more than they ask for aid in foodstuffs. They ask only that their environment cease to be destroyed, that they cease to be deprived of natural means of production (land, water) and that they be paid a fair price for their products. In short, they want to be allowed to get on with their work.

To this indictment must be added the fact that the peasants of the South want above all to be themselves, for what is involved here, apart from economic and political imperialism, is cultural imperialism.

Thus, many cultural communities in the Third World refuse to undertake just any development, to adopt just any form of progress. Such notions are even alien to some of them. Certain others would gladly do without them altogether. Furthermore, the term 'progress' has itself become more and more dubious. Associations engaged in solidarity with the Third World and, indeed, left-wing organizations in general, would do well to cross-examine themselves regarding this widely-used term according to which they themselves are seen as 'progressives' as opposed to convervatives. When one thinks of the type of progress diffused by capitalism, and that which neo-conservative co-operation agencies claim to bring, one notices that the latter blindly cling to the myth of progress and one can gain some idea of the outdated, inappropriate and ultimately 'conservative' aspect of the term, under whose banner the left-wing continues, however, to march.

But if NGOs have to 'de-mythologize' current notions of development and progress, this does not mean, as has already been said, that they should withdraw their solidarity and 'leave the Third World alone'. Western influences are omnipresent, with their positive qualities but also with all their destructive elements. There is, therefore, a great need for solidarity with the resistance movements and the work of social reconstruction currently being undertaken by Third World peoples. Traditional forms of solidarity, which must take the cultural element into account, must be coupled with new forms of solidarity that will sometimes perfect and strengthen, sometimes rectify or even lead to replacing the solidarity and partnership projects previously undertaken.

By solidarity defined and practised on the basis of the awareness of peoples' right to be different, is meant:

1. respect for a certain withdrawal into oneself, when this proves necessary to safeguard identity; this cultural withdrawal is to take its place within a wider framework of socio-economic and political strategies of 'delinking';
2. support for projects involving research into indigenous skills and values and the dissemination of the resulting information, for, to avoid unnecessarily damaging indigenous cultures, one has first to know them;
3. all concrete forms of solidarity of the North towards the South, including those undertaken through 'development projects', but always respecting cultural differences;
4. increasing the awareness of the Western public to the different forms of imperialism that hinder the well-being of the peoples of the Third World, and to the search for the cultural and spiritual values that the peoples of the South offer them;
5. the sharing, by the peoples of the North, of their own experience regarding alienation and cultural reistance, as a new kind of 'aid to the Third World'.

In short, it is a question of complementing and sometimes rectifying existing projects and solidarity actions by means of what could be called 'intercultural solidarity'.

Delinking

The process of re-personalization which the peoples of the Third World are forced to undertake must be allowed to take place without the interference of harmful external influences. The Burkinan historian and politician, Joseph

Ki-Zerbo, advocates a certain withdrawal: when the confrontation is that of scissors and paper, the victor is clear. It is best avoided.[2] This withdrawal phase will necessitate a great deal of patience on the part of those who are Westernized and, in some cases, will entail the risk of fanaticism. The risk is in inverse proportion to the extent of the preceding destructuration. Iran, as we have seen, offers a tragic example of this.

The withdrawal into oneself should last only the time necessary to rally round. Humanity has ensured its evolution and developed its civilizations by means of cultural exchange, in other words by the complex processes of inculturation and acculturation mentioned earlier. Let us take, in an area of more immediate interest to development, the example of Gandhi. The fact that it still has relevance today is not so much because he was able to call on 'pure' Oriental wisdom to solve social problems, but rather that he managed to combine within himself both East and West, drawing practical conclusions from this strong personal synthesis. Contacts between different cultural communities are beneficial but they must be established on a basis of relative equality, between partners sure of their own identity, knowing what they do and do not want. There are, therefore, cases where a relative isolation is called for in order to build self-confidence and encourage the free expression of cultural identity. One has only to think of certain tribal communities in Asia, of the American Indians, of certain countries, such as Iran, traumatized by brutal acculturation. In certain cases, therefore, support for any development project at all must be completely withheld. Programmes aimed at encouraging this aloofness *vis-à-vis* the outside world should perhaps receive aid.

If such a withdrawal deserves to be respected, it must not, on the other hand, lead to some innocent naivety. There may well exist internal mechanisms of domination that are favourable to the culture of those who dominate and detrimental to that of the dominated. A respect for cultural isolation would then amount to deferring to the misrepresentation of a community's culture by a privileged minority who are not its natural expression. We touch here on a crucial and complex problem that is faced by anyone seeking to understand a given culture and by every funding agency trying honestly to establish real intercultural solidarity. In fact, there is no such thing as culture in itself, there are only human communities that inherit and reproduce culture. Obviously, such communities are not always homogeneous. Most are steeped in class struggle or some kind of confrontation that is exacerbated by the monetarization of the economy, by the introduction of private property, wage-earning and foreign domination. It will, therefore, always be necessary to ask ourselves what culture we are speaking of, and if it is really that of the majority and not an elitist culture in the service of a dominant class. On the other hand, one must not see class conflict where it does not exist and project, yet again, Western classifications on to societies unlike our own. In one village, the chiefs and elders may have become despicable profiteers. In another, they may genuinely be the result of a harmonious social consensus. In the first case, a distinction has to be made between the culture of the dominators and that of the dominated. In the second case, such a distinction would have no meaning.

Local efforts of withdrawal are part of the larger problem with which this book is concerned, namely cultural identity and independence. But it should be pointed out that these efforts must be seen in a wider context. This context is what Roy Preiswerk and others have called delinking strategies.[3] These strategies encompass all aspects of the life of a community or country: they signify the need for partial disconnection on the economic, political and technological levels as well as in the field of culture. In fact, dealing with cultural independence while ignoring economic life, political conditions and the impact of technology would make little sense. What do these delinking strategies mean? They try to put an end to the domination imposed by international and local 'centres' on the 'peripheries'. They advocate 'self-based development': production based on the needs of the majority and the optimal use of local resources. They call on national economies to 'delink' from the international economic 'order'. The dominant economic theory, along with its official watchdogs, namely the International Monetary Fund and the World Bank, disseminate (and, if necessary, impose) the now sacrosanct law of 'relative advantages' according to which each country must try to break into the international market, due account being taken of the advantages at its disposal. The myth of export-led development leads not only to what the progressive Egyptian economist Samir Amin has called unequal exchange on the international level but also, on the domestic level, to an exchange that benefits the local bourgeoisie. This law is in direct opposition to the priority of local needs and, when strictly applied, has brought about sometimes criminal absurdities. Thus, famine-ridden Sudan exports bird seed to Europe and the undernourished Brazilian peasant is forced to grow soya beans to feed the cattle of rich countries.[4] The elites in power will plead the need for foreign currency as justification for such practices but the disastrous social reality of their countries contradicts their fine monetarist theories. The international division of labour advocated by the champions of the law of relative advantages is the antithesis of self-reliance, of endogenous, self-centred development, of the satisfaction of local needs and thus of independence. The 'delinking' theory is based on the necessity to refocus on local needs in the context of local resources.

This theory challenges strategies of 'open door' development and those based on the idea of an ever-increasing share of the international market. Obviously, this does not mean absolute autarchy, in other words total withdrawal from all commercial, financial and technological exchanges with the outside world, but rather a refocusing and the refusal to continue submitting the economy and politics to the imperatives of 'interdependence', 'co-development' and 'global village' illusions. Contacts with the outside world are not rejected a priori but subjected to the logic of a 'nationally based' economy with 'popular content'.[5] Obviously the problem of the combination of products for export and those for domestic use is extremely complex and cannot be resolved by ideological means or in a uniform way for every country. Macro-economic theories are not the subject of this book. They do, however, suggest that the relations of Third World countries ought to be based on selective delinking strategies. Likewise, local communities must invent means to guarantee themselves a relative economic and political autonomy when confronted by the centralizing, and often plundering, national state. We have cited the case of Brazilian peasants producing soya beans for export. But other Brazilian peasants, particularly those of the north-east, are forced to grow nothing but sugar cane whilst famine and malnutrition are rife in their area. This sugar cane serves the interests of the big local landowners and the industrial centres of southern Brazil. For the peasants of the north-east it represents an economic, social and ecological scourge. In such a case, internal delinking strategies within countries are also called for. The delinking theory is generally invoked at state level. But it must be applied by regional and local communities as much as by national bodies. Thus one sees emerging in Latin America parallel economic circuits linking grass-roots communities who buy each other's products. In this way these communities manage to by-pass official channels of commercialization, which usually function at their expense. The phenomenon is spreading, to the extent that there is now talk of the emergence of the *economia de los pobres* (the economy of the poor) as an alternative system that must be reckoned with.

The period of withdrawal with which we are concerned here applies to the cultural and ideological realms. But it is governed by the same logic as that of delinking strategies. It constitutes an essential component of this logic, for such strategies can define themselves only when they start from a specific cultural context.

A deeper understanding of indigenous cultures

The efforts of the Third World to repossess its values, institutions and technical skills must be respected and, if possible, encouraged. In this respect, certain significant projects are starting to be funded by some European and American NGOs, alive to such a need. We shall return to this point with examples.

This endeavour, especially when funded by public agencies, has sometimes remained the act of a social elite interested in its own culture. Now, certain elites, not necessarily acculturated, tend to ignore or look down on popular culture. They are in collusion with the economic and political powers-that-be in their country, which can influence their mentality. It is vital, therefore, for every cultural community, that this repossession also be accomplished by the masses; it must be a complementary fusion between popular know-how, creativity and interests, and (if they are not too corrupt and alien to their own people) those of elites, whether the latter be modern or traditional. Indigenous cultures must, therefore, be taken to mean concrete, present-day cultures of the people at the base of society. NGOs must not hesitate to fund research in this domain. They will, however, have to be careful to include everything currently existing within a people, amongst its masses, rural or urban. In principal, it is not a question of applying exclusively theoretical research. As much as possible, the aim will also be to make available, especially to grass-roots groups, the concepts, tools and facts that help, in the most concrete manner possible, to reaffirm threatened identities and, if necessary, to make innovations based on their own identity. This is why we speak of research–action. This is preferably practised in the form of participative research, where the cultural communities in question are allowed to control the conditions of the research and amend its methodology and content.

In certain cases, however, it is necessary to support more basic research projects, even when they are not of immediate use to a given community.[6] This is particularly true in the field of anthropology where it is necessary to maintain a certain distance towards immediate action. One touches here on one of the main flaws in the projects undertaken by many funding agencies caught up in a short-term, and ultimately disappointing, pragmatism.

Initiatives aimed at reanimating local knowledge and skills, or attempting to encourage cultural resistance and revival, therefore deserve close attention and concrete support from organizations involved in 'development aid'. Such a suggestion may seem out of place to those who have an essentially quantitative idea of the problems of the Third World, based on economic and material considerations, as well as to those whose analysis relies too heavily on the notion of class conflict and on infrastructure in the Marxist sense of the term. Some, concerned only with the urgent, neglect the important. Yet others, again obsessed by the urgency of the problems, end up tackling them only in the short term and sometimes sink into a brash, often harmful activism. One day, no doubt, they will realize how right Joseph Ki-Zerbo is, when he calls on those involved with the Third World not to destroy it culturally under the pretext of trying to nourish it physically.[7]

We touch here on an area that demands, on the part of NGOs and development and solidarity organizations, a considerable effort of self-criticism and imagination. Already, some NGOs are going in this direction. The examples quoted later are taken from lists of projects recently supported.

An extremely wide range of projects is, in fact, proposed to representatives of funding agencies who are aware of the cultural dimension of solidarity. It is to be hoped that one day the idea of intercultural solidarity will be given *carte blanche* in the world of NGOs. After all, this world has shown proof of a commendable open-mindedness and a critical faculty that many of the more bureaucratic governmental institutions might envy.

New criteria for development projects

The different forms of support given to research and dissemination of indigenous culture must be complemented by more classic forms of solidarity, including initiatives that could be called, for lack of a better term, projects and programmes of 'development'. Such projects must, however, pay more respect to cultural pluralism. A project funded by a Western agency is valid only to the extent that it is consistent with the over-all 'project' of the local community it is supposed to be helping.

There is no question of turning a blind eye to poverty and injustice when they bring about living conditions that are unacceptable to any culture. But the methods of supporting the fight against these evils will be free from cultural imperialism and become effective only if they correspond to the values of each people and are based on these peoples' own potential for creativity and struggle. NGOs must therefore continue their current solidarity work in Latin America. The defence of human rights in Salvador, support for Brazil's independent unions, the funding of certain social projects in Chile, are all important and tangibly help men and women to stand on their own feet. Common origins and values help solidarity and mutual comprehension between Western NGOs and the populations of Latin America. On the other hand, these NGOs must not lose sight of the fact that at least one-fifth of the inhabitants of the American continent is composed of non-European minorities and that even the so-called Latin populations are currently developing forms of struggle that may seem baffling.[8] The difficulties and disappointments of these same NGOs in various parts of Asia and, especially, of Africa, show an urgent need for a reappraisal of their activities. In the first place, priority ought to be given to schemes involving cultural reanimation and research such as those just mentioned. Such efforts will furnish new perspectives. At all events, we must hope so, since the alternative is to resign ourselves to either continuing along the same old lines or giving up altogether.

An important caveat must be raised here. Some people are currently speaking of 'basing development on tradition' and of considering culture as 'a tool for development'. Such an approach is well-meaning but ambiguous for it is an invitation to manipulation. By means of anthropological data, the values and rationality of other societies would be used to shape the members of these societies into the monocultural development mould. This would involve my making use of *someone else's* culture in order to include him or her more easily in *my* project.[9]

Finally, it is important to mention that solidarity is not limited to munificent financial aid supplied by relatively wealthy Westerners to projects of development, liberation and people's organiztion in the Third World. There are other, fundamental forms of solidarity that must not be overlooked. These are the ones that directly attack the virtually omnipresent mechanisms of economic exploitation and political oppression. Thus, the workers of a multinational based in Europe can, by strike action, express their support in forceful, concrete terms for the demands of workers of the same company's factories or plantations abroad. NGOs have instigated or encouraged the development of such actions. Although not the subject of this book, the latter remain of crucial importance. Whereas those who control political and economic power have at their disposal (ranging from telex to international conferences by way of missions, training programmes and the specialized financial press) all kinds of facilities to keep themselves informed and maintain their contacts abroad, the great mass of agricultural labourers and factory workers do not know each other, even when they work for the same 'boss' and are exploited by the same system. Fostering relations between trade unionists and grass-roots communities in the Third World and those in the West constitutes one of the most important tasks of NGOs who take seriously the need for solidarity amongst the masses when confronted by the power monopolized, too often for their exclusive profit, by the economic and political 'elites' of the world. There is one example that is worth quoting here, particularly since it also touches on the cultural problem. The Marcos government in the Philippines had decided to install on the ancestral land of the Kalinga ethnic group a hydro-electric dam that would mean the evacuation of the population and the submerging of their land.[10] For the Kalinga, such an uprooting meant virtual death: both spiritual, for the ancestral burial grounds would disappear beneath the water, and cultural, since their admirable, millennial terraced rice-fields would have to be abandoned for different, unknown land, and perhaps even physical, given that, decultured in this way, the Kalinga would probably be unable to ensure their survival. Contacts between activist Filipino groups and the Irish NGO, Trocaire, brought about an exemplary course of action. Since the dam was supposed to be built with the technical aid of the Irish National Electricity Company, the NGO in question organized trips and contacts for the company's unions, to allow their militants to meet the Kalinga communities and make their own judgement regarding the general system of oppression in the Philippines. The unions organized massive mobilization against the signing of the contract with the Philippines, and the company ended up (through the joint pressure of the workers, the press and governmental milieux themselves, alerted by the NGO in question) withdrawing from the project.

NGOs can and must act as pressure groups towards their respective governments as well as to the World Bank, the European Community and major UNO organizations and multinational corporations. It is an important, concrete and often very effective way of putting their solidarity into practice. Careful monitoring of Belgium's policy towards Marshal Mobutu's regime, of the French government's attitude in the Pacific and toward the government of Niger, of British policy regarding apartheid and sanctions on South Africa, of the EEC's attitude towards Brazil's gigantic Carajas project in the Amazon, which it is helping to fund, all this must be the responsibility of NGOs. They possess, thanks to their contacts with the local populations and political milieux (at times in power, at times in opposition), information that their own governments and other interested official bodies often lack, as do those who prefer to ignore it. This unique and valuable knowledge must be put to good use, through public campaigns, political lobbying, and so on.

Beyond 'development pornography'

NGOs take pains to inform their respective publics about the harsh reality of the Third World. Some have no hesitation, to shock minds and open wallets, in showing photographs of starving children, stomachs swollen, skeletal hands outstretched towards generous donors. Inside the Third World, such highly offensive images arouse strong reactions. Some people speak of *development pornography*, the reduction of human suffering to an object used to make money. Luckily, most NGOs have long since given up this style of presentation. And the most clear-headed of them have denounced the economic mechanisms that cause and explain (at least to a certain degree) the situation of the countries of the South. They have acted on the famous quote attributed to Che Guevara (albeit complementing it with hard facts and concrete evidence):

'What are you doing to stamp out hunger in the world?'

'I fight against imperialism!'

These NGOs know, and try to make the general public understand, that certain basic needs, especially regarding foodstuffs, could be satisfied locally in virtually any part of the world, providing neither their land nor their produce be snatched from the peasants and misappropriated for the purpose of consumption by local elites or for export. The starving peoples are quite capable of feeding themselves. But they must be allowed to do so. Local governments, big international organizations and private national and multinational companies, however, create obstacles that prevent people satisfying their hunger. The big question then is not 'how to feed the world?' but 'how do these obstacles come about?' Since they often stem from Western countries, to challenge imperialism is a concrete contribution to the solution of the problem of hunger. Neither must we forget the very real imperialism of the so-called socialist countries of the northern hemisphere. This is all the more deserving of denunciation now that it is no longer possible to harbour any illusions about the policy of Eastern countries towards the Third World. Ethiopia is a good example of imperialism and incompetence on the part of its 'socialist' friends from the North.

But, economic and political mechanisms apart, the cultural aspect must be tackled more frequently and more effectively in any development education campaign geared to a Western public. In NGOs' publications aimed at backing up their campaigns, this theme is still treated as a poor relation, often in a final paragraph, when 'the real message' has already been written. A deeper analysis and a constantly up-dated understanding of cultural imperialism must be reached. Such imperialism must become one of the major themes of NGOs, yet without creating unnecessary boundaries between the economic, the political and the cultural.

Finally, international solidarity is fundamentally reciprocal. In their education campaigns therefore, Western NGOs ought not only to highlight increasingly the damage caused by cultural imperialism, but also to invite their publics to look to Third World cultural communities for a spiritual message of which the West has such need and of which several examples have been given earlier. Interesting experiments already exist in this domain in the form of 'exposure programmes', visits by small groups of three or four Europeans, accompanied by a local person, to villages or districts located in some Asian, African or Latin American country. More than just 'alternative' tourism, these visits are 'immersion programmes' in a different world. One eats and sleeps like the indigenous inhabitants. One experiences with them the ups and downs of their daily life. One can feel the weight of the oppression they undergo, but also the vitality of their struggles, the wisdom of their culture and the depth of their religious experience.[11]

Of course, it is not necessary to go abroad to have an intercultural dialogue and drink at other sources. There are plenty of Third World nationals in the West! Rather than embitter their lives with endless, more or less racist harassment, one could invite them to 'the table of giving and receiving' and benefit from their presence to practise an intercultural dialogue that is rewarding to both partners. Some people are already doing this. There is also, through books and films, dance and physical disciplines (martial arts, yoga, Zen, for example) countless ways of getting to know other cultures. Should not NGOs think about facilitating these processes of learning and intercultural apprenticeship? Some already organize visits by their partners from the Third World to local communities and groups in Europe. They are invited for this purpose for a few weeks.[12]

A touch of modesty for Western donors

Westerners have much to learn from the peoples of the South in terms of basic values and the arts of life. Nonetheless, their own contribution is also a considerable one, by no means confined to the realms of science, technology and institutional and juridical organization. They can, however, usefully share their knowledge of such matters, as long as they make public the harmful effects of certain highly praised scientific discoveries. But the West also has an original contribution to make in human terms provided it is stamped with modesty. Firstly, because the West, too, is clearly the custodian of a rich cultural and spiritual heritage. But also because it has already experienced the effects on people of pan-economic and pan-technological civilization. Its experience in this matter is greater than that of most other peoples. Westerners currently involved in trying to inject new life and vigour into their own threatened culture must share their successes and difficulties in this domain. In matters of cultural resistance therefore, Westerners also have the right to their say! Another part of this book deals with the crisis in the West and the seeds of revival to be found in certain alternative experiments in the areas of science, economy, politics, culture and religion. Westerners have a duty to inform friends and partners in the Third World of such things, for the latter might be able to learn certain lessons from it and would certainly gain much encouragement. The prospect of global changes seems a little less distant when the West ceases to appear as a monolithic block, self-confident and all-conquering. The men and women of this world in crisis need to reveal their vulnerability and need. In this domain too, NGOs can facilitate contacts and help raise levels of awareness.

Part Three:
A New Generation of Projects

Introduction

The present work has tried to demonstrate that a specifically Western cultural model has been the basis for most of the operations undertaken so far under the generic term of development. Most official projects are permeated by this model and convey to the remotest corners of the planet Western values, institutions and objects. A great many NGO projects also contribute to this process. To a certain extent this is no doubt inevitable. Even projects that are genuinely inspired by indigenous cultures contain elements of Western origin. In itself the wish to control time (by a plan extending over two, three or five years) and space (the rural development of an area), and the way of envisaging changes in mentality (by conscientization) and structures (by political or trade union action) are — for better or worse — decidedly Western ways. It is one more reason for claiming that solidarity which is truly respectful of indigenous vitality must not limit itself to the funding of projects. The latter retain their importance, as long as they do not impose or uselessly suggest foreign concepts or deny the identity and skills of the people they are addressing. The seduction exercised by foreign funding can turn to rape, and NGOs must constantly be aware of this and exercise great caution.

It is time to give some illustrations of the general propositions made in the preceding chapter regarding projects. Here are some concrete examples taken, with a few exceptions, from the lists of projects supported or currently in preparation by Broederlijk Delen, a Belgian Christian NGO. It is relatively typical of those Western funding agencies who try, through their solidarity campaigns and certain partnership relations, to support groups actively involved in development seen as socio-economic liberation and human growth. Organizations such as Christian Aid, CAFOD, OXFAM or War on Want in England, SCIAF in Scotland, Trocaire in Ireland, Development and Peace in Canada, *Brot für die Welt* Misereor in the Federal Republic of Germany, Danchurchaid in Denmark, ACR in Australia, *Vastenactie*, ICCO, *Novibor* or CEBEMO in the Netherlands, *Entraide et Fraternité* or CNCD/NCOS in Belgium, *Oikos* in Portugal, the American Friends Service Committee, the Mennonite Central Committee, the Ford Foundation in the USA, or such international bodies as the Lutheran World Federation sometimes support the same projects, sometimes very similar projects. Many of them are members of international co-ordinating bodies such as CICARWS (a unit within the World

Council of Churches in Geneva), CIDSE (a working group of Catholic Lenten Campaign), or ICDA (a non-denominational international co-ordination based, like CIDSE, in Brussels). But each NGO preserves its own character.

We will look in turn at projects for research and information gathering (Participatory observation) and then at more traditional and directly operational development projects (Safeguard and adapt). Lastly, we shall suggest certain projects, imaginary this time, that illustrate the difficulty of the question (From solidarity to perplexity) and formulate certain concrete propositions (Getting off the beaten track).

10. Research and Participatory Observation

When it comes to *research projects*, a distinction must be made. The reality of culture is so enormous that it may be useful to distinguish between the symbolic aspects (myths, legends, religion, representations, language, customs, law, and so on) and the more practical aspects (agricultural skills, trades, medicine, pharmacopoeia, architecture, for example).

Here then are a dozen examples of projects dealing with *cultural research, information and diffusion* and the subject of *practical skills, techniques and knowledge*.

1. At Ho-Chi-Minhville, the 'Centre for Paediatric Research' of the Childrens Hospital has undertaken research in the villages in order to collect from traditional healers their ancestral knowledge in matters of natural medicine. It has also called upon ancient medical literature such as treatises dating from the fourteenth century. It now produces in its laboratory, on an experimental basis, a series of ointments, creams, powders and syrups based on medicinal plant extracts. These allow it, on the one hand, to treat undernourished children in the hospital and, on the other hand, to circulate throughout Vietnam the concrete, conclusive results of their research and experiments. During the war, South Vietnam had been inundated with American pharmaceutical products and doctors who received their training during this period still have difficulty in acknowledging the effectiveness of traditional medicine, which they see as 'old wives' remedies'. The theory of Yin and Yang, the five elements (earth, water, fire, metal and wood), the study of the five movements and the six energies, the influence of evolution and seasonal energy on the human body, the principal and secondary meridians, the longitudinal and transversal vessels, the six perverse energies and the seven passions, the eight diagnostic rules (yin/yang – interior/exterior – cold/hot – emptiness/fullness), the eight therapeutic rules (sudatorification, vomification, purgation, regularization, tonification and dispersion), all these millennial ideas seem at once complicated and unscientific to doctors used to the medicine taught in medical schools. But, the official policy of socialist Vietnam recommends the co-ordination of Eastern and Western medicines and particularly encourages the preparation of plant-based medicines. This is due to the fact that they cost infinitely less than producing, and especially of

importing with hard cash, synthetic pharmaceutical products.[1]

2. *Terres et vie*, a Belgian NGO run by African and European agronomists, aims to create, publish and circulate works on African 'agricultural systems', in language understandable to literate peasants, students in secondary schools and technical colleges, as well as rural extension workers. These works illustrate and explain on the one hand peasant skills and on the other, what Western agricultural science has to offer in the way of useful, appropriate and appropriable knowledge. The means of production typical of peasant and rural mentalities are not well enough known, despite the performances they sometimes achieve in particularly difficult economic, institutional and political contexts. Since the prevailing ideology favours urban, foreign life-styles, it is important to circulate in rural areas books valorizing peasant life and the economic possibilities it can offer. Works have been devoted to agricultural techniques in the strict sense, to the 'water trades' practised by the artisans of the Sahel (micro-dams, manual wells and boreholes, reservoirs), to indigenous vegetables and condiments and the market garden sector (in this case, founded on the techniques of the women of the Cameroons). Written in French, these works are translated into African languages and are widely read.

3. In the same spirit, IRED (*Innovation et réseaux pour le développement*) runs an international network of local Third World groups and companies who exchange experience and information on endogenous techniques and methods. In particular, it encourages trips by peasants to neighbouring countries or overseas. In this way, East African peasants and rural tradesmen can become familiar with indigenous techniques in India. Its bulletin and the meetings it organizes circulate all kinds of useful information in the fields of agriculture, food production, land management (soil conservation, compost, irrigation), the manufacture of tools and the building of equipment such as silos, wells, ovens, basic load-carriers, fires, for example. As for GRET (*Groupe de recherche et d'échanges technologiques*), it is concerned with revalorizing traditional techniques and skills in the building trade, suggesting alternatives for dwellings less dependent on imported materials and technology and for optimizing local production factors. The English Intermediate Technology Development Group (ITDG) is playing a pioneering role in this domain just as E. F. Schumacher, (the author of *Small is Beautiful; Economics as if People Mattered*) was himself a pioneer and a man of great vision.

4. In the Philippines during Marcos' reign, the poor districts of the big towns were overrun by the army, but the enormous shanty-towns hummed with life and creativity. Guitarists, singers, dancers and street theatre groups infused the prevailing atmosphere of suffering and menace with a sense of vitality and joy, and that natural distinction that poverty can confer when it is experienced in dignity and confidence. A local NGO, 'Creative Dramatics of Cagayan de Oro City', has undertaken the study and continuation of all this activity in the aforementioned town. It has since tried to circulate these musical and dramatic skills to other, less militant districts. The project is backed up by a

conscientization programme aimed at stimulating artistic creations that depict the causes of suffering and arouse active commitment. It also intends to set up theatrical workshops for those who want training, and hopes in this way to develop a popular culture capable of mobilizing people against the violation of human rights and in favour of justice and democracy.

5. In the Cameroons, there is talk of creating a centre whose outlook is perhaps a portent of a real transformation in terms of grass-roots development. This centre, the *Service d'études et d'animation pour le développement* (with such people as Jean-Marc Ela and Achille Mbembe), would bring to light new forms of self-management and experiments in alternative development. The founders, African intellectuals in close contact with villagers, say they are aware that, all over West Africa, a whole host of small indigenous initiatives are seeing the light of day. NGOs, churches and their missions no longer have the monopoly of 'micro-projects', claim these intellectuals, and those that are thriving today usually do so without external funding. They are self-financing, responding directly to emergencies, yet remain unknown to traditional NGOs. People from town and country, intellectuals, civil servants, peasants, white-collar workers, among others, come together to build a road, a school, a clinic, install a water supply or take charge of 'social services' (mutual aid funds for families, to be allocated in cases of need, for funerals, celebrations, for example). These new types of project seem imbued with a different understanding of development, the role of foreign NGOs, the state, and particularly of the utilization of local resources and a new relationship between culture and development. The centre envisaged by these committed intellectuals would be a place where reflection would be possible, the lack of reflection and information being, they claim, 'one of the factors that currently explains the drying up of creativity in Africa'. This centre would collect the words and actions scattered throughout the villages and working-class districts of the big towns. As the expression of a genuine popular associative movement, these activities could be studied and compared in the centre, leading to the creation of a pool of information on indigenous vitality and creativity.

6. At Belém, the capital of North Brazil, 60% of the inhabitants live in *baixadas*, huts perched on stilts above the flooded, unhealthy land. These often poverty-stricken districts are full of life and, almost everywhere, tenants' associations have been formed for the communal organization of certain services (crèches, adult education, drainage of marshlands), and to put forward united demands for public transport, waste disposal, health services and, above all, ownership rights to the land occupied for years by these people but from which they could be expelled at a moment's notice. The neighbourhood committees of Belém finally resorted to the formation of an extremely dynamic association, the CBB or *Comissão dos bairros de Belém* (Belém Districts' Commission). At the last annual general meeting of the CBB, there were more than 750 delegates representing over 45 neighbourhood committees. The CBB does not confine itself to the short-term and obviously crucial goals that have just been enumerated. It is also involved in a cultural campaign aimed at

revalorizing the habits, ways and customs, techniques and artistic expressions of the slum dwellers. It believes that popular culture constitutes a unique breeding ground for resistance to the dominant ideology propagated by the classes who share the economic and political power. The project aims to revalorize popular culture as an instrument of social change. This is how the CBB presents this idea to those attending its annual general meeting:

> We, the exploited class, are making more use, in our everyday lives, of the practices, customs, beliefs and values of our own class. This is what we call Popular Culture. We are aware that we are all descendants of the black race that is indigenous to these parts. Almost all of us come from the interior of the country where the notorious mass culture (radio, television, cinema) is not yet so powerful, although, nowadays, we cannot claim that our culture still has the same influence on us that it had on our grandparents. Today, many of us prefer to dance 'rock 'n roll' rather than the *carimbo*, value a pharmaceutical medicine more than a traditional remedy and are often even ashamed to say where we come from, to talk of African dances, blessing, herbs and prayers. And when we think about how our grandparents used to live and how we live now, we can see that our habits and customs have changed a lot . . . . Now we have to go forward and believe in ourselves. We must retrieve our culture and demonstrate our wisdom . . . . These popular practices have always been resisted, as is the case with Afro-Brazilian cults . . . . The ruling class does everything in its power not to lose control of the ways people think and act, because this is very important if it is to continue giving the orders, amassing profits and exploiting the working class. And the rulers will not easily give this up: television, the press, radio and cinema all belong to them and transmit what they want, what interests them. So it is hard for the working class to bring back the many popular practices (Patron Saint Days, *carimbo*, quadrille, *batuque*, the use of medicinal plants, etc.) that have been manipulated by the ruling class, although, as we have already seen, the essential substance of these practices can also lead to resistance and constitutes for the people an attempt to avoid totally losing its way of being, its culture . . . . In the popular movement's struggle in Belém, several of these practices have been used, as in the case of the serpent that appears in our marches as a method of denunciation, and also a way of enlivening demonstrations; — our national dishes: *maniocoba, tacara, vatapa, caruru, acai, pato no tucupi*, etc . . . ; our dances: *samba, frevo, carimbo, siria*, carnival, the bird dance, quadrille, *Bumba-meu-boi, Lundum*, etc. . . . ; — our beliefs: processions, blessings, the Evil Eye, black magic, etc. . . . ; — our instruments: *bumbo, surdo, atabaque, birimbau* . . . ; — folk medicine: plants, drinks, *unga*, etc. . . .

The CBB project's attitude is that the participatory research to be achieved in the aforementioned spheres must be used for popular conscientization, and for the organization of the marginalized masses in their struggle against the structures that oppress them. Popular culture here constitutes a springboard for resistance and popular mobilization.

Still in the domain of *cultural research, information and diffusion*, let us now look at *projects that deal with the symbolic aspect of cultures*. Here is a second set of examples.

1. One project, and an exceptional one at that, consists of distributing *Buddhist literature in the pagodas of Kampuchea*. In this way, Bonzes who survived the Khmer Rouge bloodbath hope, in the absence of trips to Thailand or Sri Lanka, to re-establish contact with the international Buddhist community and rebuild libraries destroyed under the Pol Pot regime. This project helps to strengthen the capacity for cultural resistance and the spiritual vitality of the Khmer people who have survived this ordeal, but whose identity remains threatened. This is a quite exemplary project since, the crucial physical rescue of an entire people apart, it helps restore its heritage, allowing it to thrive and regain its strength by 'drinking at its own sources'. For this particular project, the socialist regime of Phnom Penh has certainly done nothing to facilitate contact between NGOs and Buddhist monks, but if it does not support it (and does not see it as 'development') neither does it oppose it.[2]

2. The *Conselho indigenista missionario* (CIMI) is the main organ of defence, in terms of their identity, of the Indian populations inhabiting Brazilian territory. Victims of a lingering genocide (there are now less than 250,000 of them) and of the ethnocide imposed on them by policies encouraging integration into Brazilian society, these ethnic groups are unable to carry alone all the weight of the struggle to resist economic, political and cultural oppression. In this respect, their situation differs from that of the Indians of Andean countries (Peru, Bolivia, Ecuador, among others). The latter are able to resist by their own means since they constitute a considerable proportion of the population of their respective countries. The CIMI therefore tries to raise the level of awareness among the rest of the Brazilian population to the problems of marginalized ethnic groups. In particular, it tries to redress the ethnocentric and paternalistic, not to say racist nature of the conceptions spread and justified by school text books, through publishing alternative text books and making educational films which they distribute at annual campaigns, called 'The Week of the Indian', in universities, schools and to the general public. The works of the CIMI highlight the profound wisdom of Indian culture and encourages other Brazilians to gain inspiration from it. In a Brazil totally ignorant of everything to do with its first inhabitants, these works disseminate their conception of divinity, nature and society. The CIMI prefers to ask NGOs for financial help for this sort of enterprise rather than for all kinds of 'development' projects. Indian ethnic groups have become aware they will owe their survival to a certain retreat into what is called in Brazil *refugio cultural*, in other words retreat into its own lands, in the geographic and cultural sense of the term. While on the subject of the revalorization of the non-white cultures that have gone into the making of Brazilian society and that contribute to its richness, mention should be made of the action-cum-research undertaken by ISER (*Instituto de estudos da religiao*) of Rio de Janeiro based on the concept of society that underpins the different religions practised by

Brazil's black community, and on the sort of social commitment to which they inspire or inhibit their followers. Brazil's Blacks are becoming increasingly aware of their contribution to their country's history and of the subtle, but all too real racial discrimination to which they are subjected. The 'black consciousness movement' (one result of which is the organization *Uniâo e consçienca negra*) is concerned to instil in Blacks the sense of their dignity and identity, and to demand for them a role in national life in keeping with their importance. It also tries to encourage in the black community religious practices that lead to liberation. In the United States and South Africa, the churches and religious movements that have sprung up from the black population have been working towards this end. In Brazil however, such a phenomenon is not immediately apparent. Groups of Blacks have therefore asked for participatory research to be set up on the subject. Research will be done on the Catholic and Protestant churches, as well as on Afro-Brazilian religions such as *Macumba*, *Umbanda*, *Candomble*, for example. As far as Catholicism is concerned, research will mainly be concerned with the role of the 'black brotherhoods' where various kinds of worship and healing rites are practised, and on the apparently restricted space accorded to the spirituality and theology of Blacks in basic Christian communities and their liberation theology.

3. An information exchange programme has been launched by basic Christian communities in South Africa to familiarize anti-apartheid activists with the thoughts, spirituality and popular culture of politically committed Christians in Salvador, Nicaragua and Peru. Visits and lengthy stays in working-class communities in these countries are organized by the movement 'Theology Exchange Programme'. The aim is to help South Africans define their own theology and religious practice within the growing atmosphere of civil war prevailing in their country and increase exchanges on these religious questions between Third World countries.

4. The Haitian peoples' information bulletin, *Bon Nouvel*, is a conscientization and educational tool that could easily be seen as a relatively classic project. It is, however, also an important project for the diffusion of popular culture. In fact, under Duvalier, this periodical was one of the rare means of diffusing the Creole language. The latter, along with everything else authentically Haitian and popular, was an object of contempt for the authorities. Creole has always been considered a patois or, worse still, as a non-language. The inferior status accorded to Creole was a way of attacking the people themselves. In this way they were refused the right to speak, and denied all social and political impact. Yet this language represents one of the few things the people possess in their own right and from which they can draw pride, self-confidence and resistance to the collective oppression that crushes them. Let us also mention, in an entirely different political context, the Tanzanian review *Kiongozi*, a national people's information broadsheet written in Swahili rather than English, which is the only one of its kind to reach the most remote villages.

5. When Zimbabwe became independent, the Ministry of Justice undertook the revalorization of the indigenous law of the African population. This policy, happily in direct contrast with those of other African states, gave birth to a project of *research and professional training in customary law* for magistrates courts. Although an exclusively governmental enterprise, this project has been considered so important by Broederlijk Delen that they have given it their support. The partnership relationship that NGOs look for in all projects — and which is precisely what many government projects lack — existed here, for bonds of solidarity were born, if not between magistrates and this NGO, at least between it and the Minister, who had been a protagonist of the liberation struggle and, in that capacity, a privileged partner: at that time he represented the Patriotic Front and promoted educational projects funded by the NGO in question. This NGO thought it reasonable to suppose he had retained from this period the desire to remain close to the people, although experiments in this field had often been disappointing in other countries which have gained independence through a liberation movement. This programme of practical instruction in indigenous law gives the Zimbabwean court system a quality of accessibility which it had profoundly lacked under Ian Smith's white supremacist regime.

6. PROCAR or *Programa de cultura e capacitacion rural* is a Panamanian NGO particularly involved in what it calls a programme of 'cultural recuperation', with the collaboration and for the benefit of the Guaymi people. A group of twenty 'cultural promoters' of this Indian ethnic group has been trained to collect its stories and legends, and to form an indigenous theatrical company who stage traditional material. PROCAR also publishes a traditional epic tale, the writing of which — from the collection of the material down to the illustrations, and including the actual writing — was undertaken by the Guaymi themselves. This project has been accompanied by the creation of a marketing co-operative, local projects of communal production and conscientization efforts for the economic, political and cultural defence of this 80,000 strong Indian people.

There are exceptional cases where a project of cultural research–information–diffusion is supported by an NGO without the participation of those concerned, and without the research being directly linked to activities taking place at grass-roots level. These are projects of 'pure' research, often attached to academic institutions. Nonetheless, such projects deserve to be supported by NGOs. Here are three examples.

1. The Quawasquar are an Indian ethnic group living in the extreme south of Chile, whose livelihood is fishing. There are now only fifty of them, ravaged by disease and alcohol, apparently threatened by imminent physical extinction. A team of anthropologists has taken an interest in them, producing a serious ethnological monograph informing the outside world of the cruel alternative confronting these Indians: either to resign themselves to physical death, or to

integrate completely and without delay into the world of the whites and
endure a cultural death. These researches might eventually lead to an
intermediate solution. Whatever the conclusions of the research, the level of
apathy to which the Quawasquar have been reduced scarcely allows them to
take an active part in the proceedings. We are, therefore, not dealing here with
operational research nor with participatory research, and even less with a
development project, but rather with a piece of classic academic research,
albeit concerned with the survival of a human group.

2. African theologians belonging to the extremely dynamic EATWOT
(Ecumenical Association of Third World Theologians) are anxious to
inculturate Christianity and are particularly interested in the *Orthodox
Churches of Ethiopia and Egypt*. The history of these churches goes back to the
very first centuries of our era. They therefore offer very old and authentic
examples of inculturation. A project of research and communication aims to
get better acquainted with them in order to help strip African churches of their
excessively Western character. It may be that Orthodoxy is better suited to
African tradition than the secularized forms imported from Western Europe.
The role of the body in prayer, dance and song, the proximity of the elements
(the veneration and kissing of icons, the importance of incense, of the
symbolism of fire, water, and so on) and the sense of mystery in Ethiopian and
Egyptian liturgies makes African Orthodoxy a field rich in teachings and ideas.
Orthodox theology also seems closer to the African religious spirit, notably in
the importance accorded to Genesis, to the sacred character of nature and the
cosmos, as well as the divine energies that dwell within them. And finally, its
theological and pastoral discourses are founded less on reason than on spiritual
experience, as was the case for the first Church Fathers whose universe was,
furthermore, nearer to the world of contemporary African peasants than that
of modern Western theological faculties. Remaining with the important subject
of inculturation of Christianity in Black Africa, one project consists of
supporting the publication of the *Bulletin of African Theology*, an organ of
Zaire's Faculty of Theology, the only independent university institution within
the regime. This Faculty is a centre of creativity in matters of theology,
philosophy and liturgy seen as expressions of Bantu culture and as a way for
Africans to affirm, not a fake 'authenticity', as Marshal Mobutu had tried to
impose, but a means of regaining their inner identity in the light of 'the Christ,
both brother and universal ancestor'.

3. The Asia Partnership for Human Development (APHD) undertakes
studies and *research on the social function of Asian cultures and religions*. APHD
wants to discover what 'development', 'progress', 'liberation', 'oppression',
'social struggle', and so forth, mean to people who are Hindu, Buddhist,
Muslim or Confucianist, or who respond to shamanist or 'animist' religions.
What positive or negative role do these religions play in peoples' resistance to
exploitation and deculturation? What is a 'better life' seen from the perspective
of an Indian farmer, a Malay fisherman or a Taiwanese factory worker? A
working group within APHD has undertaken to study both sacred texts and

current religious practices. It hopes in this way to understand the original inspiration of these religions, and the many transformations or adulterations they have undergone under the influences both of the elites in power and the people at the base. This work party has the responsibility of formulating suggestions for evaluating and amending the analyses of APHD and its member agencies and their criteria for selecting projects. The discussions on Hinduism and development reprinted in this book are a small contribution to this work. A similar research programme takes place in the Asian Cultural Forum on Development (ACFOD), a centre based in Bangkok involved in research and reflection on the great Asian religions and culture and their relationship to current social problems. A meeting place between Buddhists, Muslims, Hindus, Christians, Marxists and free-thinkers, all anxious that the East should have a future of its own that is nourished by its rich past, ACFOD brings an important contribution to NGOs.

All of these projects of cultural research, information and diffusion are of the utmost importance and deserve priority. All NGOs should make a point of having some to their credit and would do well to make them known to their constituencies. The latter must give up wanting to fund only 'concrete' and supposedly more useful projects. They ought to accord a less reticent welcome to this relatively new generation of projects. The Western public must be encouraged to become aware of the character, at once unrealistic and ethnocentric of certain remarks sometimes expressed regarding projects that are less immediately operational, such as 'it's too theoretical', 'it's not profitable', 'we must feed and educate first' and 'produce more' or 'raise peoples' income: that's what it is all about!'. Such remarks may sound pragmatic but are in actual fact sadly counter-productive.

11.   Safeguard and Adapt

The most important projects, certainly in numerical terms, if not qualitatively, are still those most readily associated with the role of funding agencies and NGOs concerned with development. Development projects aimed at action in the field must, as has been said, draw as much as possible on all that is positive in indigenous skills and values. Some examples of this have already been given within the framework of our survey of projects of cultural research–information–diffusion: some research led to concrete action. Let us now look at the area of development projects proper.

There are projects aimed at safeguarding existing cultural elements while breathing new life into them. Other projects attempt to adapt certain elements in order to make them evolve. The latter therefore overtly envisage change. In fact, one must sometimes be able to change in order to remain faithful to one's true identity.

To illustrate the type of development project that aims to *conserve aspects of the indigenous culture in order to revive it*, here are three examples.

1. It would be safe to say that, under the reign of Haile Selassie, the Ethiopian Orthodox Church was hardly very active in the area of development. Its social activities were largely confined to schools run by monasteries. Those people in Ethiopia concerned with development and justice found the Church singularly lethargic. Its high clergy were in league with the imperial regime and enjoyed the same exorbitant privileges as the rich landowners. The revolution of 1974 and the land reform that followed were to capsize the life of this ancient Church. Dispossessed of much of its land, its 850 monasteries and 20,000 parishes had to find new means of subsistence. Through the joint influence of the new Patriarch installed by the revolutionary state, and the World Council of Churches whose headquarters in Geneva maintained some links with the more cosmopolitan of the Ethiopian bishops, the Orthodox Church of Ethiopia slowly awakened to the idea of development. Today, there is a department dealing with this question. The Development and Interchurch Aid Department (DICAD) is responsible for raising the awareness of the 250,000 orthodox priests and monks and, through them, of some twenty million followers. In reality, the priests and monks of the lower clergy have always been very close to the peasants. Many cultivate the land themselves and are involved in other

typically rural activities. Micro-projects are now being conceived and submitted for foreign funding that aim in particular to develop old techniques in which the monasteries have always excelled. Particularly important in this respect is *apiculture*. Training courses are organized by parish priests and deacons, new types of hive are introduced and today the honey flows more abundantly than ever. It is an extremely nutritious food substance and perfectly adapted to the northern part of the country (what was once Abyssinia, with its ancient Coptic tradition) where the land is overpopulated and drought-stricken. Its production takes up very little space and needs no water. Of course, one must not project the European experience on to Africa. Nonetheless, the support given by medieval monasteries to the spiritual and technical culture of Europe's populations might find its equivalent in Abyssinia where the Church and its monasteries play a vital role in the lives of the people.

2. In the depths of the most remote regions of north-east Brazil, in the state of Pernambuco, agricultural workers have managed to get themselves elected to the management of the *rural trade unions of the municipalities of the Amaraji region*, which, for decades, had been in the hands of shady, *arriviste* leaders who were trade unionists only in name. The political and financial powers of Brasilia and São Paulo had committed the region to the intensive monoculture of sugar cane, whose juice is used in the manufacture of a fuel to replace imported petrol. The result of this was the often violent eviction of peasants from their lands, their proletarianization on the plantations and in the towns, and the disruption of ecological harmony. The integration of this region into a system of production slanted towards the national market has brought about a brutal break with the traditional structures of family and community life. The outcome of this is an increasing dependence, due in particular to the reduction, or even the disappearance, of subsistence farming, and the impossibility of controlling production costs. The choice of crops and technology and the marketing system being out of the hands of agricultural workers, their union has undertaken, on top of its normal union duties and the defence of human rights, a project of market-gardening and health care based on indigenous knowledge and skills. It involves, on the one hand, encouraging a healthy, balanced diet, using locally grown food. It is a known fact that the outcome of famine, endemic to this enormous north-east area, is a generalized phenomenon of anaemia and *nanism* (dwarfism). The project aims to revalorize the skills of the peasants of the north-east, by developing their potential for self-subsistence. Moreover, it intends to encourage the cultivation of medicinal plants well-known in these regions since time immemorial, in order to supply small, community pharmacies with a stock of assorted herbs produced locally. Health officers are specially trained to be completely familiar with the cultivation, collection, drying and preparation of these medicines whose origins are firmly established in the secular culture of this people so rich in tradition. So rich also in various other contributions, for it is the melting-pot of Brazil, where the blood and the culture of Indians, Portugese and Africans are mixed.

3. The Sri Lankan movement *Sarvodaya shramadana* has already been mentioned. The origins of this peoples' movement offer a good example of the interest of projects aimed at conserving a tradition in order to revive it. Its founder, Buddhist and former high-school teacher A. T. Ariyaratne, has taken as his goal the economic and social regeneration of the Singhalese rural world, by reconstructing the pre-colonial village community imbued with spiritual values such as the *shramadana* (from *shrama*, time, work and *danaya*, sharing, exchange). Ariyaratne believes the culture of Singhalese Buddhists is symbolized by the temple, a veritable centre of development, and the water tank, indispensable for the irrigation of the rice fields. Having imitated the Western model, the country has lost the moral and technical basis of its economy. He has, therefore, launched a broad movement of *Sarvodaya*, which means the awakening of the consciousness of everyone, thus of an entire village. With no discrimination between caste or class, the aim is to make villagers aware that, working and consulting together to solve their problems, they can achieve Buddhist ideals. From the outset one thing was necessary: the repairing of water tanks, whose water conveys fertility, self-reliance and dignity. The movement was amazingly successful and now affects more than 3,000 villages. It claims to be gradually evolving into a national socio-political force capable of offering the country an original alternative based on Buddhist principles. The movement and its leader, considered to have become authoritarian, are currently under criticism. For some, *Sarvodaya* is based on a conservative idealism. Its ideology, denying the existence of class struggle in their pre-colonial society, is seen as an attempt to bar the way to Maoism, which was briefly very popular with the country's youth. In reality, it is claimed, *Sarvodaya* benefits the existing regime and village leaders. Much of the communal work undertaken is actually for the benefit of the latter. If, for example, a communal work-party is organized to improve a road, its real purpose is in fact the utilization of the labour of the poorest people (the leaders supervising and, at most, serving food and drinks), for the benefit of the well-off (they own the trucks and cars that will use the road). For the rest of the people, there is the possibility of spin-offs (the delivery of merchandise, for example, a communal work party is organized to improve a road, its real Buddhist socialism perfectly suited to the Singhalese and their needs. (But what about the Hindu Tamils of Central and North Sri Lanka?) *Sarvodaya shramadana* and its founder have perhaps been the victims of their own success. NGOs most open to ideas of 'alternative development' and indigenous cultural values have found in this movement an exemplary prototype. They have blindly granted it enormous sums of money, which means it now relies on foreign help for 80 per cent of its budget and finds itself in glaring contradiction with its stated aims of self-reliance. This Buddhist movement in which Schumacher was involved is no longer either 'small' nor altogether 'beautiful'. This experiment contains a serious warning. NGOs, whatever the extent of their openness and understanding, can swamp, in a flood of dollars, popular movements that would normally be expected to spread like bush fires. Another lesson to be learned from this example: the ideas expressed in this book have to

be handled with as much caution as determination, and an idealization of the past must never be allowed to replace lending an attentive ear to the oppressed in their current, concrete situations. We shall return to this at the end of the chapter, for it is an essential point.

The three preceding projects were designed to safeguard indigenous cultural elements (the production of honey, the use of medicinal herbs, the repair of water tanks) while trying to breathe new life into them. Other projects aim for more deliberate change. They attempt to *adapt certain existing cultural elements in order to stimulate socio-cultural and technical change*. The degree of change introduced by such projects may vary, as the three following examples show.

1. The project *Lijjat* was launched by a Gandhian organization linked to the Indian *Sarvodaya* movement. This organization, the *Shri Mahila griha udyog lijjat papad*, came about through the initiative of some women of the overcrowded district of Girgaum, in the outskirts of Bombay. Their extremely low standard of life along with their isolation in the struggle for survival, led these women to join forces in making the famous *popadum*, the flat bread that accompanies Indian meals. They prepared the dough, rolled it out and baked it together, no longer each alone in her kitchen. To increase production and package the *popadums* for sale, a small working capital was needed. Not having a penny between them, the women got a loan. They choose to be temporarily in debt rather than ask for outside help for, faithful to Gandhi's ideas, they wanted their project to be self-reliant from the outset. Their desire for autonomy and self-development was so great that they even turned down the offers of financial help that were made to them. (This project therefore does not come from an NGO file.) Today, the organization is thriving, the loans having been paid back and groups of women formed, first in several other Bombay districts then in other towns. Today there are more than twenty groups and almost 6,000 members. Thanks to its substantial profits, it now possesses its own premises, transport, and so on. Thus, a traditional cooking technique has been successfully adapted to become a productive business concern. Yet the ideals of *sarvodaya* have apparently been scrupulously observed. The women themselves own the company assets and are responsible for its management. Decisions, particularly those relating to the way profits are divided and shared out, are taken by consensus. All members must be in agreement, no decision being enforced by a majority vote. Men are not eligible for membership to the association, but may be consulted or employed as drivers, accountants, and such like. The association is based on three concepts that are seen as fundamental: business sense, the sense of familyhood and that of devotion. Thus, a foreign cultural element — efficient, pragmatic management and organizing for maximum profit — is combined with traditional indigenous values. By a sense of familyhood, the association means the atmosphere of mutual caring and help that must exist between fellow-workers, as if they were one big family. The sense of devotion is explicitly religious and implies that *Lijjat* cannot be reduced to its purely commercial aspect. It is more than just a

means of livelihood; each kitchen–workshop in which the *popadums* are prepared and packed is 'a temple, a church, a mosque, a *gurudwara*, a place of prayer where one offers up one's energies not for the profit of the individual, but for the profit of all. In this business, work is a cult'. To join this association, the women must sign an agreement which, in translation, states:

I solemnly swear to abide by the principles of our association of *sarvodaya*, the *Shri Mahila griha udyog lijjat papad*.

1. I shall undertake all jobs within the assocation as sacred tasks and accept all payment with joy as though it was a consecrated offering (*prassadam*); . . .

4. I shall consider the association as the temple of God, and conduct myself accordingly; . . .

6. I shall abide by the broadest conception of communal property. Nobody counts how many pieces of bread they eat at the family table. Likewise, I shall not be calculating when it comes to dividing tasks and duties, in other words I shall not try to see what extra gain I might acquire but rather I shall try to make sure others do not receive less than me; . . .

10. If I should leave the association I shall relinquish all rights regarding it, for the temple of God and the divinity that dwells with it cannot be broken up and divided into pieces. . . .

So here is an experiment in cultural adaptation leading to profound change, if not of traditional religious values, at least of attitudes towards such things as money, the economy, urban life and decision-making. The methods of preparing and baking the bread have also been adapted to suit the virtually industrial scale of production, and are thus transformed. Is *Lijjat* a brilliant example of dynamic and innovative cultural adaptation? Or is it all perhaps a bit too good to be true? Probably. For in reality, *Lijjat*'s principles and decision-taking rules are apparently not always perfectly respected. Furthermore, men play a part in the association, which contradicts the basic ground rule. These defects are hardly surprising. They are part of life and no doubt the fate of all successes. And *Lijjat* is certainly a success story.

2. *Nomadep* is the name of an NGO set up in Ethiopia whose French organizers are dedicated to defending the cultural integrity and *economic interests of the Afar* herdsmen, nomads who inhabit the Ogaden desert. Their project, however, goes further than *Lijjat* in terms of cultural change. NOMADEP aims to adapt not only the behaviour but also the Afar's traditional way of life to external conditions.

The Afar with whom the project is concerned occupy the semi-arid zone traversed by the River Awash. They survive there by animal husbandry, the best way of turning this hostile environment to account. The seasonal movement of the herdsmen and their livestock allows the grazing lands to regenerate. It ensures that water supplies and grass do not get used up, and thus prevents the region becoming desert. The Afar survive almost entirely on their dairy produce. They estimate that a nuclear family (an average of 6.4 people) needs for its survival a herd of one hundred goats, forty head of cattle and ten dromedaries. Until very recently, vegetables were virtually unknown to them. It is difficult for the Ethiopian leaders, who usually belong to the peasant world with its attachment to its farms and fields, to understand and accept that the pastoral, nomadic way of life is in fact an economic system in its own right that has, over the centuries, maintained the difficult ecological balance of vast territories. The Ethiopian authorities, have, therefore, generally shown incomprehension if not contempt for the Afar and their economic system. Already, in the time of the Empire, their region was officially decreed 'vacant land' which allowed the state to set up any development project whatever there. Thus, the River Awash basin is seen as future agricultural land. Huge sections of it have already been allocated to large state farms and to the resettlement projects for which the present government has a fondness. Year after year, official development projects have led to the reduction of grazing territory, leading in turn to 'over-grazing' and the start of a process of 'desertification'. The NOMADEP project is trying to make the planners in Addis Ababa see that, without the Afar and their cattle, the entire region, on both sides of the river, would be utterly unusable and unproductive.

To the pressures caused by a socio-centric mentality have recently been added others, stemming from the demographic growth brought about by the introduction of health services and, above all, those resulting from the climate itself. The drought that affected the entire Sahel belt in 1984–85 brought with it terrible famine. Grass became scarce, wells dried up. People and cattle perished. Today, the Afar realize that their ancestral way of life is under threat, and that to survive they must evolve. Whilst local authorities, almost all unfamiliar with the Afar, see the future only in terms of permanent settlements and agricultural development, NOMADEP is trying to support the Afar in seeking solutions more in keeping with their own culture. Following a lengthy process of discussion and decision-making among the survivors of the famine, many Afar clans have ended up accepting certain agricultural pursuits to supplement their stock-breeding. The foodstuff they produce should enable them to accumulate reserves to bridge the gap that precedes each rainy season. This work should also supply extra fodder for animals returning from the traditional seasonal migration. Thus, for the first time, the Afar have begun to work the land. In 1985, with the project's help, groups of nomads sowed around 400 acres of corn on the banks of the Awash. With their traditional 'milk pails', they watered their crops. They have become familiar with ploughs and the possibilities of animal draught. With the shepherds' help, NOMADEP has even invented a harness for dromedaries.

All this of course constitutes a revolution in many respects, but one that seems to be appreciated by the Afar. When one thinks that basically they undertook the first clearing and tilling of the desert with nothing but knives, hoes and oryx/animal horns, it is easy to imagine the interest that ploughs and draught animals could inspire. Similar innovations elsewhere, however, often encounter opposition that is both strong and complex, as a project to be dealt with later shows (the introduction of animal draught among Bantu peasants living around Masuika, Zaire).

In the case under question, why does the transformation appear to have succeeded? In the first place, it does not affect the foundations of the Afar way of life: farming is only a supplementary activity to cattle-breeding. Innovations are more readily adopted when they do not threaten traditional means of survival or upset the existing economic culture. Moreover, NOMADEP took care that the Afar were closely involved in the planning and implementing of the project. The land was marked off according to their own ideas and it was left to each clan to share out the plots between the different families. Lastly, NOMADEP came to the attention of a group of Muslim religious leaders who now take an active part in the project, thus giving it their seal of approval. The Afar, who are Muslim, thus feel supported in their evolution by their most traditional religious and social leaders.

The project is currently spreading. If it represents a hope, it is also certain to encounter many difficulties such as land questions, division of labour, social and economic organization. In the meantime, the introduction of farming offers another advantage that is far from negligible: that of having the Ethiopian authorities finally recognize the Afar territory. For where the land is under cultivation, the desert steppe is no longer considered vacant and undeveloped. The law accords local powers of authority to peasant organizations. Even if they do not work the land with the same attitude and mentality as peasants in other regions of Ethiopia, the Afar have nonetheless become officially recognized as part of the rural scene. This recognition by the state has become indispensable to their survival.

The NOMADEP project is a good illustration of what was said previously on the need to change in order to retain one's basic identity. NOMADEP has brought about a great change in the Afar's life. But their fundamental cultural traits, whether on the symbolic level (the relationship with the desert, cattle, Islam, for example) or the technical (stock-breeding, seasonal cattle migration, and so on) have not been negated. Change has been grafted on to elements that already existed. Obviously, it is too early to draw definitive conclusions from the NOMADEP project. Its evolution, however, encourages the hope that it will manage to respond to new challenges and introduce the necessary changes without the destruction of the Afar's values or way of life.

3. Finally, let us look at a project that openly aims to bring about change. It has undertaken to introduce to the Bantu peasants of Masuika in Kasai (Zaire) nothing less radical than *animal draught*. Its aim was to help the peasants to remain farmers by allowing them to obtain bigger harvests from their land. It was, therefore, a question of adapting existing life-styles and agricultural techniques in order to effectuate profound technical and economic changes. Socio-cultural change was also part of this project's objectives since it planned to overturn the traditional division of tasks between men and women within the family. Let us look at the results.

From the outset, in 1972, the project's main objective has been the promotion of the plough and animal draught (using oxen). This had already been introduced during the colonial period but had gradually been abandoned.

The peasants had turned once more to the traditional hoe. It was hoped not only to increase agricultural production but also, by introducing carts, to lighten the heavy work done by women (carrying wood, water, and so forth). From the outset, the organizers (three Europeans and two Zaireans) had felt that upgrading the status of peasant women and improving farming techniques would need a change in mentality and that 'in most cases, secular customs have been a hindrance in such matters'. Although claiming they wanted to introduce harnessed animals into farming 'while safeguarding the authentic richness of Bantu tradition',[1] the organizers basically concentrated on the technical aspects of the project rather than the cultural (the breeding of oxen; stabling; constructing carts, ploughs, harrows and weeding machines; the substitution of intensive, perennial crops using organic manure for itinerant farming using the traditional system of fallow land, among others).

At the outset, the technical innovations had attracted around fifty peasants who set about applying the new farming system. After several years of striving, however, the project has made little progress. Only five peasants (out of seventy) obtained better harvests than those using traditional farming methods. The others had lost interest and, according to the report, one gets the impression that the extension workers (called *encadreurs*! — literally, picture-framers!) had grown impatient: 'Some peasants were dismissed, that is, we confiscated their cattle and equipment. After having disposed of these idle peasants, we are now left with thirty-nine peasants'. But the team was worried about the reasons for the failure and decided to look at the cultural dimension. A survey was done amongst the peasants and their respective clans 'in order to reach a better understanding of the mechanisms that come into play and encourage or prevent peasant men and women from assimilating the new techniques we want to introduce'.[2] A year later, the team had to bow to the evidence. The technical aspects of the project, which it had studied with care and competence, 'are only a small part of the overall problem and it is above all socio-economic factors that prevent vigorous development and the definitive acceptance of animal draught in the region.' The team came up with a new strategy. 'We would like, through discussion with the peasant men and women, to evolve a new model of organization, better suited to the local situation, not only from the technical but also from the social and organizational points of view. These forms of organization would have to take into account the division of tasks between men and women, as well as family relationships'.[3]

Thus, it took the project ten years to discover the fundamental role socio-cultural structures play in people's economic life and in their relationship to technology and profit. The organizers of the project readily admitted their mistake and, in 1983, made the following assessment, the frankness and clarity of which are to be commended:

From the beginning of the project in 1972, one of the governing ideas was that the technical improvements brought about by the project should also be agreeable to women, since, traditionally, they perform the greater part of agricultural work. For this reason, one of the conditions of acceptance for new candidates was that the peasant's wife take part in the training session. The aim was to encourage men and women to work together with the oxen and together create the new-style farm.

Another decision that was taken at the project's inception concerned the ways and customs operating within the clan. Candidates were recommended to pay the requested down payment with their own money and to avoid turning to members of their family for financial aid. They were advised to use the increased profit from their land to pay for installation costs. The basic idea was the following: if members of his clan helped the peasant pay his debts, the members of the family would consider this aid as an investment, and there would then be a danger that they would demand a share of the profits (without having contributed to production). To avoid endless discussions, the project team decided at the time to approach each peasant individually and it prudently avoided broaching the delicate subject of family ties. It was also implicitly agreed that, at the proper moment, the peasant's son would succeed his father and thus guarantee the farm's continued existence.

During recent years, we have become more and more aware that the above strategy did not correspond to the reality before us. Although all peasants had attended the training sessions accompanied by their wives (to facilitate matters we had pretended to be unaware that most of the peasants were polygamous), the majority of the latter are reluctant to help their husbands. . . . The women who do not help their husbands in the work concerning the oxen all had their own fields, which they cultivated with hoes in the traditional way. The few women (three) who did help their husbands in the setting-up of the new agricultural system belonged, without exception, to the same clan as their husbands. Owing to the fact that the women refused to help their husbands . . . and that the members of the clan have never been involved in our peasants' activities, the latter are isolated from their peers and the lack of labour-force becomes a major problem. An investigation into this subject was very revealing. When a woman marries, she leaves her own family group to join that of her husband (patrilocality). There, she is granted the use of a piece of land and may dispose of part of what she produces as she wishes. Normally the surplus she produces in this way goes to her original family group. In theory, the woman marries under a regime of separation of property. . . . In such a system, it becomes clear why the woman has no incentive to work a piece of land jointly with her husband. In fact, the animals and equipment belong to her husband. If the woman is to work with her husband's tools on land belonging to him, she becomes [reduced to] cheap labour since the income from this land goes to her husband. In this way, the woman loses her independence, along with the few privileges she had!

In the area concerning us, the matrilineal system (in which family membership is determined through the mother's lineage) predominates. The result is that the uncles on the mother's side play a major role in social life. The whole dowry system, for example, works through the mediation of these uncles. Likewise, the sharing out of wealth or inheritances is settled by the maternal uncles. We must not forget that our peasant, possessing a capital of around 15,000 zaires, lives inside this social system. He, too has obligations towards his family group whose same uncles are the principal representatives. If he does not show enough solidarity with the group, confining himself to working exclusively with his own animals for his own advancement, this may lead to reprisals on the part of the uncles. . . . Seen from this point of view, it also becomes clear why the peasant's children have no incentive to help their father on the farm. In fact, the son knows that in the event of his father's death, he will not inherit the equipment, since the animals and equipment will be divided amongst his father's uncles and nephews.

Another reality that we must take into consideration is the fact that, in a society where family relations play an important role, the individual never takes a decision without consulting the members of the group. Now, introducing the use of animal draught and changing a time-honoured cultural system is no small matter![4]

Here then is clear proof that a development project that ignores the reality of local culture is doomed to failure.

The astonishing and significant thing is that, while the project only ever managed to interest 7% of peasants on a long-term basis in Masuika itself, animal draught spread spontaneously in Mbuji-Mayi and other areas 200 km away from the project. Yet this region is not included in the project's scheme. It is trainees sent to Masuika by very go-ahead indigenous co-operatives who brought back the necessary information and succeeded back home in what was largely a failure at Masuika. These co-operatives came into being spontaneously and most of them grew out of African sects such as Kimbanguisme and the indigenous Christian movement, Jamaa.

This phenomenon must apparently be attributed to the fact that, at Masuika, the peasant found himself isolated in an individual undertaking limited to the family in the European sense of the word. For such an undertaking he received no mutual aid, whereas at Mbuji-Mayi animal draught was adopted spontaneously by an existing community structure united by membership to a common religious group.

In the most recent account of the project available, one finds that '90 per cent of the difficulties encountered are of socio-cultural nature'! This text goes on to say that it would be useless to continue with the individualistic approach at Masuika, that the local peasants will have to devise their own approach, where family ties would serve as a stimulus rather than a hindrance to development and where the peasant woman would benefit from animal draught without losing her independence. It is only on this condition, concludes the document, that it will be possible to claim that 'animal draught has genuinely contributed to their liberation'.

The project and its unexpected developments at Mbuji-Mayi illustrate many of the observations made elsewhere in the present book:

— Culture is a coherent whole encompassing economics, technology and societal matters; it is illusory, even destructive, to try to change one of its aspects while ignoring the whole. At Masuika, socio-cultural resistance paralysed the desired technological change.

— The development that many projects try to introduce often contains preconceptions and behaviour patterns of Western origin that are inconsistent with the value system and the social organization of the people for whom it is intended. The individualistic approach adopted at Masuika doomed it to failure whilst the communal values prevailing at Mbuji-Mayi allowed the spontaneous adoption of a foreign technical contribution of an extremely innovative nature.

— When a project tries to introduce preconceptions and behaviour that are not consistent with the indigenous culture, it risks not only failure and hence a waste of the time and money invested, but, more serious still, the demoralization of the target population. It is likely that the peasants of Masuika feel devalued by the negative qualities attributed to them by the organizers. The self-image of those who were dismissed from the project is unlikely to have been improved, and this must surely have contributed to the process of deculturation already in progress. According to the organizers, the failure of the project also brought about great disappointment and a particularly distressing feeling, namely the loss of the prestige conferred by the possession of an ox.

— Indigenous cultures are weakened but resist being totally crushed. One form of cultural resistance is the inertia and non-participation opposed to a project seen as a threatening innovation or, at the very least, whose validity has yet to be proved. At Masuika, this inertia succeeded in opening the eyes of the project's organizers to the cultural dimension of development.

— Cultural changes are frequent in many societies, and they can take place under good conditions and have positive results when there is a complex, reciprocal process of inculturation and acculturation. At Mbuji-Mayi the foreign input of the Masuika project was adapted to suit the local culture, which in turn adapted to the innovation.

— The fact that the introduction of animal draught was successful amongst groups who felt united by an indigenous religious movement illustrates the important role played by spiritual matters in development.

— The African peasant is not a *homo economicus*; he makes decisions according to a precise rationality that encompasses elements other than the cost–profit relationship (but not necessarily excluding the latter). If the relational and communal dimensions are safeguarded and, if his security is not threatened, if other elements such as his value system are not brought into question, if, furthermore, the advantages to be gained from an innovation have been well established, the African peasant is perfectly willing to change his techniques and increase his productivity. The failure and success described above perfectly illustrate this assertion.

12.   From Solidarity to Perplexity

As a result of this general survey of several projects, it seems possible to gain some idea of the attitude of NGOs and other development organizations. The degree of open-mindedness shown by such organizations towards cultural realities other than their own ranges from complete ethnocentric blindness and monocultural inflexibility to the most nebulous, even dubious, cultural relativism. To demonstrate this range, and the growing complexity of the questions facing NGOs, here are some concrete cases, more or less imaginary, corresponding to each level of receptiveness.

At the rock-bottom level of intercultural open-mindedness, an NGO can confine itself to supporting groups whose philosophical *inspiration*, *analysis and concept of society* as well as whose *projects* themselves, correspond closely to its own mental world. This would apply to Western NGOs who send abroad their own technicians and volunteers and fund only projects devised by themselves. The deculturation and destruction that can be caused by such a form of generosity have been sufficiently dealt with in this book not to need repeating. It would also apply to European NGOs belonging to a very specific philosophic or political obedience who fund abroad only local groups, including trade unions, who belong to the same political movement as themselves, share their beliefs, have a social programme in keeping with these beliefs and launch projects that fit in with them. Let us take the hypothetical case of an NGO attached to an American Protestant, fundamentalist movement with close government connections, that supports near La Paz a technical college run by its own missionaries, all foreign to the country. This college gives excellent technical training and produces the best turners, fitters and welders in the country, introducing them to the world of capitalist productivism and advanced industrial technology. As workers, these young people contribute to the smooth running of factories set up in their country without, however, having received the slightest training in politics or trade union matters that might encourage them to defend their rights. Here, the beliefs of this conservative NGO are perfectly reflected in the inspiration, the social vision and the goals of the project. This project would be justly criticized by 'progressive' NGOs. But let us imagine another case, one that is no less unreal than the first. These same socially committed NGOs are supporting in La Paz a training centre for political analysis and action. The rigidly Marxist presuppositions of the training leave little space for preoccupations other than those of economic exploitation and class struggle. But, the majority of the local population is Indian. They remain close to their traditions and are as concerned about the loss of their cultural identity as their oppressive economic situation. The training they receive therefore does not entirely meet their needs. In absolute terms, these two programmes should not be placed on the same footing, but from the cultural perspective we have adopted, it is quite clear that we are dealing here with projects of extremely Western inspiration, based on a monocultural conception, one right-wing, the other left-wing.

Other NGOs, or these same ones, may display greater openness and support many other groups that do not belong to the same church or political movement as themselves. On the contrary, these NGOs are interested in partners of diverse religions or philosophic tendencies, such as a Kimbanguist group in Zaire or a Buddhist co-operative in Thailand. Our NGOs, however, insist that their partners, whatever their *inspiration* (political affiliation or religious motivation), share their *analysis and concept of society* and organize *projects* that conform to the criteria and priorities they have established. This is probably the case with most NGO projects today. Their declared intention is to support anyone, without religious, partisan or national discrimination, as long as the goals and methods of attaining them have been agreed. This seems perfectly reasonable. But it must be pointed out that, in practice if not in theory, this attitude principally fosters relations with Western, or very Westernized organizers. Thus, the militants and 'developers' supported in Asia are generally very Westernized, whether they be Marxists, Christians, or promoters of capitalist modernization. In India, it is estimated that barely 15 per cent of those who organize projects supported by Western Catholic NGOs are Hindu. Non-religious NGOs are apparently little better in this respect. In black Africa, half of the projects supported are still instigated and run by whites and this, twenty-five years after the era of decolonization.[1]

One can imagine an NGO with an even greater intercultural open-mindedness. This consists of accepting that the inspiration and the vision of society can be different, as long as the *projects* are in keeping with its own criteria. Think of the projects proposed by the Singhalese movement *Sarvodaya shramadana* dealt with earlier. Inspired by the Buddhist sense of compassion, aiming not at capitalist or socialist modernization but at the restoration of a society based on *dharma*, this movement nonetheless proposes projects that are classic in the eyes of Western NGOs, such as the building of multi-purpose community centres or the repairing of water tanks. Other, more concrete development projects referred to earlier also fit into this category.

Let us take one step further into this intercultural adventure and imagine a Western NGO trying to exist in genuine partnership with every person or organization, whatever the inspiration, social analysis, vision of society or even the projects themselves. Let us take as an example a Muslim group, trying to safeguard a society based on Qur'anic values and advocating Islamic schools for the poor. This is, in fact, what the *Pesantren* movement is doing in Indonesia. Think, too, of the Gandhian movement in India, which is motivated by Hindu values, in particular, respect for cows (symbol of fertility) which has an anti-productivist social ideal, and which is engaged in a struggle opposing the modernization of a slaughter-house. Supporting such projects poses ever more complex problems. Is a Western NGO ready to accept Islam as a basis for children's education? Perhaps, but it will probably want to know beforehand the social implications of such teaching, particularly in matters concerning the status of women and the application of corporal punishment (amputating the hand of a convicted thief). In the case of the Gandhian group, our NGO would be rather unenthusiastic about the project, unless it were explained to them that it is not only a question of 'sacred' cows but of opposing the buying and slaughtering of cattle whose meat is destined for export whereas in the villages they serve as draught animals, furnish milk and skins, and contribute to endogenous development.

Let us push our problematic questioning further still. Here are three purely hypothetical examples, ranged in an order that tries to demonstrate the extremes to which the revindication of peoples' right to cultural difference can lead. A Hindu development organization, located in Benares, proposes the funding of an education centre that, while respecting the rights of the untouchables, is nonetheless based on the duties, obligations, rights and positions associated with the caste system. A 'Bantu consciousness movement', straddling Zaire and several other neighbouring states, combats the regimes in power there, and asks for political and financial aid from NGOs and movements involved with the Third World for their struggle aiming at total self-withdrawal. Their campaign sees the only solution in a return to traditional peasant culture, the rejection of states, retreat from the market economy, the rejection of Christianity and Islam, and the discontinuing of all common action with other opposition groups. A medical project proposes the construction in the Sahel of a well-equipped clinic where excision and infibulation operations can be carried out on young girls under hygienic conditions. How would any NGO that was approached respond to these three cases? Would it fund something that fostered the caste system? Would it agree to fund a policy of withdrawal, a policy, what is more, handicapped by a basic contradiction in that it is dependent on outside aid? In any case, the NGO would have to bear in mind that, not long ago in Cambodia, a policy of total, radical withdrawal, based on the desire to revalorize peasant culture and free the people from all oppression, led to a nightmare. Would they agree to fund a clinic where customs as repugnant as the sexual mutilations in question are performed?

So there we have a general picture of the various attitudes possible *vis-à-vis* potential partners in the Third World. The cases may be hypothetical, but the range they cover is very real. The aim here is not to decide what is the correct attitude, but to underline the importance of cultural differences, the inevitable difficulty of choice resulting from these, and the fact that decisions taken are the result of criteria that are not always as obvious, objective, technical or 'progressive' as one may think. The position, more or less conscious, of the funding agencies concerned regarding the cultural question will influence decisions at least as much as the conscious, explicit criteria regarding politics, economics and technology.

The ambition of this book was defined in the introduction: to examine the present state of affairs regarding culture and development and formulate some certainties and a great many questions. If it can cast some doubt on what hitherto seemed perfectly evident, it will have attained its goal. The author will thus have been allowed to share the state of perplexity in which he sometimes finds himself and, who knows, to rouse the reader to enter into a dialogue so that, together, we can see more clearly.

One thing is certain, awareness of cultural differences has often been sadly lacking. Happily, such awareness now seems to be increasing. NGOs have a role as pioneers in this field.

13.   Getting Off the Beaten Track

In conclusion, here are three concrete suggestions addressed to Western NGOs and, by way of example, a suggestion on how to improve one of the tools of their trade.

Funding agencies, whatever the extent of their openness to the outside world, tend to support familiar partners who, by force of circumstances, become regular 'clients'. In black Africa, these clients are still too often Whites; missionaries or volunteers. Generally speaking, development agencies usually support groups whose conceptions are very close to their own. Without abandoning such relations when they are advantageous, is not there a need to diversify contacts, to get off the beaten track? One must beware of getting into a rut and of the mild but nonetheless real self-satisfaction that, even in this field, tends to set in. When they are visiting a country, NGO project officers tend to stick to a familiar circuit of projects, partners and development organizations. But what sometimes happens is that the latter involuntarily act as a screen to the indigenous grass-roots communities. This is particularly true in Black Africa, or in such countries as Haiti, India or the Philippines where Whites are numerous and very active in the field. Whatever the quality of such projects (and the respect they may even show for local cultures) one must finally recognize that it is the indigenous population who will have to take over the reins of their society. The role of Whites (or of indigenous but Westernized 'developers') can be only temporary and more and more unobtrusive. Many missionaries, volunteers and experts are already convinced of this. It is, therefore, essential that NGO project officers visiting Third World countries make an effort to meet indigenous communities, even if it means cutting short their usual round of mission posts and development centres that are in the hands of Whites or Westernized agents. Active research, sometimes difficult and lengthy, will be necessary to help them discover more indigenous partners and to inform those of them who are unaware of it, that in the West there exist NGOs ready to enter into partnership relations that respect local identities, methods and rhythms. In the conditions of oppression under which some of them live, such an offer of human solidarity, sometimes political, sometimes financial, could be very welcome.

As a second suggestion, agencies must use every possible means to facilitate contact between Third World communities and thus help to ensure that the ever-increasing North–South. contacts are complemented by South–South contacts. There is a huge and extremely fruitful area to be explored and encouraged here. NGOs can help promote such contacts by means of the funds at their disposal and also by putting partners from the same, or even different continents into contact. Two examples of South–South contacts have already been mentioned (Theology Exchange Programme and IRED). Certain NGOs have become aware of the role of go-between they are being called upon to play. They regularly offer their own premises as a place where overseas partners can meet each other.[1] This is excellent, but perhaps it will be necessary to stop thinking of themselves as the 'centre' where others meet, and facilitate such meetings in the Third World itself.

A third suggestion, or reminder rather, for many NGOs are in fact careful on this point: beware of over-funding! All agencies should bear in mind experiences like those of *Shramadana sarvodaya* in Sri Lanka, whose success abroad seems to have compromised its popular, radical character. Sharing the points of view defended in this book does not mean one should automatically pour money into those who promote or put them into practice abroad. Excellent initiatives can be killed at birth by granting them excessive funding. Money is a source of power and causes jealousy, misappropriation of funds and conflict. It leads to the use of expensive techniques and equipment from abroad. It encourages technocratic, authoritarian behaviour and damages existing communal instincts. NGOs must not fall into the bad habits of official development organizations who too often allow themselves to be seduced by what seems grand and impressive, by what is verifiable and, if possible, quantifiable (a building, a piece of equipment, etc.). Modest projects are often preferable even if, for a certain public, they seem less attractive and convincing. They are more easily mastered by marginalized, grass-roots communities, whether they be peasant, urban or ethnic. It is these communities that must remain the primary recipients of NGO solidarity. As NGOs well know, the best way to avoid falling into cultural elitism is, above all, to have solidarity with those at the bottom of society. Indeed, being attentive to indigenous cultures should have nothing to do with political conservatism. The most oppressed and exploited groups are also usually those who are voiceless and most in need of solidarity in the cultural domain. The cost of their projects is usually quite modest.

One basic change in NGOs' tools could be the adoption of analytical grids for projects and questionnaires less exclusively directed towards politics, socio-economics and technology. By way of an example, here is the questionnaire sent out by one NGO to applicants for funding.[2] This sort of questionnaire has a slightly off-putting bureaucratic quality and is scarcely in the NGO style. They are only sent to applicants who have been unable to formulate their project themselves. They are, in any case, only suggested as memory joggers, so that the main aspects of the projects are not omitted in the description. But whether the form is sent or not, the questions contained in it must be clarified by funding agencies so that a decision to support can be taken in full knowledge of the case. It is to this end that the text of this questionnaire is reproduced here, with the addition, in italics, of questions that would have to be added to it to take into account the issues raised in this book.

Vade-mecum for the Presentation of a Project

(In *italics*: questions to add to take more account of the cultural 'dimension' of development.)

1. General information
a) Name of the project or object of the request.
b) The person in charge, name, address; *does (or did) the applicant, originator or person in charge of the project belong to the same cultural community or the same religion as the people concerned by the project?*
c) Country, region, etc.

2. Circumstances, and stated aims
a) Give a short description of the region, i.e. from the social, economic, health, political, dietary, religious, cultural, etc. points of view.
b) What about the local people?: their felt needs, mentality, openness to progress, customs, cultural or other conditioning, favourable or unfavourable to genuine human development (this in relationship to the stated aims of the project).
In your opinion, what are the most important characteristics of the culture and religion of the community or persons concerned?
N.B. By culture is meant ALL aspects of life: practical skills, technical knowledge, food and clothing customs, religion, mentality, values, language, symbols, socio-political and economic behaviour, indigenous methods of taking decisions and exercising power, productive activities and economic relations, etc.
c) Aim of the project, progress or change sought in the way of life of the persons and groups, in their attitude to the existing situation. Change sought in existing socio-economic structures.
Does this aim spring from local culture as described above? Did the analysis of the situation, the chosen strategy and the concrete methods to be undertaken grow out of the local people, and are they in keeping with their cultural values and traditional skills? If not, say why.

3. Realization of project
a) Concrete action envisaged to achieve the above aims.
b) Origins of the project: whose idea was it? What individuals have participated in the preparation and how?
c) What part of the project has already been implemented?
d) What do you now hope to achieve and how? (stages, methods, etc.)
e) Those responsible: who are in charge and what are their qualifications? Who is legally responsible? Who is in charge of the financial

management? Who will own the assets acquired by means of the requested subsidy?

f) Local resources used: people — voluntary work — premises — financial contributions — subsidies or loans obtained within the country . . . *abilities and knowledge (e.g. in agriculture, health and family-planning, education, passenger and goods transport), indigenous know-how (e.g. in the manufacture of tools, in building).*

g) To whom, and how, will the project be useful, directly and indirectly? How many people are involved? What effects will it have on the local situation?

Does the project help to strengthen the cultural identity of the people concerned? If it introduces foreign values, attitudes, objects or techniques, explain why this is necessary and if, despite these foreign inputs, cultural up-rooting can be avoided.

h) The project's place in a wider framework:

— links between the project and other changes and/or achievements in progress in the region;

— forms of collaboration envisaged with other official or private enterprises.

i) What are the possibilities of the project being extended by those concerned beyond the period covered by the requested subsidy? (technical capabilities, expenses for staff and maintenance, etc).

j) How will the project help free the people concerned from economic exploitation and oppression? And how will it help to change the situation? *Are these efforts directly inspired by the culture of those concerned? If this is not the case, is it because their culture does not contain liberating elements? Please explain.*

k) *What side effects and other repercussions could the project have on the indigenous culture? Would these affect the capacity of those concerned to resist the loss of their culture (e.g. for the benefit of the dominant culture of those in power)?*

Will the project weaken or reinforce the respect felt by the people concerned for their own culture and religion, and for their own identity as author of their own history?

l) *Does this culture contain a spirituality capable of mobilizing social action? Has the energy inherent in such a spirituality been harnessed for the project?*

4. Financial details: (indicate the currency used)

a) Total budget.

b) Exact sum requested.

Part Four:
The Right to be Different

14.   A View from the Ashram

The preceding pages contain the reflections of a Westerner regarding peoples' right to be different. Here now is a series of interviews illustrating the way this theme is tackled in a completely different cultural context, namely that of the Hindu environment or environments strongly influenced by Hindu spirituality.

The texts that follow are, as far as possible, faithful accounts of conversations that took place in three different Indian states on the theme of the links that exist between development and Hinduism and the various forms of spirituality based on Hinduism. It is offered as a document[1] to be added to the ongoing file on the question of the relevance of cultures and religions to development opened by a consortium of Asian development organizations, called APHD (Asia Partnership for Human Development). As an international non-governmental organization APHD is rather unusual, since it brings together, on a basis of strict equality in matters of decisions, Western funding agencies and Asian organizations which are more used to being on the receiving end of development aid. The organizations in question are, on the one hand, Catholic development organizations (for example *Entraide et Fraternité* and *Broederlijk Delen* in Belgium, the CCFD in France, *Développement et paix* in Canada, and, on the other hand, SEDEC (Socio-economic Development Centre) in Sri Lanka, NASSA (National Secretariat for Social Action) in the Philippines, and Caritas in India. It is a unique way of making relations of solidarity and partnership more real, since the Western NGOs thus shed some of the power conferred on them by the money at their disposal. In fact, Asian and Western funding agencies take joint decisions regarding the granting of funds to the many projects that are submitted to them each year.

APHD hopes to push the idea of partnership with the Asian peoples as far as possible. But since APHD is made up of Christian NGOs, this desire runs the risk of remaining somewhat theoretical since, the Philippines apart, the Far East is not Christian but Hindu, Muslim, Buddhist, Animist, and so on. Because those Asians who are Christian usually belong to the most Westernized circles of their respective countries, one may well wonder what sort of development and type of society they have in mind. Are they sufficiently attentive to the values inherent in the dominant religion or religions of their respective countries? Are they able to conscientize populations whose spiritual and religious conceptions they do not share? Are they not, by force of circumstance, the means of Westernizing their countries, and is this not an alienating process?

The members of APHD, well aware of these questions, set up a sub-committee to look into them. In this sub-committee, I am the representative of European NGOs. The interviews that follow were conducted by me within the framework of the studies undertaken by this group in January 1985. Two Indian friends organized a trip that allowed me to visit temples and ashrams (meditation centres), and meet groups and personalities who are well established figures in the cultural, spiritual and explicitly religious Hindu world. This inquiry, therefore, deals principally with groups other than those with which progressive Western NGOs normally come into contact. In this sense, it is not concerned with the work done by countless progressive *action groups* who are already supported by APHD. This brief survey was directly concerned with the following questions:

* Is it true, as is often claimed, that Hindu spirituality, wisdom and philosophy and Hinduism as a religion, are irrelevant to the problems of society? Is it possible, on the contrary, to derive from them a spirituality leading to active social commitment?

* In what way do Hindu spirituality and philosophy and Hinduism itself embody a model of society that differs from the one currently prevailing in modern India? Is there inherent in them a different conception of socio-political action, even of development, than that of Western modernity?

* Are the teachings and methods of Mahatma Gandhi an illustration of this, and does the Gandhian movement offer India a viable alternative today?

* Are the identity and values of the Indian people threatened by Westernization and does the latter contribute to the oppression experienced by the vast majority of Indians? What forms of cultural resistance to this aggression exist today?

* In what way might foreign solidarity organizations contribute to popular cultural resistance in India? And what about Indian development organizations?

No particular scientific methodology dictated the methodology of the inquiry. The questions were posed according to the requirements of the contacts and the evolution of the discussions. There is no question of attempting to draw general conclusions from these few interviews. There is, however, a lot to be learned from them and they offer useful food for thought and pose particularly interesting questions for Westerners in general and NGOs in particular. Certain interviews deal with ideas that will be strange to readers with no prior knowledge in this field. References are made to the Vedanta[2] and ideas associated with it, such as *maya*, *advaita*, and *satya*. An attempt has been made to clarify these briefly as they occur. The same goes for typically Gandhian terms such as *satyagraha*, *swaraj*, and *asangraha*. The interviews close with a few personal observations. Once again, there is no question of conclusions. These interviews are only insights — albeit particularly penetrating ones — into a vast area of contention that is currently the object of an intense debate in India itself. As some of those interviewed pointed out, however, these questions are rarely tackled by representatives of Western development organizations.

1.   Interview with Sri Balaram Reddia, a high caste Hindu, well versed in Vedantic philosophy and a disciple of Ramana Maharshi. The interview took place in Ramana Maharshi's ashram, the Ramanashram, at Thiruvanamalai, in the southern state of Tamil Nadu.

Ramana Maharshi (who died in 1950) was one of the most respected and beloved saints of modern India. He combined Vedantic philosophic thought of the highest order with a great personal love for all beings. The ashram lies at the foot of the sacred Mount Arunachal, considered to be the embodiment of Lord Shiva. Today the ashram is run by Brahmin priests who, by definition, are upper caste.

Q.   What was Ramana Maharshi's teaching on love and compassion? Can it be relevant for people engaged in social action in India?
A.   Our Guru taught that compassion must begin with oneself. It will then automatically flow to others by a process of identification, for there is no difference between the other and self. This belief is based on *advaita* [non-duality]: the other is me, I am him. This is the basis of Vedanta. As for social action, it is acceptable. Krishna (Vishnu in earthly form and a divinity much loved by the people) performed deeds. If you have read and meditated on the Bhagavad Gita you will understand what I mean. So, you may act, provided you are detached from your ego and beware of *avidya*, in other words ignorance and illusion. That is the main thing.
So you think the philosophy of Vedanta and Ramana's teachings are relevant to solving India's problems? Do Vedanta and the doctrine of non-duality have real meaning and practical application for ordinary workers and peasants?
Vedanta is the perfect answer, for India and the whole world for that matter! The world is suffering from *maya* [the illusion caused by dualism]. Neither science nor politics can solve this problem. Only when the mind retreats into its innermost recesses, descends into its deepest sources, will things get better. Look into yourself, not outwards! Then you will discover that the entire world is *maya*, a mere reflection of Ultimate Truth. No external action will solve problems while the ego is a prisoner of illusion and is not purified. The solution is *satya*, truth! I must discover that my ego is only an illusion of the mind. This discovery is *jnana*, in other words illumination, enlightenment, profound judgement, real knowledge.
Is Mahatma Gandhi's way a good example of what you have in mind?
No, not really. Gandhi followed the path of action, of *karma*. According to the philosophy of Vedanta, *karma*-yoga, or union with the Ultimate Reality

through action, is a relatively inferior way. It is followed by *bhakti*-yoga which signifies union through devotion and love of God. This, in turn, merely prepares the way to *jnana*-yoga. *Jnana* is the best way, but is reserved for a select few.

Ramana helped people to achieve *jnana* by clearing their minds. Gandhi helped people by *karma*, in other words acting on behalf of the poor. It is fine, but does not grant the same degree of elevation as *jnana* which offers the highest bliss. *Karma* is like primary school, *jnana* like a PhD . . .

But, isn't seeking my own bliss an egocentric undertaking?

No, because it is not a question of my bliss. The ego dissolves into the divine bliss. *Tat tvam asi*, as we say in Sanskrit, which means 'You are That', you are part of the godhead. Your *atman* (soul) is *Brahman* (God). The important thing is to become aware of this, then live it.

If those who follow jnana*-yoga are the finest, why do they not get involved in socio-political questions so as to solve the world's problems?*

We cannot. We would be contaminated by the world! I cannot save a drowning man if I cannot swim well myself. I must first perfect my path to *jnana*, strip myself of all illusion, of my self-centred mind.

So, according to your philosophy, you can offer the poor neither solution nor help? . . .

You see, what matters is to have a pure heart. Material well-being is secondary. Who is lower? The poor man who is good or the rich man who is bad? Is it not the latter who is the most miserable?

2.   The extremely Brahmanic spiritualism of Sri Balaram left us flabbergasted. For this reason our guides had organized a second interview intended to bring us back to more familiar territory. This interview took place in Pondicherry, . with **Mr Baskaram Ramdas** and **Mr Shankar**, who introduced themselves as social activists, Hindu-born though non-practising. They run a very active conscientization-cum-organization programme among fishermen, a marginalized and underprivileged group. The project receives no outside funding. It finances itself through a printing shop which they run themselves. They also run a school for the fishermens' children. Their project is on the same level as those supported by NGOs. Yet they have no contact with the latter and receive no financial aid.

Q.   Is it Hinduism that motivates your social commitment?

A.   No, my basic motivation is not any scripture but life itself and my solidarity with people. That having been said, nothing prevents me looking in sacred texts for corroboration of my commitment and an extra incentive. And, in fact, I happen to be very receptive to the Baghavad Gita and its call for disinterested action, with no thought of personal reward.

The detachment of the ego in socio-political action is a very important factor! It is one of the great lessons one can learn from the Gita.

Westernization seems to be creeping in everywhere in India, maybe at the risk of people losing their own values and their sense of identity. What are your

thoughts on this and do you have a strategy to combat it?
Your concern is valid. But, no, we have no strategy on that score, nor an alternative model to offer. We react to specific problems as they arise. We confine our activities to trying to curb some of the worst effects of capitalist exploitation and all that goes with it. In India, above all, we must bring to an end the system of capitalist exploitation. Afterwards, we may be more free to explore our own way, which need not be the same as either the West or present-day communist countries.

Would Mahatma Gandhi's message mean anything to contemporary India?
His social models are inapplicable and nowadays his followers are isolated and unable to face up to reality. India is not an ashram! But Gandhi still has an impact through his spirituality. We can draw much relevant inspiration from the man himself.

What about the Aurobindo ashram here in Pondicherry and the communal life-style practised at Auroville? Are these experiments relevant?
They are islands of intellectuals living in a world of ideas. The local population does not even understand what they say. The whole thing is very alien to the place where it has set itself up.

In fact, the local population resents the presence of the ashram. Auroville is a flop. We have nothing to do with it.

Foreign funding agencies support certain projects in India, yet you do not make use of their funds though you could very easily qualify for it. Why is that?
Development workers in India should aim at self-sufficiency and should not accept foreign money. People working for Western NGOs may well be prompted by genuine feelings of solidarity; but they are still so very Western! For instance, the first thing they do here is look for a project lasting one to two years, as though life can be put into a strait-jacket!

We prefer to keep our distance from foreign NGOs and their ideas. If you Westerners really want to help us, you should take up the struggle in your own countries first, because many of our problems stem from your system.

3. A Benedictine monk of British origin, Bede Griffiths runs the Saccidananda Ashram, established on the banks of the sacred River Kaveri at Shantivanam near Kulitalai by his predecessors, Father Monchanin and Father Saux. The latter is known there as Swami Abhishiktananda. The ashram is concerned with the inculturation of Christianity into the Hindu tradition.

The spirituality (including yoga, taught by Swami Amaldas), the liturgy and thought all demonstrate a marriage of Occident and Orient. Bede Griffiths is in fact the author of a book entitled *The Marriage of East and West*.[3]

Just before communal prayers, celebrated in the Hindu manner and based on extracts from the Upanishad, Bede Griffiths, swathed in the saffron robe of renunciation, replied to our questions.

Q. Do India's many great swamis [sages] have much to offer in terms of social action and finding a solution to the problem of India's poverty?

A.   Both Swami Chitananda of the Divine Light Society and Swami Nityananda are holy men, as of course was Sri Aurobindo. But I feel they have little to contribute when it came to solving the problems of society. They confine themselves to teaching that we all live in a dream world of *maya*, illusion. What people must do, therefore, is to become aware that everything is one [this is *advaita* or non-dualism], and that external elements are only dreams, illusions.

Such pure Vedantic philosophy is not much use to action-oriented Hindus, which is a pity since these *swamis* really are extremely holy men. In reality, there is a current lack of leaders. Personally, I believe that Mahatma Gandhi's teaching is still very relevant for India today. He bridged the gap between spirituality and active commitment to justice, between the vertical and horizontal dimensions. He applied the Gita and the Sermon on the Mount to politics.

Do you think that other philosophic or religious systems than the Vedanta would be more appropriate to unite spirituality and action?

Most certainly. Vedanta can be very stultifying and *advaita* can be socially sterile. I think that *bhakti*, the least intellectual path to enlightenment, is really the people's religion.

In our ashram, we try to combine *jnana*, enlightenment through meditation based on Vedantic teachings, *bhakti*, devotion, and *karma*, concrete action. For me, the here and now is real. I interpret the term *maya* not as mere illusion but as one aspect of Ultimate Reality. At that level, all is one, certainly, but the differences of the everyday world are also real.

But isn't this bhakti *you speak of the love of God and not, properly speaking, love of one's neighbour?*

Indeed. But when you love God, you implicitly love everything in Him. This is *bhakti*'s strength and interest. *Bhakti* has also freed the Indian people from the rigidly hierarchical caste system and the sterile intellectualism Brahmins often expound.

Mahatma Gandhi did not reject the caste as such, only the concept of untouchability. What do you think of this?

The caste system can be valuable, but nowadays we find this difficult to accept. We want equality, egalitarianism. But this is not feasible, and modern societies do not function well. In the human family, everyone is different but each has their place. Everyone is needed: priest, warrior, farmer, merchant and worker. There is nothing essentially wrong in differences. Reality is based on complementarity, not total uniformity. Of course India is currently suffering under the caste system because many people have lost the sense of *Dharma* [law, order, virtue, religion]. We ought to go back to Gandhi's *Ram-raj*, a system whereby the god Ram is the lord and chief of the village. That is what *Dharma* is all about.

Unfortunately, instead of complementarity of castes, there is now competition between them. There is often no interdependence any more. The caste system may have degenerated, but the West has nothing to teach India in matters of equality. In the caste system, inequality is recognized and acknowledged. In Europe, a great deal of inequality and hierarchies certainly exist, but these inequalities are not openly admitted. They are more or less hidden.

4. The interview that follows throws more light on the question of castes. It took place in Kulithalai (Tamil Nadu) with a Hindu-born intellectual, Mr Jeyaraj, who works for a voluntary organization called SPADE (*Société pour l'action et le développement populaire*, Society for Popular Action and Development). An Indian NGO staffed entirely by Indians, SPADE is involved in the conscientization and organization of the oppressed peasants.

Q.   Conscientization is a method of Latin American origin. It seems to me to be used in India by Christian and Marxist NGOs raher than Hindu. Is this a valid impression? And, if so, how did you, as a Hindu, come to be working along such lines?
Friends whom I trust suggested I join their group. Prior to that, anything to do with voluntary development organizations and movements engaged in conscientization of the masses was, to me, Christian, Western. I felt it did not belong to our tradition. And I was afraid Christians would try to convert Hindus, using their funds and activities. I was more politically minded and worked for the JP Party [Jayaprakash Narayan] which propounded Hindu socialism. For me, there could be no distinction between politics and the Hindu religion. Gandhi had combined the two, and so did JP.
Are you still a Hindu?
Let's say I am agnostic. For me, the question of God is a mystery. I have distanced myself more and more from religion — or rather, from the church. The reason was the caste system. You see, I belong to the upper caste and, according to Hinduism, I am not supposed to mix with *Harijans* (the untouchables). This code of pure and impure imposed by Brahmin priests is inhuman and stupid but still applied. Actually, you shouldn't really ask people if they are Hindu. It doesn't really mean anything. If you ask them what their religion is, they will tell you they belong to such and such a class. You will be very hard put to find social activists who are 'practising Hindus', in other words who go to church.
At the end of the last century, such great spiritual figures as Ramakrishna and Vivekananda tried to modernize Hinduism. Didn't this Hindu renaissance lead to social action?
Vivekananda and other saints spoke of altruism and charity, but not in the same sense as Christians. They never really got through to the people. Even the Ramakrishna Missions based on Western monasteries have little impact on the villages. Their monks are first and foremost philosophers who perform an act of social work in order to achieve a higher degree of personal spirituality.
If Hindus are not socially committed, how can India hope to change? Can social change be left entirely to non-Hindus? Wouldn't that lead to failure or to cultural and political oppression on the part of an avant-garde that does not

share the spiritual values and concerns of the people?
Yes, this is a problem. But let us not exagerate. As an agnostic, it is true that I do not entirely fit in with the mainstream of the Indian people. I do not fully share the spiritual world of the people whose awareness I am trying to raise. But these people are not strangers to me either! I know their values and want to change some of them, those I consider destructive.
Do people equate happiness with material wealth?
Yes and no. Certainly they want more money and more goods. But what also makes them happy is going to the temple, celebrating a village festival and, especially, visiting relatives and friends in other towns and villages. Simple things that cost nothing are still important. But, nowadays, villages are threatened by commercialization. Before, the villages had wonderful dances, now this has been replaced by commercial things such as films and pop music.
You are currently involved in conscientization work, helping people fight exploitation and obtain more social amenities, more money and goods. Do I understand that you yourself find this work slightly ambiguous?
Yes, but there is no alternative! People are not happy; they want change, a good job, decent housing that is cheap, health facilities . . . So we help them to meet these new aspirations.

You see, whether we like it or not, the Western model is here. We are neither completely traditional nor totally Westernized. Your Western model is no good for us but I have no other model to offer. It is a terrible problem.

5. In Bangalore, the capital of Karnataka, a session was held with members of ICRA (*Institut pour la recherche et l'action culturelles*) and those of 'Pipal Tree'. The latter seeks to examine the links between religion, culture and development and has made possible many contacts reported here.
The first conversation was held with Mr Nagaraj, a well-known playwright. He is professor in Kannada and comparative literature at Bangalore University. Hindu by birth, he was born into a so-called low caste.

Q. Does Hinduism contain elements conducive to socio-political commitment?
A. Yes, provided we do not confine ourselves to its various philosophic systems, in particular to Vedanta. These systems offer no solutions to society's problems and, in certain cases, are downright harmful.

For me, even the Gita leads to a certain callousness, an indifference in the face of suffering. It leads to a rather elitist kind of stoicism.

But Hinduism encompasses many movements, sects and beliefs. It has enormous variety and this somewhat anarchic pluralism is its saving grace!

Take for example the 12th century Virashiva movement, a radical, anti-Brahmanic [upper caste] movement which argued for spiritual equality, which implies social equality. Take Mahatma Gandhi, who was both a great holy man and a social and political leader whose ideas and non-conformist actions constituted a profound critique of the established order. Nowadays,

Gandhism has unfortunately sunk into complacency. Its criticism of the social injustices and repressive aspects inherent in Hinduism lack moral sting. It has lost its prophetic character, the 'spiritual anger' that was its strength.

Take Sai Baba today, a demi-god who performs all sorts of miracles. He does not belong to the Brahmin caste but to the lower *Sudras*, the manual workers. Admittedly, Sai Baba does not actually challenge society's values, but the very fact that a *Sudra* should be recognized as a *Bhagwan*, a demi-god, indicates a defiance of the dominant Brahminism. Jainism also contains interesting social values based on non-violence and concern for the ecology. And do not forget Buddhism, a mine of alternate social models. We look for philosophic system under the influence of Western thought: this is a mistake.

Existing movements and sects are not based on the sort of grandiose intellectual constructions proposed by the various schools of philosophy. We need to adhere to the entirety of religious practices and beliefs, in order to achieve a global, holistic understanding of the relationship between popular religion, social action and economic development. One thing is certain; above all one must not confuse Hinduism with Vedanta.

Isn't the plurality of India's creeds and cultures under threat today?
Yes, indeed. As I have already pointed out: Hinduism and Indian culture are not monolithical. India is a vast mosaic of different groups, traditions and creeds. Yet, today, we are being threatened by an approach to development that is socio-economic, unilateral and monocultural.

The central government has become the medium for this process. Once, when Nehru was opening a huge hydro-electric dam, he made this terrifying statement: 'These dams are the temples of modern India' . . .

We must reject anything that threatens the plurality of our culture. We must construct different models of society, of relations between human beings and between them and nature.

At 'Pipal Tree' we are about to start an inquiry into the various notions of justice contained in the different Indian traditions and religions.

6. The second interview at 'Pipal Tree' was with Mrs Shanta, a practising Hindu involved in conscientization work with ICRA in Madras. A third interview with another member of 'Pipal Tree' closes this series.

Q. Is it in your religion you find the motivation that pushes you to social action?
A. Of course. Listen to this religious poem: 'Whenever I see a plant dying from lack of water, I feel that same thirst.' If you can feel such compassion for a plant, why not for a human being? There is no difference between me, the plant and my neighbour. I am him. He is me. We have the same *atman* [soul] in *Brahman* [God]. 'To serve others is to serve God' says an old text of the Siddhas, who were Tamil holy sages. According to them, 'unless you can see God in people, you will never see God at all'. The Siddhas combined

jnana [enlightenment] and *karma* [action].
Do you know many Indian groups involved in development and conscientization?
Only a very few work along lines familiar to you, using conscientization and
organization of the people.

Conscientization is seen as typically Christian. When I, a Hindu, go into a
village to do conscientization work, the villagers automatically assume I am
Christian!

At the moment, there are committed Hindu groups, but they do not work
along the same lines as we do. They act with more discretion, do not use
foreign funding and employ different analyses and strategies than those
used by Western-inspired agencies.

In my region, for example, there is a small ashram of ten to fifteen people.
Each has a job and, on top of that, is involved in some social work. They
object to the attitude to castism preached by many Westernized groups and
are afraid that conscientization of the oppressed may lead to inter-
community clashes.

They, too, are against the oppression caused by the caste system but they
employ a model based on harmony and not on conflict. In fact, they try to
conscientize the dominant castes as well. It is rather like the Gandhian
model.

7. The next visit was to the Chinmaya Mission, run by Swami Chinmaya, a
sage involved in both *jnana* (enlightenment through meditation) and *karma*
(work as service to others). In the modern-looking temple of this urban-based
Mission the following conversation took place with a Brahmin devotee of the
temple, Mr Narayana Menon.

*Q.   What is Swami Chinmaya's doctrine and what is its relevance to the
solution of India's current problems of poverty and oppression?*
A.   The Swami teaches that the self is nothing and that God is everything.
My mind and my body are only instruments to serve God. To serve God and
to reach Him, one must undertake the path of *karma-yoga*, in other words
selfless action on behalf of the poor. I must work for God, for example by
caring for the sick, the underprivileged and the oppressed.
*Can anyone reach God through work, even those considered of low caste and
untouchables?*
Of course. The humbler your work, the better you will be placed to destroy
your ego and accommodate God. Look at Gandhi. You should see God in
everything and then, having rid yourself of all attachment, serve Him.
Does God expect us to do social work?
Certainly! Everything is *maya* [illusion] except service to others. Love of
God and love of people is the same thing.
*What difference is there between the Chinmaya Mission and the Ramakrishna
Mission whose monasteries are both devoted to social work?*
We are both followers of Vedanta, trying to help the poor. But the

Ramakrishna monks stay inside their monasteries and social service centres, whereas we go out into the community to preach and do social work.

8. After our visit to the Chinmaya Temple, we ran into a group of red-clad trade unionists organizing a solidarity demonstration for their union, the All India Trade Union Congress (AITUC). This union is allied to the Communist Party of India (CPI). We spoke to one of the demonstrators and learned that they were employees of the Chinmaya Mission's hospital.

Q. Are you satisfied with the working conditions in this hospital?
A. No, they really exploit their workers. Ten or more hours work a day, and very poor wages! Recently we went on strike.
But Swami Chinmaya teaches that he wants to help the poor . . .
Yes, of course, and he really is a great man, wise and generous. But he cannot keep an eye on all his welfare institutions. The hospital is run by middle-men who exploit the workers while claiming to run a charity organization.
As a communist trade unionist, can you accept the Swami's teachings on God, jnana *and* karma?
Personally, yes. I used to be one of his followers. Then I discovered Marxism and exploitation. But I think you can combine spirituality and revolution.
Do many militants think like that?
Not all of them agree with me! Many of them are hard-line Marxists. But there are others who feel that religion will always be important and that leaders like Gandhi and Jayaprakash Narayan (JP) understood this.
Today you are leading a demonstration. Will you also pray?
Yes, every day I say my *puja* [prayer, worship]. It is very important to me.

9. *Shanti Kutir*, the House of Peace, is a simple three-roomed flat of Gandhian austerity, situated on the outskirts of Bombay. Thanks to the unique hospitality shown by its inhabitants, the place has become a meeting place for peace activists and Gandhians from all over the world. This establishment has close links with the Bombay Sarvodaya Friendship Centre. Sarvodaya, meaning the awakening of all, is the name generally used by Gandhian institutions and movements. Mrs Hansa Mazgaonkar is the soul of *Shanti Kutir*. She shared the following observations with us.

Q. You have been involved in social work with the Sarvodaya movement for more than thirty years. Do you think the social situation in India has improved since Gandhi's day?
A. No, it's worse. Independence has been accompanied by a rising demand for goods, not just on the part of the poor who need them, but also on the part of the middle class. Today, there is more social tension, more exploitation, a greater concentration of wealth and land in the hands of the rich than before. Values of *asangraha* [sober life-style, non-accumulation of material goods] are disappearing. We are in the age of money! But there are

people who react. I'm thinking particularly of the groups of women I organize.

What religious denomination do these women belong to?

They are mostly Hindu but they are against the caste system. Some are devotees of Chinmaya, some are Jain and others are followers of Swami Muktananda or some lesser known *swami*.

Then there are those women who go on retreats to listen to a young, socially-committed *swami* who establishes links between the Ramayana [a traditional Indian epic] and social justice. He speaks out against government corruption and in favour of the rights of the *Harijans* [outcasts] on the basis of the history of the god, Ram, who was forced to abdicate and leave his kingdom. He was an example of *asangraha* [non-accumulation]. 'The Ramayana is the story of your life', says this *swami*.

What you say about this swami *raises an important question: could one not promote a social conscience and sense of justice via the Hindu temples? Why not train Hindu priests,* swamis *and* sadhus *[ascetics] in a socially-oriented philosophy and practice?*

With very few exceptions, they would refuse to listen. Many *pujaris* [those who perform the *puja*: rituals and prayers in the temple] are Brahmins, greedy for money and power. They maintain a watertight division between worship and social concerns. Most people who go regularly to the temple are the same. *Puja* is often a very self-centred affair.

Vinoba Bhave asked the *Sadhusamaj* [association of ascetics] to act for the poor, but this request was turned down by the majority.

10. Mr Daniel Mazgaonkar, Hansa's husband, took part for many years in the Bhoodan Movement led by Gandhi's most outstanding disciple, Vinoba Bhave. This crusade, which mobilized thousands of enthusiastic followers, aimed to solve the terrible land problems through voluntary gifts of their land by landowners to village committees who then redistributed it on the basis of needs. (The climax of the Gandhian movement, the crusade was unsuccessful in fundamentally transforming land-ownership structures.) Daniel Mazgaonkar's life is devoted to training Gandhian activists, based on the principles of active non-violence or *satyagraha* (strength of truth–strength of soul). He is also co-ordinator of the International Network for a Society Overcoming Domination (originally a Brazilian initiative, now a decentralized inter-communication network linking grass-roots groups, social activists and pacifists from all over the world) and is heavily involved in the anti-nuclear movement.

Q. When all is said and done, what impact have Gandhi's ideas had on post-colonial India?

A.   Leaders like Nehru only used Gandhi's ideas and methods to achieve political independence from British colonial rule. Gandhi's ideas regarding economic and political non-violence were not followed. There has been no decentralization towards the villages, no village-based industries or crafts, no promotion of organic farming, no firm insistence on people being self-reliant, using their own initiative, no policy of production and consumption based on local resources. In fact, Gandhi envisaged a new society, a completely different way of life, based on the voluntary curbing of needs. The basis of Gandhian analyses and strategies is religious. Gandhi called for *Ram-raj*. This was not taken up by the Congress Party.

What exactly is meant by Ram-raj?

Literally, it means 'the reign of Rama, or God'. *Ram-raj*, or *Gram-raj* (village power), refers to village life organized along lines of spirituality, goodness and truth, therefore with no hunger, no unemployment, no caste barriers. Such is the will of God, whom Gandhi invoked in the incarnation of Ram. We are for a secular state but secularism has come to mean equal distance from all religions, rather than equal proximity to the essence of all religions.

Why have Indian leaders not followed Gandhi's principles?

Their heads were all stuffed with Western concepts. They wanted to speed things up and turn India into a world power capable of competing with other great powers. So, against the advice of Gandhi and Vinoba, they opted for a centralized state, heavy industry, economic planning along Soviet lines and massive foreign aid. Gandhi, on the other hand, identified with the Indian masses and their needs, ideas and values.

Although he also was educated in the West, his feet were firmly planted in Indian soil . . .

What aspects of modern India would you criticize most?

The centralization of political power and the rampant introduction of alienating technology. Our constitution is based on centralized government and on decision-making by majority. Mahatma Gandhi wanted clusters of village republics, joined in a federation to form an Indian nation built, directed and organized from the base up. Instead of this, India has reduced the human and material potential of villages as well as their capacity for self-government and self-reliance. Too much power has been given to central organs. And this has been further reinforced by the centripetal tendency of mega-technology. Gandhi was against machines when they impose their own logic and rhythms on people. He foretold the devastation of nature and the dehumanizing of people that mega-technology would bring about.

Now that India has been following this Western path for more than thirty years, how do you see the country's future?

Frankly, I feel rather depressed. Gandhians have failed to have the necessary impact on government. Now I think India will follow Western models to the bitter end. There will be still more exploitation and the gap between rich and poor will continue to grow. Outbreaks of violence will occur which, in their turn, will provoke police repression and closer links between the state and the rich. India will feel the full lash of Westernization. It is only after this shock that it will understand that an alternative exists, namely the Gandhian model.

At the moment, are many people interested in the Gandhian model?
The famous film on Gandhi aroused interest among the young. Many groups are now springing up, seeking non-violent social change. They don't necessarily refer to Gandhi by name, but that is unimportant.

As far as we, the Gandhians, are concerned, we ought to open the dialogue, accept these new militant socio-political forces while, at the same time, making our position quite clear.

Do you think it is possible to combine Gandhian spirituality and Marxist analysis?
You see, India needs harmony and co-operation, not more division and class struggle. Of course we recognize that exploitation and social conflict exist. But, for us, the exploiter is a human being, not 'the enemy'. I must combat his oppressive, exploitative role, but, at the same time, try to change *him* as well as social structures. We struggle by means of *satyagraha* [the power of truth] against the rich in order to achieve not only external but also interior change. We aim to convert the rich, not to snatch something from them. This requires the co-operation and mutual help of all men and women, just as all the fingers of the hand must co-operate, irrespective of the fact that one is longer than another. Struggling for higher wages and more rights alone is not enough. Society also needs more love and co-operation. Only then can there be happiness. You Westerners may have realized this yourselves after taking a good long look at your society . . .

At first sight, it may look as though Marxism and Gandhism have the same goal: justice and happiness for all. But there are fundamental differences. First of all, the *satyagrahis* [militant Gandhians] will relinquish power when their goal has been achieved, whereas communists will retain leadership after the revolution. Secondly, the end never justifies the means for us, as it does for communists. Thirdly, we ask people to look inward and discover why evil exists in society. We insist on the oneness of external and internal change. Communists, on the other hand, want to apply pressure by external force. For them, all evils stem from external social structures. Since their ideology is dualistic, they insist on conflict and division.

Was Vinoba's approach different from Gandhi's?
Vinoba put slightly less stress on political action and more on spiritual change. Of course both Gandhi and Vinoba used *satyagraha* [power of truth, strength of soul]. But Gandhi used it more for 'resistance' to oppression and Vinoba more for 'assistance' to society, to win hearts and change society through spirituality, personal purification and meditation. Personally, I tend to believe there is a connection between my impurity [individual soul] and the social impurity that surrounds me [collective soul]. All is one.

When I act on myself, I act on society. That is why personal change is not just a self-centred activity. It concerns society.

Are non-violence and self-sacrifice really rooted in the culture of the Indian people?
In a way, yes. People cherish values of tolerance, love, spiritual life, co-

operation and sharing with others. The ideas of renunciation and self-sacrifice are still widespread amongst us. As a matter of fact, people are unhappy with the individualism, materialism and competitive spirit that reign in Bombay. I know many families who have returned to the villages they came from. There, they can experience friendship, peace, serenity and, above all, solidarity. People like to think and act collectively.

You travelled in the West recently, making contact with peace movements there. What were your impressions?

I think the West has lost what I would call the village-spirit. It should renew traditions of co-operation and sharing and rediscover the sense of harmony between human beings and nature.

This in turn would help India, for here many people think that everything Western is good. Today, the examples set by the West are inadequate. In fact they are positively harmful.

11. A school, a large farm, some fields and a few hermitages go to make up a Gandhian ashram where socio-political action is combined with a life-style based on austerity, autonomy and prayer.

One feels away from it all, in an idyllic India full of wisdom, tranquillity and beauty. Yet the indigenous tribal population of the region has to sell its labour power in town where it is outrageously exploited. Material and human misery are starting to make their appearance.

There, we met Dr Vasant Nargolkar, who used to be one of the leaders of the Gandhian 'Quit India' movement. He and his wife later joined Vinoba Bhave's *Bhoodan* (land-gift) campaign. They both faced imprisonment because of their non-violent but radical political commitment. Commissioned by the *Sarva Seva Sangh* (Association for the Good of All), a national organization combining various Gandhian *Sarvodaya* groups, they visited China and Israel and have written books on the communes and kibbutzim of these countries. Dr Nargolkar believes that these experiments in life-style and communal methods of production are part of a general movement on the part of humanity towards a more convivial, harmonious society.

Q. Many people think the Sarvodaya *movement is no longer relevant in India. You run a* sarvodaya *ashram here amidst a tribal population. Do you see this as an example of what Gandhians ought to be doing?*

Not really. The *Sarvodaya* movement ought never to have given up political struggle. Vinoba was not aggressive enough and allowed our movement to grow soft. Jayaprakash Narayan tried to give it new impetus but at the moment the movement lacks real power. It is really only the *Vahini*, the student and youth movement, which has taken up conscientization work and organizing the masses with anything like the necessary militancy and anger. Here, in this ashram, our involvement in development projects (irrigation, reforestation, and so on) is really very makeshift. I am not happy about it. That kind of thing ought to be left to government.

Do you think the Gandhian movement is a spent force, that India needs other

strategies, other models of society?
Absolutely not! On the contrary, I am very optimistic. In the long run, the whole world will come to recognize the validity of *Sarvodaya*, its non-violent methods and its social, economic and political vision. This will come about through force of circumstances, as society evolves towards greater spirituality. I believe, like Aurobindo, that humanity is involved in a grand process of improvement, caught up in an immense spiral that leads towards ever-greater scientific, material and spiritual growth.

But what do Gandhian ideas have to offer in concrete terms, to solve the current problems of exploitation, pollution and poverty in India's constantly expanding cities?
As we grow spiritually, we will give up these madmen's cities. They will be abandoned and will serve as monuments to a bygone stage in human evolution. Today we see only what goes wrong: the Bhopal tragedy, massacres of Sikhs in Delhi, violence, exploitation. Of course, these are undeniable facts that call for immediate action and I believe *Sarvodaya* should be much more involved in active resistance to all forms of oppression. We must struggle, but, at the same time, we must recognize the existence of subterranean currents of goodness and growing planetary solidarity. Humanity is growing, believe me. Progress, true progress, is inevitable, but we must play our part in it. I am not just speaking about progress in ideas, but of progress that is both spiritual and material, of global evolution.

What particular values of the Indian ethos will influence this process of change?
I will name one, a central one. This is renouncement, self-denial. Beneath the outer shell of greed and indifference promoted by the mass media exists a profound propensity for detachment, which is the core of our identity.

Having visited China, do you think the Chinese Revolution has been part of this process of change taking place in humanity?
Undoubtedly. What I like in China is that there is employment and food for everyone, and an active role for women in society. Women in China are fearless. All of which is very good. The problem is that much of it was achieved through coercion, not through willing self-sacrifice and *Sarvodaya*.

Only self-sacrifice on the part of all citizens will bring about a successful revolution. And it will come, believe it or not! As a Christian, you should know that humanity is progressing towards God.

12. Mr Siddharta is the founder and secretary of ICRA, the Institute for Cultural Research and Action, based in Bangalore, and was, at the time of this interview, international co-ordinator for INODEP-South, a well-known institute, operating in various countries, specializing in popular organization and political education based on the pedagogy of Paulo Freire.
Siddharta is an Indian Christian who belongs to the Syriac Church of Kerala. Lawyer and anthropologist, he also participates in 'Pipal Tree', a research group (mentioned previously) that studies the links between religions and social change in India.

Q. Are there signs of growing 'deculturation' and Westernization in India? Is the country going to lose its cultural and spiritual roots?
A. There is certainly a process of Westernization in India, some aspects of which are terrible, some positive. For instance, consumerism is creeping into our villages, spreading vulgar materialism. Admittedly this is very worrying. But I do not think there will be generalized, total acceptance of Western values. Individuals react in different ways. For example, those who hold with fundamentalist religious beliefs totally reject Western values. They would like to carry on as though nothing has changed over the last hundred years, but they find themselves constantly on the defensive and consequently have little power. Others try to accept certain aspects and reject others. For example, they use chemical fertilizers on their fields but wear clothes made of traditional cotton rather than synthetic fibres. Others again accept Western modernity in its entirety, but remain very strict in matters of caste and food. Retaining the purity of blood lines and hence marrying within their caste are crucial to them, but other aspects of the caste system code of conduct are allowed to die out. For example what it prescribes one must do, whom one may touch, with whom one may eat, what profession one may take up, and so on. I think a blending process is taking place, characterized by a fusion of acceptance and resistance regarding foreign values. A specifically Indian synthesis will come out of this blending process. The interaction of new and traditional values will continue and go on to produce a new ethos that will be truly Indian.

When one questions Africans, American Indians or people on the Asian continent about these issues, many seem less optimistic than you. Do you think India has a greater potential for cultural resistance than other countries?
The strength of Indian tradition is formidable. You have only to look at the relatively meagre results of Christian missionary work here. Very few Indians have genuinely been converted to Western-style Christianity.

To what do you ascribe this strength in cultural resistance?
India, like China, is basically a proud society. They are both literate societies, with traditions of literature, poetry, philosophy and science going back to the beginning of recorded history. In recent times, India allowed itself be dominated by a colonial power because Indian society has never attached the social status or importance to power accorded it by other societies. Moreover, the doctrine of *maya*, which is an ahistoric world-view, has led Indians to adopt a certain distance towards concrete temporal issues. Indians are very conscious of the fact that a social order of the highest level existed here long before anything approaching civilization appeared in Europe.

In the same way, the Chinese have always thought that they are the centre of the world. And indeed, many predict that the Pacific area around Japan and China will soon be the new economic and political centre of the world. But national pride is no bad thing. It can also help the West to realize that it possesses no intrinsic superiority.

Countries such as Japan and Thailand would appear to have adopted Western values much quicker than has India. Why is this?

Although India has opened up considerably to capitalism and technology (albeit at a slower pace than Japan), it has retained a solid cultural continuity. This relative resistance to the aggression of capitalism stems from Indian attitudes to ideas of history, the individual and competitiveness. These ideas have little currency with us. The analytical element is less powerful than the mythical. Because of its slower pace, India is able to change in accordance with its own ethos, adopting one thing, rejecting another. I think India is going to become a bi-cultural nation, in the same way that I see myself as a bi-cultural person. The blend of cultures is a blessing. I actually think that monocultural Westerners are missing out on this experience.

What about you personally, an Indian educated here in a Catholic school who studied and worked in Europe for several years — do you feel completely Indian?

I have a definite sense of being completely Indian and of being very different from Europeans. I realized this when I was working in Paris. I don't suffer from the tension and stress that troubles Europeans. And I don't hold with their work discipline, which seems very rigid to me. Nor do I agree with the apparent need to see time only in terms of money.

Can Indian development workers and foreign NGOs concerned with social problems do anything to strengthen the Indian people's capacity for blending new and traditional values?

We can and should bring more cultural elements into our development work. Even the training centres for development workers that exist here in India attach little importance to this. They tend to confine themselves to a strictly sociological analysis of culture and religion. Obviously, sociology is useful, but its scope is simply not broad enough to allow it to tackle the reality of India in all its complexity (or that of any other country for that matter).

The approach of such centres, and the committed action groups trained by them sound like a typical Latin American approach. Consequently, their projects easily get the support of progressive Western NGOs. The analysis and proposed action, the language used, all this is very familiar to Western ears and Eurocentric mentalities. In the final analysis, I think that ninety per cent of the project applications addressed by Indian groups to foreign funding agencies, use terminology that was born in Latin America.

What can a centre like ICRA do to foster cultural resistance and collective creativity amongst the people and those who work alongside them?

I feel that our training here at ICRA should include a serious consideration of the cultural factor. We must put the accent on the concept of 'indigenous resources', and try to infuse in villagers a pride in their own cultural heritage. At 'Pipal Tree' we have been involved in studying traditional religious festivals to see if they contain anything that might help to mobilize people and offer new directions for social action and alternative models of society. In the same way, we should study folk dance, poetry and other traditional forms of expression in order to devise more adequate methods of conscientization and organization. We should also be thinking of including a serious introduction to Mahatma Gandhi's thoughts, for example. His concept of militant non-violence is a tremendous wealth, though it remains largely unexplored.

Do you think India should return to Gandhi's teachings?

I see Gandhi as a point of departure, not of arrival. There is no point in turning back the clock, whatever the reason. I don't believe in 'restorations' of any kind, nor of fundamentalist religious revivals. What is needed is renewal, rather than restoration or revival. The revivalist fundamentalism of a Khomeini turns a blind eye to some of humanity's major achievements. Certain members of the RSS [the Hindu nationalist movement], although not as narrow-minded, also seek a return to tradition instead of promoting a well-balanced interaction between secular and religious values. It's a dead end.

What advice would you give Western NGOs and other agencies involved with the Third World?

Firstly, foreign NGOs ought to examine the extent to which their own people resist the tremendous wave of cheap Americanization that is sweeping over the whole world. They may find that the West, too, has its problems of deculturation. To take Europe as an example, one should look into what remains today of Danish, German, English, Scottish and Basque cultures . . . Explore your own situation and how you yourselves resist; then you might have a better understanding of what is happening in the Third World!

Secondly, raise these issues in your educational campaigns. Help your public to be more aware of their own culture and this in turn will give them a better understanding of the dangers of deculturation and standardization, in their own countries as much as in the Third World.

Thirdly, encourage as many people as possible in the West to get to know at least one foreign culture, Chinese for instance, or American Indian, or Bantu. Help Westerners become at least bi-cultural . . .

Western NGOs' actions in the Third World would be much more positive if they relativized their own cultural model. It strikes me that many Westerners still think they are superior. You find this attitude even within Western NGOs involved with the Third World. Their militants and experts may well want to prove their solidarity through mutual respect, but a deep-seated Eurocentrism is part of their make-up. It has become unconscious. Funding agencies must therefore study and learn to appreciate other cultures, lest they impose their own values. They certainly have the money to do this! Many NGOs in the West have acquired a sound socio-economical analysis, but they are not yet equipped or trained to be sensitive to cultural factors.

You are probably right. But the Third World hardly helps us to become aware of our ethnocentrism. Our Indian partners, for examples, scarcely ever raise these questions!

This is the result of a long process of cultural domination that has its roots in colonialism. Western NGOs must raise these questions themselves if their Third World partners do not. But to be able to initiate a dialogue, you must first get to know the culture of the place in question. If you do not, it is obvious that you cannot raise meaningful questions.

In bringing these interviews to a conclusion, some general observations spring to mind. They will of course have to be verified and studied in greater depth in the light of new contacts and more systematic studies. One fact must be borne in mind: these interviews were conducted with only one section of the Indian population, namely the Hindu milieu, involved in development matters or not.

In the world of socio-political action and development, India has a great variety of options and methods, notably those of Marxists and those of action groups (often Christian-inspired) resorting to conscientization and peoples' organization. These do not fall within the scope of the investigation undertaken here, any more than the links between Islam and development. Here then are a few observations:

*   The common denominator linking the individuals encountered during these interviews is their adherence, some to Hinduism as a religion, some to the social and spiritual values that underpin it. Several of them refer more or less explicitly to some aspect of Mahatma Gandhi's message, some even belong to the *Sarvodaya* movement and militate within it.

*   A fundamental distinction must be made between these speakers. There are those who seek to bring about social change by means of socio-political action, and then there is the Brahmin, Sri Balaram Reddia (the very first interview) for whom only self-purification can solve social problems. This fundamental distinction, a veritable *summa divisio* for anyone involved in social action and development, brings to mind the one made by Arthur Koestler between the yogi and the commissar.[4] The first seeks social change through inner means, the second through action on the outside world. Clearly, those who confine themselves strictly to personal growth, like Sri Balaram, do not allow us to go much further in our reflection on socio-political action for development. But this sensibility must not be ignored, for less extreme versions of it crop up again in many other speakers for whom personal asceticism is a necessary — but not sufficient — dimension of social change. If Sri Balaram conforms to the stereotype of the yogi described by Koestler, none of the other speakers can really be said to be pure 'commissars'. For these, we would have had to search in milieux less touched by spirituality, in particular amongst Marxists (and even amongst some heavily secularized progressive Christians?). But the latter are not the object of this modest investigation. It is interesting, however, to note that the Marxist trade unionist encountered at Bangalore is also a practising Hindu for whom prayer and political struggle are indissociable.

The yogi–commissar distinction was not made by those we met. Several of them evoked instead the three ancient paths of yoga open to people, *jnana* or meditation, *bhakti* or piety and *karma*, selfless action. For some, the latter means no more than performing one's duties of caste and worship, but others extend it to include all aspects of life, including socio-political commitment. It is possible to combine two of these paths, or even all three. In the latter eventuality, one can say that Hindu spirituality, far from being disincarnated and irrelevant, leads directly to social action. This was the attitude adopted by Gandhi who apparently practised *jnana*, *bhakti* and *karma* simultaneously.

* A second important distinction should be made between those involved in social work based on a model of harmony and those whose struggle is based on analyses and strategies that acknowledge conflict. The first do admit the existence of social problems and acknowledge situations of oppression and exploitation but, like Vinoba Bhave, they fear actions that would exacerbate existing conflict and seek instead a wholesale conversion of the population. Thus they speak of the 'conscientization of the rich'. This is a contradiction in terms, however, for militants who practise the pedogogy of Freire. Those who believe, on the contrary, that society can progress only if the oppressed masses stand up against the minority that exploits them, may not all be unaware of the benefits of harmony. But they level accusations of naivety or even objective complicity with injustice at those who refuse to accept the need for social struggle.

It is interesting to note that these two approaches rub shoulders in the same movement, *Sarvodaya*: within it, Gandhi had declared the necessity for non-violent but radical struggle. But Vinoba later preferred social action emphasizing harmony rather than confrontation.

The debate between the protagonists of 'resistance' and the champions of 'assistance' (to society as a whole) is not over and apparently divides the Gandhians we interviewed.

* Still on the subject of Gandhi, all of those to whom we spoke were agreed in according him a certain relevance. His vision of society, as well as his personal behaviour, which combined personal change and political commitment, are seen as *idées-forces* of the Indian character. The visions of the future and the alternative social models described in these interviews are often inspired by Gandhi, either directly or implicitly.[5] The present-day Gandhian movement, *Sarvodaya*, on the other hand, came in for much criticism. It is generally considered to have been overtaken by events and is no longer seen as a contender in the spectrum of social and political forces existing today. Some Gandhians, who partly agree with this critical analysis, are aware of the situation, but still believe that in the future a revival of Gandhism, both as a philosophy and a movement, is inevitable.

* Does the Hindu religion and the various forms of spirituality inspired by it breed a certain callousness and indifference to one's neighbour? Are they irrelevant in terms of socio-political commitment? These interviews make such opinions, widely held in the West, difficult to maintain in any generalized way.

First of all, there are many Hindus, prompted by the sight of human misery, who are struggling to create a better society. In certain cases, this attitude stems from their innate sense of justice and love, rather than primarily from any sacred scripture or religious principle. But it should also be noted that, throughout history, there have been numerous interpretations of these texts and several new contributions. So Hindu India now has philosophic and religious texts that lead to the idea of loving one's neighbour and even of engaging in social action. This is particularly true of the Bhagavad Gita, a text referred to by many of those we interviewed who believe, as so many modern thinkers before them have done, that this little book contains a powerful spirituality for social and political action.

*   Amongst the militants we met, many feel sustained by the spiritual values of Hinduism but do not identify with any organized religious body. They desert Hindu temples, their rituals and priests and claim that, when it comes to social matters, they expect very little from Hindu clergy and holy men. It seems that in this respect Hindu *pujaris* and *sadhus* differ from Buddhist monks and Christian clergy, some of whom are involved in development and social change.

*   India's contact with the most vulgar, materialistic aspects of Western modernity has led to an alarming process of deculturation. Some of those we spoke to were nonetheless confident of India's ability to resist cultural alienation. Seeing religious, ethnic and cultural plurality as an extremely valuable Indian characteristic, they believe that a unique, authentically Indian synthesis will ultimately emerge. But suitable measures need to be taken now to reinforce India's cultural resistance to the violent attacks on its values. NGOs, both Indian and foreign, can play either a negative or positive role in this matter. Here, then, is an urgent, specific challenge addressed to NGOs and all other solidarity and development organizations.

*   The latter are reproached for approaching the reality of India with concepts that are foreign, and strategies evolved to meet the realities of other continents, in particular of Latin America. There, progressive Western funding agencies are involved in intense, significant solidarity work. But they have a tendency to want to repeat this experience elsewhere. They are on the lookout therefore for projects that make use of analyses and strategies that are familiar to them and whose success has been proven in Latin America. Such projects do exist, and may be perfectly valid but it might very well be that others also exist, equally valid and more deeply rooted in the spiritual and cultural reality of the Indian people. And ultimately, the latter projects may prove more effective and durable.

*   A look at projects supported in India by Western NGOs shows that, amongst their organizers, there is a disproportionate number of Indians who,

for one reason or another, do not, or no longer, belong to the dominant religious, spiritual or even cultural world of the country. Some are Christians, others Marxist, and there are, comparatively speaking, too few Hindus, Muslims, and so on, amongst them. Funding agencies who profess to be concerned with the spiritual and cultural dimension of development, and with maintaining solidarity with Indian efforts at cultural resistance will, therefore, have to get off the beaten tracks and diversify their contacts. They will have to seek out other Indian groups and movements who, though involved in active social struggle, nonetheless remain squarely planted in the cultural world they hope to conscientize, energize and organize. This is not to say that foreign NGOs should be forced to instantly abandon all their usual criteria for selecting projects. But, they should take a good look at these criteria in the light of other conceptions, other analyses and other strategies.

* Many Indians involved in development work based on local values and perceptions do not mix with foreign NGOs.[6] This is particularly true of groups belonging to the Gandhian movement, which places special attention on the principle of *swaraj*, in other words autonomy and financial self-reliance. Other groups also instigate and run their projects along lines of strict financial autonomy. This can only be cause for rejoicing, since the aim of all development aid workers is to make oneself redundant and bring about precisely this independence in all respects, including the financial. The wish on the part of Western NGOs to co-operate with Hindus or Gandhians, laudable in itself, must not force those who were managing on their own into financial dependence! But there may well be groups in need of financial support or some other form of solidarity who remain isolated or thwarted in their activities through lack of access to Western NGOs. Those NGOs who are ready to venture into cultural worlds that are unfamiliar to them should at least make their presence known, and indicate that they are willing to enter into relations of solidarity. Such relations would be of particular use to NGOs in discovering, understanding and loving that deeper India that too often eludes them.

* For NGOs used to a class analysis, the intellectual bewilderment brought about by contact with certain groups of Hindu origin can prove rather disconcerting, and the socio-political activities of such groups, who seek harmony rather than struggle, may appear naive, or downright reactionary. The same goes for the disarming goodwill displayed by disciples of Vinoba who simply appeal to the sense of good in every citizen's heart, whatever their economic and social position. It is impossible to reconcile all points of view at one fell swoop and it is pointless to chuck overboard one's analyses and the fruit of one's own experience. But could not Westerners start to recognize the different social and political sensibilities that exist side by side in India and elsewhere in Asia, and open a dialogue with development workers and social activists who hold other ideas than their own? Such a dialogue can open the door to new forms of solidarity and a valuable process of mutual growth, with the 'commissar' West and the 'yogi' India inviting each other to make up the

deficiencies in their respective approaches.

* Certain people we interviewed made an essential point: foreign NGOs ought to try above all to change the dominant socio-political and economic systems in their own respective countries. They ought also to contribute towards a profound transformation in the life-style based too much on consumerism, on profit and the arms race. They should also try to help the Western public to see alternatives to the dominant monocultural model, to rediscover and revitalize their own European and American cultural and spiritual values which have also been atrophied. Such an undertaking would help NGOs to understand India's cultures better and have more respect for them. It would also help Westerners to better appreciate the current threat of deculturation throughout the Third World and show concrete proof of solidarity in this, for them, relatively new struggle, namely that of the creative, dynamic safeguarding and renewing of the masses. Progressive Western funding agencies would then add to their current attempts to fight economic and political imperialism, a genuine effort to fight cultural imperialism as well. They may then discover that this cultural struggle is no secondary concern nor an abstract and barely relevant academic exercise, but the very precondition for efficient development work and truly respectful partnership. For such a shift to be made, NGO staff will have to stop extrapolating from Latin America on to the rest of the world. They will have to recognize more clearly that the poor of Asia, Africa, the Pacific (and even of Latin America for that matter) are entitled to their own experience, their own modes of struggle and their own alternative social models and world-views.

15. Lomé III — a New Approach?

The European Economic Community (EEC) is made up of countries several of which had colonies when the Treaty of Rome was signed (1958). From their point of view, the creation of a common market in Europe was no reason to end the extremely close commercial and economic ties that existed between countries such as France, Belgium, Holland and Italy on the one hand, and, on the other, the countries that were, or had once been, under their colonial domination. When Great Britain joined the EEC, this sphere of influence was extended to the British colonies and protectorates who had recently gained independence, situated in the West Indies, the Pacific and Africa. More recently, this huge area was further expanded when Portugal and Spain joined the EEC. We shall speak shortly about the particular relations enjoyed with a group of countries called the ACP, namely those belonging to Africa and the Caribbean and Pacific regions. Over the years, the EEC signed with its African partners, then with ACP, international conventions granting them financial and technical aid. In particular, guaranteeing certain preferential conditions such as the duty-free entry of many of their goods into the European common market. Generally speaking, these conventions have helped consolidate neocolonial relations of economic dependence, though the most recent of them have added innovating mechanisms. They are one step in the laborious search for a new economic order, notably by aiming to resist the deterioration of the exchange rate.[1]

There is no space here to go into the contents of the Conventions known as the Yaoundé, then the Lomé Conventions. Innovative and exemplary for some, these Conventions are denounced by others as factors for European division and domination of the Third World, amongst other things by their perpetuation of the extraversion of economies, and of agricultural production in particular.

What does deserve our attention here is the Third Lomé Convention, which involved the co-operation of sixty-six countries from Black Africa,[2] the Caribbean,[3] the Pacific,[4] and the EEC. It came into effect at the beginning of 1986 for a five-year period (1986–90).[5] Prime importance was accorded to financial and technical aid in matters concerning the growing of food crops (but obviously without excluding agriculture for export which is one of the Convention's *raison d'être*). This placing of the accent on self-reliant development (along with the EEC–ACP dialogue on development policies and the inclusion of clauses dealing with human rights) has rather overshadowed another important innovation. This involved a new facet of the ACP–EEC co-operation: the so-called cultural and social co-operation that appears alongside co-operation in matters of agriculture, industry, energy, commerce, finance, technology, and so on. It is interesting to look at how an international treaty like this Convention can contribute to the intercultural solidarity that concerns us here. Pioneering thinkers, both on the side of the ACP (Ambassadors Raymond Chasle of Mauritius and Seydina Dumar Sy of Senegal, the Malian ex-minister Mr T. Konate, among others) and that of the EEC (Deputy Bersani and M. Charles Vandervaeren, both of the Commission, Mr Edgar Pisani, ex-Commissioner for Cooperation and Development) have understood the damages and failures brought about by the Eurocentric, 'economicist', technocratic approach of the preceding Conventions. Indeed, the preoccupations of Lomé I and Lomé II were above all economic and commercial, and the financial and technical co-operation rarely took into account the human factor in development projects or the valorization of the human resources of the ACP countries. The introduction of a cultural dimension into Lomé III was all the more audacious in that it went way beyond the traditional promotion of international cultural exchanges. It was not merely a question of encouraging visits by dance companies to the signatory countries or organizing artistic events such as exhibitions, film festivals, and so on. All of which is, of course, worthy of encouragement. But the advocates of the cultural dimension of the future Lomé III believed that culture should not be reduced in this way to a performance, an object or, even less, a luxury object. In view of the magnitude of the problems currently facing the countries involved in the Lomé Convention III, such an appendix would in any case have been rather futile, or even a ruse designed to hide the relative meagreness of the results obtained during the negotiations on economic, commercial and financial themes properly speaking. Culture ought not to be limited to an object whose diffusion is encouraged. It should be understood as the subject of the history of peoples, a dynamic process and the integrating dimension of all social and economic change. According to the protagonists of this conception, the ACP–EEC co-operation should be refocused on human beings, as active subjects, and their culture, employed in the widest sense of the term.

As Ambassador Raymond Chasle wrote, it was no longer a question of culture seen in the elitist sense of *culture–art* but in fact of culture as source of strength and a driving force, of *culture–action*. Pisani, for his part, speaks of culture as both heritage and project. In this sense it is 'the driving force and, above all, regulator of development'.[6] He goes on:

> . . . The way we eat, the way we produce, the way we distribute land, the way we organize authority, the way local communities live, the place accorded women, children and the elderly in society, are just as profoundly cultural as art objects and languages . . . . Only this double dimension will allow us to achieve something that is not artificial. There are, of course, many original

elements that have enriched the human heritage and the culture of African, Caribbean and Pacific countries must be safeguarded. But African sculpture, Caribbean music, the oral literature of the entire developing world are not, for all their irreplacable value, the heart of the matter. The real reason lies elsewhere: it is that each country can and must, in its own way, re-invent development, its development, using its own methods.[7]

In the European Parliament, interesting debates were held on this topic. Since such conceptions are scarcely common currency in institutions of this sort, it is worth quoting some extracts from the EEC–ACP report on cultural co-operation presented at Strasbourg on 7 June 1983 by the chairman, Angelo Narducci:

Nowadays, everyone is convinced that it is not the transfer of financial means, even large-scale, nor the transfer of technology allocated without due thought, nor again lavish aid in foodstuffs that will guarantee the development of the ACP countries and, even more, of the least developed countries. Together, Parliament and Commission, we have chosen the strategy of self-sufficiency in food production and integrated agricultural development. To achieve this we have tried to initiate projects that no longer come from those on-high to those below. We have tried to encourage, on the contrary, forms of self-development capable of immediately mobilizing all available human resources, and of using them with complete respect and the total valorization of their identity and their specific socio-cultural realities. This connotation may seem obvious but it is extremely new compared with previous experiments: it introduces a profoundly different typology of projects and makes use of evaluation criteria that differ noticeably from those used up to now. It is basically a question of goals and methods that change in an evolutive perspective: the starting point is based on a pool of wealth — human and cultural — that cannot be quantified in economic or commercial terms, but which becomes the essential condition for the success of any project whatever. For these countries, the goal is to achieve self-sufficiency and escape from that state of perpetual dependence, so costly for us, so humiliating and degrading for the recipients.

To this innovative argument for a development policy respectful of cultural identity, members of the European Parliament had added that a unilateral EEC–ACP co-operation that did not 'acknowledge the community values and solidarity that Africa brings to an individualistic Europe', would slide back into the old dependence policies and negate any real co-operation between equal, responsible partners. It is to this relatively new way of thinking that Chairman Narducci was referring when he concluded:

The hegemonies we are attempting to combat, whether they be economic, political or military, are based precisely on the pernicious conviction that there exist superior cultures that must be asserted whatever the cost. In placing the relations with our partners in the ACP countries on the level of an intercultural dialogue, of respect for specificity and cultural identity within a framework of an exchange that is useful to everyone concerned, we would also improve our relations within our own countries and would discover our true role as Europeans.

The third ACP–EEC Convention signed at Lomé on 8 December 1984, (called Lomé III) therefore included, for the first time, an entire section devoted to 'cultural and social co-operation'. It deserves a closer look.

It is agreeably surprising to read in the Articles devoted to the overall aims and orientations (Section 1, Chapters 1 and 2) that 'support shall be provided in the ACP–EEC co-operation for the ACP States' own efforts to achieve more self-reliant and self-sustained development based on their cultural and social values, their human capacities . . .' (Article 4), that 'co-operation shall be aimed at supporting development in the ACP States, a process centred on man himself and rooted in each people's culture' and that it supports measures taken by these states 'to promote their cultural identities . . .' (Article 10). Decidedly a good start. But two thoughts spring to mind on reading these preliminary Articles. Firstly, Articles 4 and 10 deal with the social and cultural values and cultural identities of states, and not at all with that of the people who inhabit them. One might well ask what exactly such expressions mean. What do the cultural values of the ACP states express? Are they not basically Western institutions?[8] Happily, the context of these unfortunate expressions is more reassuring, for the culture of peoples is dealt with there. All states, however, must first have the desire and the ability to promote peoples' culture. It is sometimes so alien to them! The second observation concerns the fact that the degree of reciprocity is not mentioned in the articles devoted to aims. Whereas the foreword speaks of 'complete equality between partners', of a spirit of international solidarity and friendly relations, the chapters of the Convention devoted to principles and orientations deal only with cultural co-operation in the EEC–ACP sense, as if only the countries of the South suffer from loss of identity and cultural disorientation. The Convention makes little attempt to follow up the appeal of the European MPs who claimed that the peoples of the ACP countries had a spiritual contribution (*supplément d'âme*) to offer to an 'individualistic Europe', headed for cultural impoverishment.[9] Reading these introductory remarks, one has the impression that the Convention has not quite succeeded in achieving a genuine dialogue or a mutually enriching exchange between cultures by rising above, at least in this domain, the one-way relationship of assistance to those less fortunate than oneself. Once again, the term 'co-operation' remains a euphemism denoting aid from donor to beneficiary. This shortcoming, and the unfortunate pronouncements on the role of state, are indicative of a certain frame of mind, but are no doubt also tied in with the very nature of the Convention. In any case, they detract nothing from the merit of those who, despite strong opposition, fought to make Lomé III what it eventually became. It is quite clear that many of the latter are firmly convinced of the value of the cultural contribution of the ACP peoples to

Europe. Certain ACP spokespersons have explicitly expressed the hope that the Community and the Member States will henceforth encourage education programmes aimed at the European public, dealing with the social and cultural realities of the ACP countries.[10] These shortcomings in the declaration of the Convention's general aims must not blind us to its positive contribution within the narrower field of aid. We are getting there.

Section VIII, devoted to 'cultural and social co-operation', is composed of three chapters. The first, entitled 'Cultural and social dimension', treats culture as a fundamental dimension of all development projects supported by the EEC in ACP countries. Article 116 states: 'The design, appraisal, execution and evaluation of each project or programme shall be based on understanding of, and regard for, the cultural and social features of the milieu.' This implies, in particular, an in-depth understanding of the human environment in question and an analysis of local technology and skills. The Article that follows details the factors that both project and programme appraisal must take into consideration. Under the heading of social aspects, it examines the project's impact on 'the reinforcement of capacities and structures of self-development' and on 'the methods and forms of production and processing'. Under the heading of cultural aspects, project appraisal will take into account the project's impact on the cultural milieu, 'the integration and enhancement of the local cultural heritage, notably value systems, ways of life, modes of thought and know-how, materials and styles', and the methods of information acquisition and transmission.

This brief sketch outlines a whole new policy for projects whose tone is markedly different from that to which big international organizations have accustomed us. This policy implies, for each project, the revalorization (or, at least, the greatest possible respect) of the various local ways of thinking and acting. Those working in this field will immediately imagine the impact of such a policy in the areas of agriculture, fishing, animal husbandry, arts and crafts, housing, formal and informal education, nutrition, energy, preventative and curative health-care, including pharmacopoeia, and so on. Such a declaration of intent is no doubt very positive. Of course, the EEC and its overseas partners still have to show their desire and ability to translate this into specific, concrete measures. Note, in particular, the Clause dealing with respect for the interaction between human beings and their environment. This seems to give official recognition to the fact that it is precisely the knowledge of the local populations regarding their natural habitat that, until very recently, allowed a lasting balance between human beings and nature and that programmes of reforestation or struggle against the encroaching desert are doomed to failure when one ignores the system of representation, the myths, the symbols and the skills of rural societies.[11]

Chapter 2 tackles what it calls operations to enhance: the value of human resources through education, formal and informal training, scientific and technical research (including the valorization of local technologies and the weeding out of those that are imported); information for ACP populations, 'making wide use of cummunications systems at grass-roots level'; more active contribution of the ACP countries to the international flux of news and knowledge; the participation of the population and — last but not least! — the role of women (Articles 118 to 121). This list leaves one confused, since it all depends on the type of training given and the content of the news that is to be circulated to villages and towns. Will these relate to development imposed from outside, inspired by a destructive, alienating, coercive state, or will it be a maieutic pedagogy aimed at 'helping others to be themselves'? For Pisani, it is just such an undertaking that is called for.[12]

As for co-operation in matters concerning academic education, one can only hope that the intentions will be spelled out in greater detail. The Convention speaks of 'restructuring educational institutions and systems to renew their content, methods and technology'. This is a fundamental task in the struggle against the mental colonialization of which young Africans in particular have been the victims. Can the EEC help the ACP states to develop a more adaptable teaching network, based on local knowledge and know-how and inspiring respect rather than contempt for manual work and village life? One hardly dares hope so, so often have these things been said and repeated. Already, in *L'Afrique noire est mal partie* ('False Start in Black Africa'), René Dumont had called for 'an educational revolution in the rural areas'.[13] This was back in 1962! Since then, Africa has made little progress in this domain. Chapter 2 also deals with the support to be extended to ACP states trying to ensure the close, ongoing participation of grass-roots communities in development work, in particular by encouraging co-operatives and the like (Article 122). Here, an observation similar to that made regarding training springs to mind. There is a real danger that culture could be used as a tool to manipulate the masses and force them into 'participation'. It cannot be repeated often enough: development must take place from the bottom up. If the state or the 'developer' try to impose them, failure is inevitable.

One Article stresses the importance to be accorded women, the major omission of the first two Development Decades. Lomé III sets out to enhance the work of women, improve their living conditions, expand their role and promote their status in the production and development process and give them greater access to credit facilities (Article 123). In this, Lomé III reflects the growing current awareness of the paramount importance of women, particularly in Black Africa. This is excellent, but the idea of increasing their status must not be used as a pretext to export European feminism. Projecting all over the world what the European woman rightly considers just for her, would surely amount to yet another form of cultural imperialism. What is needed in this domain is to develop and strengthen real solidarity with the women of ACP countries without drifting into more Western messianism.

In short, one can find in all these Articles the best and the worse, depending on the spirit in which the general clauses are interpreted. In fact, the practical implementation of the intentions stipulated by the Convention have encountered many difficulties.[14] Above all, many civil servants and development experts hardly know what to do about this 'cultural dimension'! They have not been trained to recognize this as an important factor and they lack the concrete tools and ideas to implement the aforementioned Articles. Others simply dismiss the whole thing as irrelevant, having failed to understand the fundamental and urgent character of cultural resistance. The EEC and the ACP countries would do well to seek the collaboration of NGOs, both European and ACP, in this matter. In the sphere of mobilization of human resources at grass-roots level, NGOs have at their disposal a rich experience and know-how generally lacking in state bureaucracies and large-scale official co-operation agencies. NGOs are themselves products of the mobilization of human resources at the base, rather than government creations. Their contribution could become a determining factor, provided, of course, that they themselves open up completely to the cultural dimension of their obligations.

Chapter 3 of the Convention concerns the promotion of cultural identities. It deals with the development and distribution of cultural products, teaching materials, audio-visual means of popularizing information, radio and television programmes, records, cassettes, and such like (Article 126). The EEC–ACP collaboration aims to safeguard and promote the cultural achievements of ACP peoples, in particular by the creation of data banks and sound recording libraries to collect oral traditions, and by the conservation of historical and cultural monuments and the promotion of traditional architecture (Article 127).

There is not doubt that Lomé III is a new departure in the long list of international conventions dealing with co-operation. To the criticisms and questions already expressed must be added a general observation. Lomé III is an instrument of international law. It was signed by states, and it is left up to ACP and EEC states and to the CEC to put it into practice. Bearing in mind the lack of interest and the rather low level of respect shown by many civil servants for the populations targeted by this social and cultural co-operation, one suspects that Lomé III may well remain a pious vow of intent. This being said, it is only fair (and interesting) to acknowledge that not all civil servants are narrow-minded technocrats. CEC's Directorate No. VIII (Development Co-operation) and many ACP ministries do have very open-minded and committed people within them. In any case, the CEC now disposes of an instrument that allows it both to avoid certain damage and setbacks resulting from ignorance of local cultures, and to actively promote projects that re-inforce local cultures.

Thus, the CEC can refuse to support projects that go against the safeguarding and promotion of local cultures and it is to be hoped that it will be willing and able to make use of this faculty. Constant attention on the part of the public and specialized NGOs is called for in this matter. This is one of the goals set by the South–North Network on Cultures and 'Development', created during the Chantilly Conference, which we shall deal with directly. This network, made up of people and NGOs from both Third World (including ACP) and European countries, will raise awareness of development agencies and the general public regarding the role of culture in development, notably by publicizing projects and studies that foster development based on indigenous peoples' culture. It will also ensure that the directives of Lomé III in cultural matters are effectively put into practice. The network will see to it that the concern for culture is not reduced to some kind of elitist entertainment, but that it underpins (and thus strengthens) any action against oppression and exploitation of the poor. It will see to it that the ongoing debate on culture and development comes to grips with concrete situations, hard facts and specific projects. Its theoretical reflection must lead to action.

As for the active promotion of cultures, the EEC cannot impose programmes or projects on its ACP partners. In fact, the practical implementation of the Lomé Convention, unlike bilateral aid, depends on initiatives stemming from the ACP states, and is therefore dependent on the development policies pursued by their governments. The CEC does not have power of initiative concerning the projects and programmes it funds. The ACP states themselves must therefore propose development projects that take into account the culture of the peoples in question. On the other hand, the CEC can play a more active role through European NGOs. In fact, it is free to support NGOs who undertake, either in ACP countries or within the European Community, projects that actively safeguard and promote the identities of peoples. The procedure of co-financing, established some ten years ago by the CEC, allows it to provide a crucial financial contribution (usually fifty per cent of the budget) to projects submitted to it by European NGOs. It is now up to these NGOs to act, to help the CEC implement the policy it claims it wishes to put into practice. Certain of its senior officials, as well as some ACP ambassadors, ask for nothing more. This became clear to those who participated in the Chantilly Conference devoted to 'The role of culture in the overall development co-operation implemented by the Third Lomé Convention', which was attended by some of the most prominent names in negotiations on the cultural dimension.[15] They called on NGOs to take on the role of pioneers in matters of de-alienation and cultural promotion, to provide concrete examples of non-technocratic approaches and to propose explicit models of projects and programmes. They believed this would offer great scope for joint action between the CEC and NGOs.

Let us not forget that, amongst the resolutions taken at Chantilly, the Conference declared itself in favour of a policy to spread information and raise awareness in Europe and the ACP countries about the role of culture in development. The CEC was asked to support and finance projects undertaken in this spirit by churches, universities, NGOs, schools, and so on. Another important subject that seems far from resolved is the restitution of art objects and archives now in Europe, objects invested with a highly symbolic value for ACP peoples. The Conference was of the opinion that certain of these museum pieces and archives are indispensable if these peoples are to recover their historical continuity and revitalize their culture. Those attending the Conference also emphatically requested that the Member States see to it that improvements are made in the material and cultural life of students and migrant workers from ACP countries. 'Immigrants', said the Europeans, 'bring ACP culture to our cities, but we ignore it'. Europeans are asked to recognize the riches contained in the cultural contribution of ACP migrant workers and students. 'This recognition could be proof of a real desire for intercultural exchange based on equality between partners', one reads in the recommendations. In the same spirit, the Chantilly Conference came out in favour of an 'intercultural partnership'. Its participants stated that it is important that support be given to the promotion of ACP cultures, but that, simultaneously, an intercultural partnership between Europe and the ACP countries should be fostered, to make European populations aware of the enrichment their own culture might gain as a result, particularly in its present state of crisis. A proposal was made for: exchanges of lecturers, teachers and artists, of school holiday camps; the joint training of European and African development workers on site in Africa; the twinning of university classes and departments; the introduction of the intercultural issue into the basic curriculum in Europe; the promotion by the media of a positive, rather than catastrophic, image of ACP countries. The importance of the latter proposal can be seen when one recalls how Ethiopia — one of the signatories of Lomé III — was represented by the media when famine struck it.

To conclude this summary of Lomé III, let us chalk up to its credit the official expression of the intention, ratified on both sides, no longer to accept development projects that do not take into account the values and skills of the communities concerned. This can have important practical repercussions, at the very least by limiting the damage and, if all goes well, by actively promoting the flourishing of indigenous cultures. Lomé III therefore employs and helps to diffuse a broad definition of what is meant by culture, no longer reduced to an object but extended to a process. This is not the least of the Convention's achievements. At all events, it offers European NGOs an interesting field of action. No doubt NGOs will have to jog the faltering goodwill and imagination of some development experts, to have the spirit and the letter of Lomé III respected and implemented. To do this, they will have to open a dialogue — a good thing in itself — with the officials concerned and encourage the CEC, or even publicly challenge it if necessary, by exercising, through the press, European MPs and the general public, the necessary pressure. Finally, they can, by means of their own projects for which they may claim CEC co-financing, break new ground in the realms of intercultural co-operation and encourage the CEC to do likewise. It is also up to NGOs to promote something that has remained in the shadows of the Convention, namely the diffusion in Europe of cultures not primarily of ACP states but of the peoples they are supposed to represent.

16.   Summary and Conclusion

> My heart is moved by all I cannot save
> So much has been destroyed
> I have to cast my lot with those who age after age
> perversely, with no extraordinary power
> reconstitute the world.
>
> Adrienne Rich

Article 15 of the Declaration of Algiers on Peoples' Rights stipulates that no people should have imposed on them a culture that is alien. The present book derives from this principle. The main elements of the argument advanced here can be summarized into the following points:

1. Today, poverty, malnutrition and violation of human rights are even more widespread in the Third World than they were in the past. Most of the many development strategies and projects have ended in failure. This undeniable fact calls for a critical examination of the theories and analyses employed up to now, as well as the development strategies and projects arising from them.

2. One can distinguish, on the one hand, strategies based on development perceived essentially as material growth, modernization and 'catching up' with the West (Rostow's theory and variations of it); and, on the other hand, those that perceive development as a global process of liberation from the mechanisms of domination inflicted by the centres of power on their peripheries (the dependence theory). The first of these strategies is employed by large, official bureaucracies. The second is utilized by progressive states and organizations, and by development NGOs, including Western funding agencies.

3. The 'catching up' theory is based on sheer ethnocentrism. It presents the Western model as an obligatory way of life, the universal goal of all peoples. The dependence theory denounces Western imperialism, particularly the exploitation of people and resources that take place in the name of 'catching up'. But it, too, is steeped in an ultimately monocultural conception of development.

4. The Third World's indigenous cultures have largely been ignored, particularly by technocratic 'developers' of capitalist persuasion, but also by

left-wing milieux and socially committed NGOs. This failure to adequately recognize indigenous cultures is one of the fundamental reasons for the failures and difficulties incurred up to now in development work.

5. Cultural analysis must not replace previous economic, social and political analyses; it should complement and amend them. Culture is understood here not as a collection of objects or a pastime for the privileged, but as a vital process that underpins all aspects of a given community's life. If necessary, a distinction will have to be made between the culture of those who dominate and that of the dominated.

6. Local communities have often succeeded in checking the alienating development that threatens them. By means of a kind of civil disobedience, they resist the obligation to develop according to Western standards. But their cultures are not only sources of resistance to deculturation, they are also the well-springs of alternative forms of society, and generate original forms of social struggle.

7. Thus, this book evokes the vitality and interest of cultural systems that are different in economic, social and political terms. Western economics stresses the relationship between human beings and objects, whereas most cultures place the emphasis on a certain sense of order that regulates the relationships between people. Political economy has been based, since Adam Smith and the like, on a narrow and therefore mistaken concept of man as a *homo economicus*, that is someone who, before undertaking anything, makes a cost–profit analysis based on strictly materialist and quantitative criteria. But, not all people react like the Western *homo economicus*. There are other economic cultures than those of capitalism and socialism. With the West currently in a state of crisis, it would surely be sensible not to impose its model overseas but rather to investigate what seeds of alternatives exist in the Third World. Attitudes to money, profit, time and land may differ from people to people and place to place.

8. Indigenous societies tackle technology differently. They have perfected a set of trades, techniques and know-how that have been overlooked for too long. Peasant communities are capable of producing a food surplus without massive technological intervention from outside. They demonstrate a real capacity for change and adaptability, as long as the process is based on the valorization rather than the denial of their own technical achievements.

9. Indigenous communities approach politics and law in their own way. Far from feeling themselves truly participating citizens of post-colonial states, they find themselves threatened by them, hemmed in by their frontiers and crushed by their alien, centralizing and unifying law. Indigenous cultures contain the seeds of models of decentralization based on polycentrism, and forms of democracy based on concensus. They have their own legal systems, which are often rich, imaginative and able to adapt to change.

10. Cultural communities have their own ways of envisaging resistance to the mechanisms of domination and their own ideas about active commitment to a better society. One has to realize that Africans and Asians do not necessarily react to exploitation and oppression in the same way as Europeans or Latin

Americans. In Black Africa one rarely finds genuine trade unions, militant opposition parties, radical peasant associations, committed human rights groups. But it would be wrong to conclude from this that Africans lack political consciousness or the ability to struggle for radical change. Other kinds of action exist there. Solidarity groups and funding agencies ought to explore these alternative types of struggle rather than think of them as out of date or ineffectual.

11. As the locus of greatest coherence, religion represents for each people a potentially powerful driving force for resistance to cultural alienation. It also leads to socio-political commitment, if its potential for liberation can be harnessed. The theology of liberation was able to achieve this in Latin America. Is it not up to other religions (and to Christians of other continents) to make a similar effort? In this way, an end can be put to the alienating character of conservative interpretations of religion and of certain dubious aspects of popular religiosity. The powers that be have often been able to manipulate religion into beliefs that are rightly denounced as opiates of the people. Yet this process is reversible. Religions will become liberating, capable of mobilizing people, not by imitating what is happening in Latin America, but by a truer grounding in the life and spiritual tradition of the people concerned. In this way, Gandhi achieved a powerful synthesis of the deepest, most liberating elements of Hindu tradition, the Qur'an and the Gospels. In Black Africa, dynamic religious movements are springing up. Buddhism also produces forms of active socio-political commitment that go largely unnoticed in the West but which offer powerful alternatives.

12. The apparent inevitability of the Westernization of the world is deceptive. The failures encountered by development prove this. Behind façades of Westernization, indigenous value systems remain intact. They are hard to kill. What is needed, is not a romantic return to an idealized past but a lucid and well-balanced combination of inculturation and acculturation. Each people will have to forge its own modernity, its own new response to present-day challenges. Yet this delicate exercise is prevented by the sheer weight of Western cultural imperialism.

13. This brings us to an essential clarification: underdevelopment is not the point of departure of the history of Third World societies. Rather, it is the outcome of a process of economic, political and ultimately cultural destructuration. When the most internalized aspects of a culture are affected, one has to expect the worse: 'the withering away of identity'.

14. The tragedy of the Third World is, therefore, profoundly cultural and spiritual, rather than merely technical, economic or political. If the cultural and spiritual basis is destroyed, one risks disaster. It is then that a society sets out on the one-way road of inertia and fatalism.

15. Development is an ambiguous concept. Obviously, it covers some great achievements on the part of the West, but it also constitutes a dreadful threat when it imposes or even suggests a change that denies the cultural identity of a people.

16. It is not a question of undertaking a simple 'return' to one's sources

(traditionalism or obsession with the past or some kind of deceptive cultural 'purity') but rather of having 'recourse' to the past, so that each people may draw from its own heritage the reasons and means for living, for reconstructing its identity and, if need be, for evolving. For it may be necessary to change in order to safeguard what is essential.

17. Cultural alienation, spiritual impoverishment and the withering of identity are evils that afflict Westerners as well. The Third World can help them achieve the cultural and spiritual re-rooting that is necessary to overcome their crisis.

18. Peoples' right to be different need not put an end to all forms of development. It does mean, however, that programmes and projects should be based explicitly on the cultural identity of each individual people. New, intercultural solidarity arises from this, perfecting and amending rather than replacing previous forms of commitment.

19. Intercultural solidarity implies respect for a temporary 'withdrawal into oneself'. If need be, funding agencies must shield communities from the development and progress that threatens them. Above all, intercultural solidarity means support for all forms of research whose goal is local regeneration, resistance to deculturation and the positive affirmation of cultural identity. One should not always seek immediate effectiveness, optimal productivity or results that are concrete and quantifiable. Allowing cultural death to take place in order to nourish physically, would be to sacrifice the important to the urgent.

20. Western funding agencies and solidarity groups are not immune from ethnocentrism. This is true even of those who have shaken off the paternalism of the past and now practise forms of partnership with groups in the Third . World. More often than not, they support the latter only on condition that they share their own vision of development, their socio-political analyses, their methods of action, all of which are Western (or Latin American) in origin. But their close contact with the various grass-roots peoples has allowed a growing number of agencies to become aware of the cultural dimension. They have adopted new tacks, as the twenty or so projects described in this book attest. The EEC has followed suit (Lomé III). It is to be hoped that other public development agencies will, in their turn, become aware of the cultural element. The South–North Network on Cultures and 'Development' may be a useful tool for sensitizing the general public, development experts and NGOs, both in the Third World and in the 'donor countries', to the cultural dimension of development.

We have been employing here the phrase 'cultural dimension of development'. Yet this widely used expression is rather unfortunate. For one thing, 'development' is an ambiguous concept, heavily loaded with Western connotations. And 'dimension' could suggest that there is a separate cultural facet to development, alongside the political, economic and social. On the contrary, development is an all-inclusive process that is, in the final analysis, cultural. *For it is the idea of culture that gives both meaning and direction to economic activity, political decisions, community life, social conflict, technology, and so on. It is in fact culture that gives development its* raison d'être *and its goal.* It is each people's own culture that must decide what, for them, is a 'good life'. It is culture that instils its rhythm on the life of a community and gives it its direction. It is clearly better, therefore, not to speak of 'the cultural aspects of development', as though culture were a more or less decorative accessory, or of 'cultural development', as though it was only a question of culture as artistic creation. Culture, in the broad sense used in this book, is, properly speaking, the basis of 'development'.

Up to now, development theories and strategies have suffered from excessive fragmentation. Most of them have looked only at the material, quantifiable aspect. Others have put particular emphasis on the political and social nature of development. Yet only the cultural dimension can give coherence and finality to development. Faced with the fragmentary nature of analyses and activities, the cultural approach tackles social reality in a way that is dynamic and holistic. Dynamic, in that culture evolves through needs, desires and external contacts. Holistic, because culture encompasses all aspects of life, whether they be material or spiritual, symbolic or technical, economic or social. In short, the cultural approach is synonymous with the human approach in all its complexity and richness. Respect for a local culture implies respect for the men and women who are both its trustees and its creators. Stressing the cultural dimension of development means placing human beings at the centre of all analyses and initiatives. In this respect, the plea for taking the cultural into account echoes Louis J. Lebret[1] and those who have been saying for three decades that the human being ought to be the goal of development. Christian churches, and other religions such as Islam and Buddhism, have been claiming this for some time now. It has to be said that their message has not always been heard or that it has been partly obscured by Western ethnocentrism. Furthermore, these religions themselves have not been able to clarify all the implications of their basic position on the cultural dimension of development. If, on the Christian side, there exists a rich literature on 'culture and evangelization', there is still a great lack of material on 'culture and development'. The same missionaries who, in their capacity as pastors, will seriously try to adapt to local culture, will often behave as Eurocentric 'developers' when undertaking socio-political activities. Furthermore, some church hierarchies display extreme reticence when indigenous members of the clergy or laymen try to put into practice official principles regarding inculturation of Christianity.

Today, funding agencies, researchers and Third World activists are proposing to reopen the debate concerning the cultural dimension of development. They could ally themselves with the protagonists of eco-development, whose theses they confirm, complement and amend. Indeed, amongst the most salient features of eco-development is the principle of utilizing the specific resources of each region. Of all these resources, the human being is the most precious. For Professor Ignacy Sachs, one of the foremost defenders of this theory, eco-development is concerned both with natural and cultural ecology. Respect for the diversity of cultures and the setting up of an acceptable 'social ecosystem' are, according to him, part and parcel of eco-development strategies.[2]

In fact, the argument contained in this book stems from the notion of self-reliance that has been mentioned several times in these pages. Self-reliance has become a key concept for many funding agencies and researchers, as well as for Third World grass-roots communities and progressive politicians. The interpretation the term has received, however, and its practical application often remain limited to the realms of politics and economics.

Thus, Third World countries try, in the name of self-reliance, to re-focus national economic activities on local needs and resources. This is what is called the delinking of 'peripheral' economies from the 'centres'. This was touched on earlier, when dealing with the economic dimension of withdrawal (selective strategies of delinking). These strategies are not only of interest to states. Local communities are trying to acquire more autonomy regarding the local mechanisms of exploitation that cause their impoverishment. NGOs support them in this. From the political point of view, states and liberation movements have both drawn from the idea of self-reliance arguments demanding sovereignty for countries still under colonial rule. It is also a key concept in the struggle against neocolonialism and superpower politics.

All this is important. But self-reliance in economic activities and political decisions depend on the existence of a cultural bedrock that can serve as its foundation. It is a people's culture, its wisdom, values, religion, skills and knowledge that justify this confidence and give it its breadth.

Self-reliance must be understood as an act of emancipation from all harmful forms of extraversion and dependence. For each people or local community, it is a question of preserving or reclaiming their liberty and, ultimately, their identity. Self-reliance implies a process of autonomization that is, at the same time, economic, political and cultural. In this sense, the distinction between the economic, political and cultural spheres resorted to in this book are artificial. In real life, these are closely intertwined. It is precisely this inter-sphere relationship that conventional development thinking has sadly overlooked. Let us not fall now into a new kind of blindness by overlooking the hard facts of economic and politics when stressing the importance of culture.

Peoples' movements, grass-roots communities and ethnic minorities are asserting with increasing strength their dignity and a profound faith in their own capacities. This is an invitation to stop bewailing the fate of the Third World and, instead, see there reasons for hope. It calls for a common commitment towards the defence of peoples' right to be different. This right to be different calls for the rejection of all conceptions and policies of imitative development. Grass-roots communities also remind us of a basic reality: it is not the privileged and often very Westernized minorities that carry the hope of the Third World, but the great mass of the poor, the oppressed, the exploited.

This book does not set out to champion some fashionable idea for intellectuals casting around for something new. The author's sole ambition was to make a contribution to a debate that is important and suggest concrete actions that are even more so.

Notes

Chapter 1

1. Cf. Goulet, Denis, 'Obstacles to world development: an ethical reflection', paper presented at the Intercultural Conference held at La Marlagne (June 1983), organized by the Centre Interculturel Monchanin (Canada) and the Université de Paix (Belgium) on the theme of intercultural co-operation.

2. Rostow, W. W., *The Stages of Economic Growth, a Non-communist Manifesto*, Cambridge University Press (1960).

3. Corm, Georges, 'Saper l'idéologie du développement', *Le Monde Diplomatique*, April (1978).

4. One had only to re-read Engels' *The Origin of the Family, Private Property and the State* to be convinced of this.

5. Mention should also be made of 'community development' projects, centred on mobilization and mutual aid. This method tries to heed local aspirations and claims to respect indigenous socio-political structures (e.g. chieftaincies, etc.).

6. Kerr, Graham, 'Indigenous development groups and their potential roles in alternative development strategies', in *Law in Alternative Strategies of Rural Development*, INTWORSLA, New York (1982), p. 167. The author quotes from a study by ONU (UNRISD) which concludes that 'rural co-operatives . . . bring little benefit to the masses of the poorer inhabitants . . . and cannot be generally regarded as agents of change and development for such groups'.

7. Mende, Tibor, Seuil, Paris (1972). For every dollar of aid to the Third World, European countries (EEC) nowadays sell it US$10 in goods and services. For the USA, it is $20.

8. 'Quelle industrialisation pour le Tiers-Monde?', IFDA, *Dossier* 20, (1980) p. 1 (27). See also in the same *Dossier* p. 2 (37): Judet, Pierre, 'Conséquences sociales de l'industrialisation dans les pays du Tiers-Monde'. IFDA (International Foundation for Development Alternatives) has published excellent contributions on the subjects we are dealing with here.

9. 'Le capitalisme périphérique', special edition of *RevueTiers-Monde*, No. 52 (1972).

10. See in particular the document prepared by the *Groupe des 77* for CNUCED in Manila, 'Arusha Programme for Collective Self-Reliance and Framework for Negotiations', UNCTAD V, Manila 1979, UNCTAD (1979). This approach aims to encourage all forms of extraversion and autonomy, without necessarily breaking entirely with the surrounding world. The term 'self-reliance' was first endorsed by Emerson, was taken up again by Gandhi and, more recently, by Nyerere.

11. Notably the dialogue undertaken between the European Community and the ACP States (from Africa, the Caribbean and the Pacific) within the framework of the Yaoundé and Lomé Conventions. These are dealt with later in this book.

12. Goulet, Denis, 'La crise dans les modèles de développement', *Foi et Développement* (Paris) No. 03 (1983), p. 2.

13. At the level of development NGOs, there are many organizations belonging to the international consortium ICDA, to CIDSE, and to CICARWS and CCPD (specialized commissions of the World Council of Churches), as well as the European amalgamation, Euro-Action Accord.

14. CIDSE, an international consortium of Catholic NGOs, changed the meaning of its initials. It no longer means 'International Co-operation for Socio-Economic Development', but '. . . for Development and Solidarity'.

15. For example, see Broederlijk Delen, *Projets et développement: voies et libération*, Brussels (roneo).

16. Cosmao, Vincent, *Un monde en développement? Guide de réflexion*, Ouvrieres, Paris (1984), pp. 20 ff.

17. Freire, Paulo, *L'Education, pratique de la liberté*, Cerf, Paris (1971); *Pédagogie de l'opprimé*, Maspero, Paris (1973).

18. Humbert, Colette, *Conscientisation, expériences, positions dialectiques et perspectives*, IDOC-France-L'Harmattan (Working document of INODEP-3), Paris, 1976.

19. The examples quoted are taken from existing projects, supported by an NGO. Generally speaking, these projects are not mentioned in publications. See, however, the recent study by Rouille d'Orfeuil, Henri, *Coopérer autrement. L'engagement des organisations non-gouvernementales*. L'Harmattan, Paris (1984).

20. But it must be added that the evils have sometimes been aggravated (as is at present the case in Brazil), for social struggles fit into a dialectic that seems endless. The impact of these struggles and of NGO projects in terms of the evolution of societies can be judged only in the long term.

21. 'Et germe l'espoir' is the title of a fine testimony published by Menotti Bottazi, one-time head of one of the major French NGOs, CCFD: Cerf, Paris (1980). A critical evaluation of some NGOs can be found in *La Revue Nouvelle* (Brussels), Vol. LXXX, No. 9 (1984), pp. 155 ff.

Chapter 2

1. The dialogue recently published between Raimondo Panikkar and Étienne Leroy illustrates the problem perfectly. As a philosopher, Panikkar casts doubts on the universal character of the San Francisco Declaration of the Rights of Man. Leroy, as a jurist, accepts the argument but fears the 'fiendish' use to which such questioning might be put by the world's dictators. See the review of the Centre Interculturel Monchanin (Quebec), *Interculture*, Vol. XVII, Books 82 and 83 (1984).

2. *Pour un dialogue des civilisations*, Denoël, Paris (1977), p. 197.

3. De Varine, Huges, *La Culture des Autres*, Seuil, Paris (1976), a definition notably taken up by one NGO that has tackled this theme: Service d'Information Tiers-Monde, *Culture cri de libération*, Berne (1978), p. 1. For the different notions of culture, see especially the useful summary made by Raymond Chasle, the

Mauritian Ambassador in Brussels: 'La culture, une notion large', *ObjectifEurope*, (Brussels) No. 29–30 (1985).

4. 'Quelle coopération internationale? D'une coopération intégrationiste à une coopération interculturelle', *Interculture*, Vol. XVI, Book 79 (1983); *cf.* also 'Ontogestion et développement, la tradition autochtone contemporaine d'onto-gestion et de solidarité cosmique', *Recherches Amerindiennes au Quebec*, Vol. 13 (1983).

5. And several others cited here, as well as the participants of the Marlagne conference (see Introduction).

6. *Lettre ouverte aux élites du Tiers-Monde*, Sycamore, Paris (1981), p. 44.

7. Commission des Communautés Européennes, *Memorandum sur la politique communautaire de développement*, Brussels (1982), (roneo) and its publication *La main et l'outil*, R. Laffont, Paris (1984).

8. Chasle, Raymond, *Les aspects culturels des échanges économiques dans les relations internationales: l'exemple de la convention ACP-CEE*, Brussels (roneo, for the African Cultural Institute). We will return to Lomé III Convention later.

9. 'Report on the symposium', IFDA, *Dossier* 13 (1979), p. 9 (7).

10. *Global development: the end of cultural diversity?*, IFDA, (1975) (roneo), author's translation.

11. *Development, Seeds of Change*, (1981) 3/4.

12. IFDA, *Dossier* 7, (1979).

13. *Main basse sur l'Afrique*, Seuil, Paris (1979), p. 26; but Ziegler maintains that the unification of the non-communist world under the reign of multinational capital is a historical fact, now irreversible.

14. It will be dealt with here in the interviews with Indian militants.

15. Thus, when one claims to be upholding 'scientific socialism', there is a risk that one is replacing the 'culture of silence' with the culture of science!

16. Chonchol, Jacques, Preface to Humbert, Colette, *Conscientisation . . .*, (see Bibliography).

17. See the practice of the Catholic consortium 'Asia Partnership for Human Development' (APHD). Non-denominational (non-confessional) NGOs seem no more able to find Hindu or Buddhist partners. It should be noted that APHD has just undertaken a study of this lacuna. A group has been formed to try to develop solidarity and 'partnership' with representatives of the dominant cultures and religions in Asia. This will be discussed in greater detail later.

18. Stavenhagen, Rodolfo, 'Indian ethnic movements and state policies in Latin America', IFDA, *Dossier* 36, (1983), p. 14.

19. '. . . the struggle lacks drive . . . class consciousness particularly inadequate . . .' claimed Joseph Ki-Zerbo on the subject of African peasant and working classes: 'Intellectuels, ouvriers et paysans: nouveaux rapports pour une autogestion africaine', the subject of his speech at the Congrès Constitutif de l'Internationale Africaine des Forces pour le Développement, Dakar, April (1975).

20. Main basse . . . pp. 195–8, (see Bibliography). Ziegler recently published his *La victoire des vaincus; oppression et résistance culturelle*, Seuil, Paris (1988) which extols the potential liberating content of tradition in Africa and clearly acknowledges the tragic shortcomings of Marxist analysis in this respect.

Chapter 3

1. Panikkar coined the term 'cosmothéandrisme' (from cosmos, theos, and aner) to denote the triple (cosmic, divine and human) dimension of human beings within the universe. See Smet, Robert, *Essai sur la pensée de Raimondo Panikkar*, Centre d'Histoire des Religions, Catholic University Louvain (1981).

2. Garaudy, Roger, 'Comment l'homme devint humain', *Jeune Afrique*, Paris (1979), p. 108. Raimondo Panikkar believes the current universal imposition of Western paradigms is a substitution for transcendence.

3. Although dominant, they are not exclusive and have not extinguished other, more spiritual aspirations that have been apparent throughout the history of the West.

4. Scheuer, Jacques, 'Le message de l'Inde d'hier au monde d'aujourd'hui', *Interculture*, Book 72, (1981).

5. If it had not been different, the problem of cultural imperialism would not have arisen in the first place. . . .

6. Arsom, 'Stratégie alimentaire d'un pays en voie de développement. Un exemple: Le Zaïre', (*Académie royale des sciences d'outre-mer*) Brussels, (1984).

7. For a discussion of Zaire's economic decadence and the responsibility of the ruling class who control and organize it, see Verhaegen, Benit, 'Classes sociales, pouvoir et économie au Zaïre', *Genève–Afrique*, XVIII, 1, (1980).

8. *Ibid*, p. 21. Elsewhere direct links between producers and consumers are developing. Latin Americans, aware of the extent of these links, speak of 'the economy of the poor'.

9. cf. Foreword.

10. That is, who has been influenced by Western culture to the extent of renouncing an important part of his or her own. The notion of acculturation is discussed in greater depth in a later chapter.

11. Bureau, René, 'L'impact de la technologie sur les cultures', paper given at the Chantilly Convention (13–15 June 1985) on 'La fonction de la culture dans l'ensemble de la coopération au développement mise en oeuvre dans la troisième Convention de Lomé', (roneo).

12. Arsom, 'Stratégie alimentaire d'un pays en voie de développement. Un exemple: Le Zaïre', Brussels, (1984), p. 41.

13. Data taken from Hugues Dupriez, agronomist and economist attached to ENDA who will be discussed later in the present work. The Bamileke, an ethnic group in the Cameroons, have their own data-processing experts. For the projects, see below.

14. Author of *Cri de l'homme africain*, L'Harmattan, Paris, (1980) and *L'Afrique des villages* and *La ville en Afrique Noire*, both published by Karthala, Paris (1982 and 1983).

15. 'Identité propre d'une théologie africaine' in *Théologie et choc des cultures*, Cl. Geffre, ed. Cerf, Paris, (1984) p. 38.

16. Notes taken during an interview the author held with Jean-Marc Ela. Regarding peasant rationality, see the work of Prof. Dominique Desjeux, in particular 'Development as an acculturation process' in *Development, seeds of change* . . . , the revue of SID (cited in Bibliography).

17. For this idea of rationality, see Gilbert Rist's excellent article, 'Relations interculturelles et pratiques du "développement" ', *Revue Canadienne d'Etudes du Développement*, Vol. V, No. 2, (1982), p. 239.

18. Bureau, René, *Le péril blanc, propos d'un ethnologie sur l'occident*, L'Harmattan, Paris (1978), p. 70.

19. Seuil, Paris (1979), p. 53–9.

20. *Ibid.*

21. 'A Buddhist perspective on Asian development in the eighties and a Buddhist view on partnership in practice', paper presented to the general assembly of Asia Partnership for Human Development (APHD), Tagaytay, 1982. By the same author, 'Buddhism and Development', *Asia Action*, (ACFOD), No. 1 (Bangkok).

22. Gunantilekke, Godfrey, 'Sri Lanka, a national dialogue on development', IFDA, *Dossier* 14, (1979), p. 9 (101) to 12 (104). Unfortunately the neo-liberal government has since opened the frontiers of this once protected country: in five years, the influx of transnational companies and their gadgets has upset many customs. The local culture is threatened, but villagers apparently remain alive to the appeal of Buddhist values. Those working in the field claim that anything is still possible.

23. *Quotations from Chairman Mao-Tse-Tung*, Foreign Languages Press, Peking, (1966), and for Guevara, MESA-LAGO, *The labour sector and socialist distribution in Cuba*, Praeger, New York (1968).

24. *Sarvodaya* signifies the well-being or awakening of all, the common good. It is also the name of the Gandhian movement in India. It will be discussed later.

25. See Ariyaratne, A. F. *Collected Works* (2 vols.), Sarvodaya Research Institute, Dehiwala (1980). The evolution of the movement (1,500,000 members) is currently attracting lively criticism from the Left. It is reproached for having toned down the radical character of its doctrine and of having been taken over by those in power. See below, Ariyaratne was awarded the Prix International Roi Baudouin pour le Développement in 1982.

26. Tévoédjrè, Albert, Éd. Ouvrieres, Paris (1978).

27. Ed. Erce, Montreal (1983).

28. In 'Quelle monde pour demain?', Association Mondiale de Perspective Sociale, Geneva (1981), p. 60.

29. De Montvalon, Robert, 'Cultures et pauvreté de pauvretés de notre culture', *Communio Viatorum* (1971), p. 1. See also the question posed by Robert Vachon 'Qui est riche et qui est pauvre?', op. cit., p. 21. See also the excellent collection published under the auspices of the Institut Universitaire des Etudes du Développement (Geneva): 'Il faut manger pour vivre . . . ; controverses sur les besoins fondamentaux et le développement', PUF and IUED, Paris (1980).

30. This author has written: *Libérer l'avenir, appel à une révolution des institutions* (1973), *Une société sans école* (1971), *La convivialité* (1973), *Énergie et équité* (1973), *Némésis médicale, l'expropriation de la santé* (1975), *Le chomage créateur* (1977), all published by Seuil, Paris.

31. Ngoc-Hanh, Nguyen, 'Sur la complémentarité de la médicine traditionelle et de la médicine occidentale dans le contexte du développement de la santé communautaire', IFDA, *Dossier* 12 (1979), p. 12 (9).

32. *Espace et liberté en Haiti*, ERGE and Centre de Recherche Caraïbes (University of Montreal), Montreal (1982).

33. Mignot-Lefebvre, Yvonne, 'Agro-systèmes paysans en crise; un projet de vidéo-communication en Haiti', interviews with G. Belkin, *Revue Tiers-Monde*, Vol. XXV, No. 98, April–June (1984).

34. The phrase is from Sheikh Hamidu Kane, in his preface to Dupriez and De Leener's *Agriculture tropicale au milieu paysan africain*, ENDA-L'Harmattan, Terres et Vies, Nivelles (1983).

35. Dupriez, Hugues and De Leener, Philippe, *Agriculture tropicale au milieu paysan africain*, ENDA – L'Harmattan – Terres et Vies, Paris-Nivelles (1983).

36. Dupriez, Hugues, *Paysans d'Afrique noire*, L'Harmattan et Terres et Vies, Paris-Nivelles (1982).

37. Hochet, Anne-Marie, *Afrique de l'Ouest; Les paysans, ces 'ignorants' éfficaces*, L'Harmattan, Paris (1985).

38. Fuglesang, Andreas, 'The myth of people's ignorance', *Development Dialogue* (Uppsala), (1984), Nos. 1–2, pp. 45 and ff.

39. *Ibid.*

40. Functional, that is, socially neutral, rather than conscientizing; being aimed at structural change.

41. Republic of Central Africa.

42. Particularly in the region of Beni-Butembo, and that of Bukavu where peasant co-operatives, now re-formed into federations (e.g. FERCOP), are flourishing.

43. 'Un miracle agricole', *Demain le monde* (Brussels), No. 1, July 1985, p. 2; translated from an article in the *Guardian Weekly*, of 16/12/84. To these examples taken from East and Central Africa, one could add those of the Sahel region of Africa cited by P. Jacolin.

44. Kadja Mianno, Daniel, 'La démocracie dans les sociétés traditionelles et dans les nouveaux États africains: recherche pour une autre voie de l'auto-développement', IFDA, *Dossier* 32 (1982), pp. 30–41.

45. See below.

46. Eghbal, Afsaneh, 'L'État contre l'ethnicité; une nouvelle arme: le développement-exclusion', IFDA, *Dossier* 36 (1983), pp. 17–29.

47. *The Challenge of world poverty, a world anti-poverty programme in outline*, Penguin, Harmondsworth (1970). Myrdal saw the weakness of States (the 'soft' states) as an obstacle in the struggle against poverty. Ten years on, François Partant hopes rather for the shattering of states: *La fin du développement, naissance d'une alternative?*, Maspero, Paris (1982).

48. Deleury, Guy, *Le Modèle hindu*, Hachette, Paris (1978) p. 244. See in particular Ashis Nandy's remarkable paper 'Culture, State and the Rediscovery of Indian Politics' *Economical and Political Weekly*, Vol. XIX, No. 99 December (1984).

49. Le Roy, Étienne, 'L'esprit de la coutume et l'déologie de la loi', in *La Connaissance du Droit en Afrique*, Deeds of the Symposium organized by L'Académie Royale des Sciences d'Outre-Mer (ARSOM), Brussels, 1984.

50. 'Culture africaine et développement. Primat de la "bisoïte" sur l'inter-subjectivité' paper given at the Chantilly Conference (13–15 June, 1985) on 'La fonction de la culture dans l'ensemble de la coopération au développement mise en oeuvre dans la troisième Convention de Lomé' (roneo).

51. Verhelst, Thierry, 'Customary land tenure as a constraint on agricultural development: a re-evaluation', *Cultures et Développement* (Louvain), Vol. II, 3–4 (1969–70).

52. Leroy, Etienne, 'Les droits africains traditionels et la modernité', *Interculture*, No. 65 (1979), p. 35.

53. See for example Verhelst, Thierry, 'Legislation on the judiciary: "Fantasy law" or programmed expectations?', *Verfassung und Recht in Ubersee* (Hamburg), 2nd Term, (1973) p. 137.

54. Verhelst, Thierry, 'Safeguarding customary law: judicial and legislative

processes for its adaptation and integration', UCLA (Los Angeles), Occ. Paper No. 7 (1969).

55. For example, legislation from the royal council, the jurisprudence of the chief, and proverbs which are a source of doctrine.

56. Paper presented at the symposium mentioned above.

57. Agondjo-Okawe, Pierre-Louis, 'L'enseignement du droit au Gabon', in: *La Connaissance du Droit en Afrique*, op. cit. A similar claim is made regarding popular law in Haiti: Despeignes, J., *Le droit informal haitien*, PUF, Paris (1976).

58. But even these countries have minorities, albeit numerically small: tribal and Muslim populations in the Philippines, the Twa in Rwanda, Berbers in Morocco, Indians in Argentina, etc.

59. It does not, however, always exclude coercion.

60. On this subject, see *Le péril blanc* (The White Peril), by René Bureau (see Bibliography) which combines the rigour of anthropological knowledge with a trenchant, invigorating humour.

61. See Hurbon, Laënnec, *Culture et Dictature en Haiti; l'imaginaire sous controle*, L'Harmattan, Paris (1979).

62. This will be dealt with in greater detail in a later chapter.

Chapter 4

1. Gandhi had been influenced by H. Thoreau, Tolstoy, Ruskin. He was familiar with the Gospels and the Qur'an, some of whose principles he applied with as much respect as those of the Bhagavad Gita. See Kantowsky, D., 'Gandhi, coming back from West to East', IFDA, *Dossier* 9 (1984).

2. Notably Adolfo Perez-Esquivel and the Brazilian Bishops José Maria Pires, Antonio Fragoso, Helder Camara.

3. Mesters, Carlos, *La mission du peuple qui souffre*, Cerf, Paris (1984).

4. Vachon, Robert, 'Pour une réorientation radicale des O.N.G.; du développement endogène à la solidarité interculturelle', *Interculture*, Vol. XVII, Cahier 85 (1984). Elsewhere in Afria there had been instances of popular resistance where women undressed publicly (e.g. a group of 8,000 women in front of the prefect of Bamenda, in 1958 in the Cameroons) or acted out the preparations for tribal war (the disturbances in the Aba Market, in 1929, in Nigeria): see, respectively Perham, Margery, 'The Aba Market Women's Riot in Nigeria, 1929', in Wilfred Cartey and Martin Kilson (eds.) *The African Reader: Colonial Africa*, Vintage Books, New York (1970), pp. 163–9 and Bruchaus, Eva-Maria, 'Animal power for easy farming', *Development and Co-operation* (Bonn), 6/1984, p. 10.

5. Houtart, François, Lemercenier, Geneviève, 'The great Asiatic religions and their social functions', Centre de recherches socio-religieuses, U.C.L., Louvain-La-Neuve (1980). But these authors show (p. 218) that the classic Marxist analysis pays insufficient attention to the progressive role played, for example, by Theravada Buddhism in the so-called socialist movements.

6. See particularly the short, fascinating booklet distributed by Entraide et Fraternité, *Va libérer mon peuple* by Carlos Mesters, Brussels (roneo).

7. *A Espada do Gedeão; a forca dos fracos,* bulletin published for La Campagne de la Fraternité (l'action de Carême brésilienne) in the North-East region, 1983; with contributions from, amongst others, Alfred Bour, Antonio Fragoso, Fredy Kunz and Margarete Malfliet, Loyola, São Paulo (1983), p. 79.

8. Various texts taken from the pamphlet *A Espada do Gedeão* . . . , op. cit.
9. 'The miracle of being awake, a manual on meditation for the use of young activists', Buddhist Publication Society, Kandy (1980). He is also the author of a book that helped open Western eyes to the horrors of the Vietnam War: *Vietnam, lotus in a sea of fire*, Hill and Wang, New York.
10. Eliade, Mircea, *Le yoga, immortalité et liberté*, Payot, Paris (1954) and Herbert, Jean, *Le yoga de la vie quotidienne; karma yoga*, Dervy, Paris (1978).
11. This is true of this theology as it is expressed in books. However, the way in which grass-roots communities live it out gives it a quite specific tonality that is better suited to these culturally very mixed populations. And one tends to forget that there is also a *spirituality* of liberation. One finds little trace of this in libraries, but it is alive and is what gives basic communities their vitality. See for example Guttierez, *La libération par la foi; Boire a son propre puits ou l'itinéraire spirituel d'un peuple*, Cerf, Paris (1985); Sobrino, Jon, 'Spiritualité et Libération', *Liaisons Internationales*, Nos. 42 and 43, (March, June 1985); Mesters, Carlos, *La mission du peuple qui souffre*, Cerf, Paris (1984), and the works of Arturo Paoli and Alfredinho Kunz.
12. For a discussion of these Asian standpoints see: 'The place of non-Christian religions and cultures in the evolution of Third World theology', in *Irruption of the Third World, Challenge to Theology*, Fabella, V., Torres, S., (eds), Orbis, New York (1983) and in particular that of the Singhalese Aloysis Pieres, p. 119. See also Soares, Georges, 'Inculturation, liberation, dialogue; challeges to Christian theology in Asia today', IMCS (International Movement of Catholic Students), Asia Document Reprint Service, 1985.
13. Innovative social initiatives from sects combining Christian and Animist elements. The repression they are subjected to (e.g. in East Kasai) shows that the authorities fear their impact.
14. On the other hand, sorcery is undeniably an often tyrannical impediment to progress, according to the criteria of Western modernity which encourages precisely this ambition, particularly in the economic domain. See Singleton, Mike, 'La sorcellerie en Afrique: qui fait quoi?', Pro Mundi Vita, *Dossier Afrique* No. 2, Brussels.
15. Information from notes taken during an interview with François de l'Espinay. See the contributions of this author to the issues of *Interculture* devoted to 'Brésil africain et autochton' Nos. 69 and 70 (1980) and Westra, Willemier, 'Religie en dagelijks overleven, hulpverlening in de Candombléreligie van Brazilie' *Internationale Spectator*, (s'Graven hage en Brussel), No. 6/3 (1982).
16. This is the sub-title of Laënnec Hurbon's *Culture et Dictature en Haiti*, L'Harmattan, Paris (1979).
17. *Ibid*, p. 37.
18. EATWOT, Ecumenical Association of Third World Theologians.

Chapter 5

1. Salomont-Bayet, Claire, 'La science moderne et la coexistence des rationalités', *Diogène*, No. 26 (1984), p. 19. The author rightly adds that to live only one of these rationalities would constitute an impoverishment, even if it were the one considered the most effective.
2. Perrot, Dominique, 'L'Occident est-il ethnocentrique ou a-t-il perdu son

centre?' *Recherche pédagogique et culture* (Paris), No. 46 (1980), p. 53. The phrase itself comes from Roger Bastide.

3. Regarding this subject and the significance of new paradigms see the following chapter devoted to the crisis in the West.

4. Their definition has yet to be finalized. I take my inspiration here from the description put forward by Nicolaas Standaert in *Enkele aspecten van 'inculturatie'*, paper (roneo) given to the work party on 'Inculturation ici et là-bas' organized at Drongen, August (1985), by the Conseil national missionnaire (NMR) and the Conseil pastoral interdiocésain (IPB) of the Flemish dioceses of Belgium. The term 'acculturation' was used as far back as 1936 by North American anthropologists, but in a slightly different sense.

5. Mbembe, Achille, 'Tensions entre Rome et les églises africaines (foi catholique et culture noire)', *Le Monde Diplomatique*, 32nd year, No. 78, September (1985).

6. Decret *Ad Gentes* on the Church's missionary activity, No. 2, (Diversité dans l'unité).

7. Mbembe, A., *ibid.*

8. A missionary, R. Jaouen, testifies to the vitality of African religions in 'Persistance visible et invisible de la religion traditionelle', *Foi et Développement*, No. 29–30, May–June, (1983).

9. Latouche, Serge, *Faut-il refuser le développement?*, PUF, Paris (1986).

Part 2:   Chapter 6

1. See Cosmão, Vincent, *Un monde . . .*, (see Bibligraphy), pp. 22 ff. Until very recently Father Cosmão was director of the Lebret Centre in Paris. His thinking, along with that of other centres both in the South and the North, has helped to sensitize certain Christian NGOs to the cultural dimension of development.

2. *Ibid.*, p. 23.

3. *Ibid.*

4. This was mentioned in the Foreword.

5. 'La notion . . .', p. 4, see bibliography.

6. Kalpana Das, Director of the Centre Monchanin, suggests using this in 'Development and international co-operation: a cross-cultural probing', *Interculture*, Vol. XVI, cahier 79 (1979).

7. Suess, Paulo, *Culturas indigenas e evangelização*, Vozes, São Paulo (1982), p. 237.

Chapter 7

1. The same assertion was made to me by President Julius Nyerere, then Tanzanian Head of State. His good humour and cordiality robbed the remark of any hint of moralizing or reproach. For all that, it retains its caustic quality.

2. Morin, Edgar, 'Pour sortir du XXᵉ siècle' Nathan, coll. *Points*, Paris (1981), pp. 26–34. See also André Gortz's plea for autonomy, self-organization and voluntary co-operation: 'Adieu au prolétariat; au-delà du socialisme', Galilée, coll. *Points*, Paris (1980).

3. The philosopher and psychoanalyst Erich Fromm has written useful works on this subject. See in particular, Introduction to *Socialist humanism: an international*

symposium, Anchor Books, New York, (1966), p. IX and 'Avoir ou être? Un choix dont dépend l'avenir de l'homme', R. Laffont, coll. *Réponses*, Paris (1978).

4. Prigent, Yves, 'L'expérience dépressive, ou la parole d'un psychiatre', Desclée-de-Brouwer, coll. *Connivences*, Paris (1978). 'Europeans look as though they eat without appetite' a Latin American traveller returning home told Clodovis Boff who reported the remark in his 'Lettre a l'église européenne', *Etude et Dialogues*, Brussels, 21st year, No. 170 (September–October 1985) p. 4.

5. On this subject, see notably Ferguson, Marylin, *Les enfants du Verseau; pour un nouveau paradigme*, Calmann-Lévy, Paris (1981), and Capra, Fritjof, *Le Tao de la physique*, Sand, Paris (1979); the works of Edgar Morin, *La Méthode* (Vol. I and II), Seuil, Paris (1977), and Prigogine, I. and Stenger, I., *La nouvelle alliance, Métamorphose de la science*, Gallimard, Paris (1979).

6. For Morin, the movement of December 1986 was ethical and cultural rather than political. It grew out of the coming together of egalitarian fraternalism and the 'vague refusal to embark on a process leading either to unemployment or to a universe where one is drawn into a world that is bureaucratic, disciplined, joyless and grey, where dreadful threats are everywhere': interview in *Le Monde*, 13/12/1986, p. 19, under the title, 'A revolt without revolutionaries'.

7. Edgar Morin defines the paradigm thus: 'It is a principle of basic differentiation/bonding/oppositions between certain dominant notions that order and control thinking, in other words the constitution of theories and the production of discourses', in 'Pour sortir du XXᵉ Siècle', Nathan, coll. *Points*, Paris (1981).

8. Ferguson, Marylin, *Les enfants du verseau; pour un nouveau paradigme*, Calmann-Lévy, Paris (1981).

9. Boff, Clodovis, 'Lettre à l'église européenne', *Études et Dialogues*, (Brussels), 21st year, No. 170, (September–October 1985), p. 4. The author speaks of 'an ecclesiastical winter that coexists with a cultural winter'.

10. Hildegard Goss-Mayr, European philosopher, non-violent activist (and the wife of Jean Goss). Joe Holland is an American activist involved in the pacifist and feminist movements, and works at the Center of Concern in Washington. See in particular the latter's excellent essay, 'The spiritual crisis of modern culture', Center of Concern, Occasional Papers, Washington, D.C., 1983. Also Hildegard Goss's *L'homme face à l'injustice; libération non-violente, spiritualité et praxis*, Académie Sociale Catholique d'Autriche, Europa Verlag, Vienna (1976).

Chapter 8

1. Certain authors date these characteristics back to the advent of patriarchy or that of towns. Thus they are part of the history of a large section of humanity. Non-Western peoples therefore are no strangers to these cultural traits, but the modern West has exacerbated them, and its technological discoveries have allowed it to magnify the consequences. See particularly Fromm, Erich, 'La passion de détruire; anatomie de la déstructivite humaine', Laffont, coll. *Réponses*, Paris (1973), and the works of René Girard and Lewis Munford.

2. Bertherat, Thérèse and Bernstein, Carol, *Le corps a ses raisons*, Seuil, Paris (1970), and for the fundamental importance of the body (and correct breathing) within Christian spirituality, Goettmann, Alphonse and Rachel, *L'au-delà au fond de nous-mêmes; initiation à la meditation*, Béthanie, Centre de Recherche et de Méditation, Meisenthal (1982).

3. Pope Jean-Paul II referred to this during his visit to the Cameroons: 'Africa can offer the world, amongst other things, the example of unflagging warmth of hospitality, of the solidarity that exists so strongly between members of the same tribe to the extent that no one is ever left abandoned . . . These are values of which the modern world has great need in order to overcome the contradictions and traps of a humanism deprived of its basic religious dimension', *Le Monde*, 14/8/85, p. 3. (Yet Rome has still to accept all the consequences of the respect it says it wishes to display towards Africa. See Achille Mbembe's article 'Tension entre Rome et les Églises africaines', mentioned in the Bibliography.

4. Morin defines 'neo-atheism' in *Dieu aujourd'hui: recherches et débats*, Desclée-De Brouwer, Paris (1965), pp. 21–5. The same Edgar Morin has said that what the Third World needs most is spirituality in the West.

5. Goettmann, Alphonse, *Karlfreid Graf Durckheim, dialogue sur le chemin initiatique*, Dervy-Livres, coll. 'Bethanie, les chemins de la profondeur', Paris, (1984), pp. 29–30.

6. Monsignor Cardijn, founder of the JOC, man of action though he was, was also a man of prayer. It is said he devoted three hours a day to it.

7. By secularism I do not mean the sane cognizance of the world, but the state of mind resulting from the materialism and rationalism described earlier. The same goes for the term 'secularization' as used here.

8. *Comme un éclair de l'Orient à l'Occident; Jésus, Gandhi et l'âge atomique*, Orant, coll. 'Béthanie', Paris (1983). This book describes the tactics employed by pacifists to protest against American Trident nuclear submarine bases and explains the central place activists accord to prayer accompanied by the giving of oneself. (They ran the risk of heavy prison sentences and a veritable social ostracism.) In this book love is presented as an enormous, revolutionary energy, capable of changing the course of history and of pitting its strength against that of nuclear energy.

9. Holland, 'The spiritual crisis . . .', see Bibliography.

10. Entraide et Fraternité, the Belgian, Catholic NGO responsible for organizing the 'Lenten sharing' has launched, a propos of this, a project which has met with great interest, especially within certain circles of young people. It involves the observance of a 48 hour total fast based on the theme 'fast for change'. For its part, Broederlijk Delen organizes 'abstemious weekends' during which families are encouraged to leave the car in the garage and not switch on the television, encouraging by these two acts more congeniality and inner calm.

11. Atheists have discovered indirectly, through the Orient, the wealth of the Judeo-Christian spiritual heritage. See for instance the spiritual journey described by Olivier Clement in *L'autre soleil; autobiographié spirituelle*. Stock, Paris (1975), pp. 87 and ff.

12. In France, the Béthanie Centre for Research and Meditation offers beginners classes in meditation and understanding one's body, as a spiritual experience to retrace one's roots. The animateurs, Alphonse and Rachel Goettmann have close links with the non-violent action movement. (Prieuré St. Thiebault, 57130 Gorze, Moselle, France). At the International Centre of Sainte Baume there are classes aimed at introducing the participants to the spiritual disciplines of other continents (Le Plan d'Aups, 83640 Saint-Zacharie, France). In Belgium, the centre, Voies de L'Orient, offers introductory classes in meditation and the significance for Christianity of oriental disciplines such as Zen and Yoga (69, rue du Midi, 1000 Bruxelles). An introduction to the 'culture of silence' is offered at Brembergcentrum (Bremberg, I, 3044 Haasrode, Belgique). The Anjali centre brings together

Christians looking for a practical introduction to yoga and prayer (rue de la Revolution, 7, Bruxelles).

Chapter 9

1. CIDSE (Coopération Internationale pour le Développement et la Solidarité), international organ within which European and North American Catholic NGOs work together. This dossier can be obtained from the Secretariat of CIDSE, 1–2, avenue des Arts, Bte, 6, 1040 Brussels.

2. 'Rencontres sur les communautés culturelles', IFDA, *Dossier* 33, (1983), p. 61.

3. *À contre courants, l'enjeu des relations interculturelles*, Éd. d'En-Bas, Geneva, 1984. See particularly its excellent table on p. 233. See also its contribution entitled 'Identité culturelle, self-reliance et besoins fondamentaux' in the anthology *Il faut manger pour vivre . . .; controverses sur les besoins fondamentaux et le développement*, published under the auspices de l'Institut Universitaire d'Études du Développement (Geneva), PUF and IUED, Paris (1980).

4. See notably Morre Lappe, Frances and Collins, Joseph, *L'industrie de la faim*, Éd. Etincelle, Montreal, (1978), and George, Susan, *Comment meurt l'autre moitié du monde*, Laffont, Paris (1978).

5. Amin, Samir, 'Note sur le concept de déconnection (delinking)', IFDA, *Dossier* 50 (1983), p. 38.

6. The anthropologist's role can be important but remains ambiguous. The best understanding of the internal mechanisms activating a society are sometimes used in a manipulative way that can lead to the violation of a people. We will return to this later.

7. 'Pour une stratégie globale de la culture et de la communication', IFDA, *Dossier* 14, (1979), p. 1.

8. See non-violent evangelical struggles, below.

9. On this subject see Goulet, Denis, 'Development experts: the one-eyed giants', *World Development*, Pergamon, Vol. 8, pp. 481–9.

10. For the action taken against the construction of this dam on the River Chico, see 'A decision for justice', APHD, *Newsletter* No. 6.

11. However, even in such programmes, the cultural dimension could be increased.

12. In such a spirit, Broederlijk Delen has played host to trade unionists from São Paulo (Brazil). 'Entraide et Fraternité' is undertaking a regular exchange programme between Wallonian and Malagasy peasants. By means of this, Wallonian villages have been able to welcome villagers whose reality, though differing on many points, is much more similar than one might have expected at first sight. The observations made by these peasants from far-off Madagascar gave rise to profound reflection and passionate debate.

Part 3:   Chapter 10

1. This project is supported within the framework of the programme undertaken in Vietnam by the CIDSE (Coopération Internationale pour le Développement et la Solidarité), a consortium of European and American Catholic NGOs.

2. This project is part of the CIDSE programme (see preceding note) in Kampuchea.

Chapter 11

1. Progress report of Nkata project, Masuika, 1980; (1981; roneo).
2. *Ibid.*
3. Taken from the request for renewal of the project's funding, introduced in 1982.
4. Progress report, January 1982–June 1983 (1983; roneo).

Chapter 12

1. Estimates made by Broederlijk Delen's partners in India and Zaire. Projects in India will be discussed in a later chapter dealing with development and Hindu culture.

Chapter 13

1. This is what is done on a large scale by CCFD (Comité Catholique Faim et Développement), a French NGO.
2. It is, in this case, the questionnaire used by the NGO, Broederlijk Delen.

Part 4:   Chapter 14

1. The interviews reprinted here were originally written in English under the title 'Cultures, religions and development; interviews conducted and recorded by Thierry Verhelst, 14–23/1/1985' (roneo), Brussels (1985).
2. The Vedanta, one of the most elevated of classical Indian philosophies, is non-dualist: according to it, all is one, non-duality (*advaita*). The external, material world, in all its diversity, is merely a reflection (*maya*) of Ultimate Reality. To attach oneself to it is to be a victim of ignorance and illusion. Only the union (*yoga*) of man with the Whole brings happiness. Through his soul (*atman*), man may participate in the Whole that is God (*Brahman*). This union is disturbed by the egocentric mentality. Man therefore needs to practise asceticism, of which classical India enumerates three major paths: meditation (*jnana*), devotion (*bhakti*) and action (*karma*). For our purpose here, *Karma-yoga* has a particular interest. This path is highly regarded in one of the books of the classical epic Mahabharata, namely the Bhagavad Gita.
3. William Collins, Fount Paperbacks, London (1982).
4. In the sense of political commissar of a revolutionary party: see Koestler, Arthur, *Le yogi et le commissaire*, Paris, Calmann-Levy, 1969, pp. 13 ff.
5. It is quite clear that, in India, Gandhi is completely ignored by some and openly rejected by others. This is true of orthodox Marxists who see him as a utopian reactionary, even as dangerously anti-progressive, and of certain outcastes

who criticize him for not having condemned and combated the very principle of the caste system. Gandhi certainly opposed the idea of untouchability imposed on outcastes. He saw this as a detestable deformation of the caste system. But he considered the latter a good thing if conformed to while abiding by the obligations imposed by *Dharma* (natural law). The opinion expressed by Bede Griffith closely resembles this.

6. What is true for Hindus and members of the Ghandian movement also applies more and more to groups attached to the communist parties, particularly the CPM which has grown very hostile towards NGOs and the Indian partners. Such groups are suspicious of the conscientization work and popular organization done by NGOs because it takes place outside the party, its directives and its control. Food for thought here for those who refer to NGOs involved with the Third World as cryptocommunists!

Chapter 15

1. These conventions place at the disposition of signatory countries who export agricultural and mineral raw materials, mechanisms for stabilizing export revenues. These mechanisms, called Stabex and Sysmin provide a sort of insurance system against the sometimes catastrophic losses suffered by countries who depend almost entirely on a limited number of export products. Through transfer of funds, losses incurred either through fall in prices or in production are covered.

2. As well as the islands surrounding Africa which are members of Organization of African Unity (OAU). Neither South Africa nor Namibia are of course signatories.

3. Antigua and Barbuda, the Bahamas, Barbados, Belize, Dominique, Grenada, Guyana, Jamaica, St. Christopher-Nevis, St. Lucia, Surinam, St. Vincent and Grenadines, Trinity and Tobago.

4. Fiji, Solomon Islands, Western Samoa, Tonga, Tuvalu, Vanuatu.

5. The complete text of the Convention can be found in *Le Courrier*, (EEC Brussels), No. 89, January–February 1985, special no.

6. Pisani, Edgar, *La main et l'outil, le développement du Tiers-Monde et l'Europe*, R. Laffont, Paris (1984).

7. *Ibid*.

8. See the section of the present work devoted to 'States without nation . . .'

9. Except for articles 127 and 128 concerning the diffusion in Europe of 'cultural goods and services of ACP states that are highly representative of their cultural identities'. It is fitting here to wonder who will have the right to judge just what is representative . . .

10. Chasle, Raymond, *La coopération culturelle et sociale dans le cadre de la Convention de Lomé III*, paper (roneo) given at the Chantilly Conference (13–15/6/1985) on 'La fonction de la culture dans l'ensemble de la coopération au développement mise en oeuvre dans le troisième Convention de Lomé', see below.

11. Chasle, Raymond, op. cit.

12. Speech by E. Pisani at the Chantilly Conference mentioned above.

13. Seuil, Paris (1962).

14. De Boer-Sizoo, Edith, 'Resources humaines et formation: racines de co-développement', working document (roneo) presented to the conference Lomé III and NGOs held in Paris, 4–6 June 1985.

15. This conference was held under the auspices of the EEC, June 13–15 1985, and was organized by 'L'Institut Robert Schuman pour l'Europe' and the 'Joint Task Force sur les questions de développement', an ecumenical organization comprised of development experts and heads of NGOs belonging to the Churches of EEC countries. This organization also acts as the secretariat of the network. It changed its name in January, 1986 and is now called 'Service Oecuménique Européenne pour le Développement' (EECOD).

Summary and Conclusion: Chapter 16

1. Father L. J. Lebret, o.p., is the founder of Économie et Humanisme, produced by IRFED (Institut International de Recherche et de Formation en vue du Développement Humain Harmonisé), instigator of the encyclical *Populoram Progressio* and author of *Dynamique concrète du développement*, Éd. Ouvrières, Paris (1961), and *Économie et Civilisations*, (Vol. 1) *Niveaux de vie, Besoins et Civilisations* (in collaboration with A. Piettre, A. Sauvy and R. Delprat), Éd. Ouvrières, Paris (1956).

2. Ignacy Sachs is Director of Studies at the École des Hautes Études en Sciences Sociales where he runs the International Centre for Research on the Environment and Development and joint founder of the International Foundation for Alternative Development (IFDA), whose excellent Dossiers have often been quoted in the present work. Sachs has written: 'Stratégies de l'écodéveloppement', Éd. Ouvrières, coll. *Développement et Civilisations*, Paris (1980).

Bibliography

1. Development in general

George, Susan, *How the Other Half Dies: The Real Reasons for World Hunger*, Allanheld, 1977.

George, Susan and Paige, Nigel, *Food for Beginners*, Writers and Readers Publishing Co-operative Society Ltd, London, 1982.

Goulet, Denis, 'La crise des modèles de développement', *Foi et Développement* No. 103, Paris, 1983.

Jalée, Pierre, *Pillage of the Third World*, Monthly Review Press, 1968.

—— 'Le capitalisme périférique', special no. of *Revue Tiers-Monde*, No. 52, 1972.

Lappe, Frances Moore and Collins, Joseph, *Food First: Beyond the Myth of Scarcity*, Ballantine, New York, 1979.

——, with Kinley, David, *Aid as Obstacle*, Institute for Food and Development Policy, San Francisco, 1981.

Lecomte, Bernard J., *Project Aid: Limitations and Alternatives*, OECD, Paris, 1986.

Pisani, Edgar, *La Main et L'Outil: Le Développement du Tiers-Monde et L'Europe*, Laffont, Paris, 1984.

—— *Quel Monde Pour Demain?* Proceedings of the first congress of l'Association Mondiale de Prospective Sociale, Dakar (21–23 January 1980), Association Mondiale de Prospective Sociale, Geneva, 1982. (Contributions by Albert Tévoédjrè, Ivan Illich, Abdellatif Benachenhou, Jacque Bugnicourt, C.A.O. van Nieuwenhuijze, Denis de Rougemont, Rodolfo Stavenhagen et al.)

Sachs, Ignacy, 'Stratégies de l'écodéveloppement', Ed. Ouvrières, coll. *Développement et Civilisations*, Paris, 1980.

Schneider, Bertrand, *The Barefoot Revolution: A Report to the Club of Rome*, ITDG, 1988.

Tévoédjrè, Albert, *La Pauvreté, Richesses des Peuples*, Ed. Ouvrières, Paris, 1978.

2. Culture and development

a) Africa

Bgoya, Walter and Hyden, Goran (rep.), 'The State and the Crisis in Africa: In Search of a Second Liberation', in *Development Dialogue* No. 2, Uppsala, 1977.

Bureau, René, *Le Péril Blanc, Propos d'un Ethnologue sur l'Occident*, L'Harmattan, Paris, 1978.

Bimwenyi Kweshi, Oscar, *Discours Théologique Négro-africain: Problèmes des*

Fondements, Présence Africaine. Paris, 1981.

Dupriez. Hughes, *Paysans d'Afrique Noire*, L'Harmattan et Terres et Vie, Paris-Nivelles, 1982.

Ela, Jean-Marc. *African Cry*, Orbis, 1986.

────── *L'Afrique des Villages*, Karthala. Paris, 1982.

────── *La Ville en Afrique Noire*. Karthala, Paris, 1983.

────── *My Faith as an African*. Orbis, 1988.

Harrison, Paul. *The Greening of Africa: Breaking Through in the Battle for Land and Food*. Paladin, London, 1987.

Hyden, Goran, *Beyond Ujamaa in Tanzania: Underdevelopment and Uncaptured Peasantry*. Heinemann Educational, London, 1980.

Mbembe. Achille, 'Tensions entre Rome et les églises africaines (foi catholique et cultures noires)', *Le Monde Diplomatique*, Vol. 32, No. 378, September 1985.

Miske. Ahmed Baba, *Lettre Ouverte aux Elites du Tiers-Monde*, Sycomore, Paris, 1981.

b) The Americas

Anglade. George, *Espace et Liberté en Haïti*, Ed. ERCE et Centre de recherches-Caraïbes (University of Montreal), Montreal, 1983.

Burgos-Debray. Elisabeth. *I, Rigoberta Menchú*. Verso, London, 1984.

Galeano, Eduardo, *The Open Veins of Latin America: Five Centuries of the Pillage of a Continent*, Monthly Review Press, 1973.

Guttiérez, Gustavo, *We Drink from Our Own Well: The Spiritual Journey of a People*. Orbis, 1984.

Hurbon, Laënnec, *Culture et Dictature en Haïti: L'Imaginaire sous Contrôle*, L'Harmattan, Paris, 1979.

Mesters. Carlos, *La Mission du Peuple qui Souffre*. Cerf, Paris, 1984.

c) Asia

Ariyaratne, A. F., *Collected Works* (2 vols), Sarvodaya Research Institute, Dehiwala, 1980.

Dietrich. Gabrielle, *Culture, Religion and Development*. Centre for Social Action. Bangalore, 1978.

Geertz, Clifford. *The Interpretation of Cultures. Selected Essays*. Basic Books, Inc., New York, 1973.

Griffiths. Bede. *The Marriage of East and West*, Collins (Fount Paperbacks), London, 1982.

Rao, O. R.. 'The Concept of Basic Needs: An Analysis', *Gandhi Marg*, (Journal of the Gandhi Peace Foundation), Vol. 4, No. 4, July 1982, pp. 459–470.

Scott. James. *Weapons of the Weak: Everyday Forms of Peasant Resistance*. Yale University Press. New Haven and London.

Sivaraksa. Sulak, *A Buddhist Vision for Renewing Society*. Thai Wattana Press, Bangkok, 1981.

────── *Siamese Resurgence, a Thai Buddhist Voice on Asia and a World of Change*, Asian Cultural Forum on Development. Bangkok, 1985.

Varma. S. P.. 'Gandhi and Contemporary Thinking on Development'. *IFDA Dossier*, No. 37, September 1983.

d) General

Cosmao. Vincent. *Un Monde en Développement? Guide de Réflexion*. Ed. Ouvrières, Paris, 1984.

Development, Seeds of Change, Village through Global Order, Review of the Society for International Development, Rome; special number devoted to 'Culture, the Forgotten Dimension', No. 3/4, 1984.

Ellis, William N. and Ellis, Margaret McMahon, 'Cultures in Transition: What the West can Learn from Developing Countries', *The Futurist*, March–April 1983.

Esteva, Gustavo, 'Alternatives to Economics', *TOES/NA Newsletter*, 1988.

—— 'A New Call for Celebration', *Development: Seeds of Change* No. 3, 1986.

Fabella, V. and Torres, S. (Eds), *Irruption of the Third World, Challenge to Theology*, Orbis, New York, 1983.

Goulet, Denis, *The Uncertain Promise: Value Conflicts in Technology Transfer*, New Horizons Press, New York, 1988.

Latouche, Serge, 'Faut-il refuser le développement?', PUF, coll. *Economie en Liberté*, Paris, 1986.

Luyckx, Marc (rep.), 'De la Culture de développement Vers d'Autres Paradigmes', Actes du 1er colloque d'Automne, South–North Network on Cultures and Development, Brussels, 1988.

Nerfin, Marc, 'The Image of the Other', *IFDA Dossier*, No. 67, September–October 1988.

Panikkar, Raimundo, 'Alternatives to Modern Culture', *Whole Earth Papers, Indian Voices on World Order*, Winter 1978, Vol. 1, No. 5, pp. 14–15.

—— 'The Message of Yesterday's India to Today's World', *Religion and Society*, Vol. XXVII, No. 1, March 1980.

—— 'Let Us Stop Speaking About the Global Village', *Interculture*, (Montreal), Vol. XVI, No. 4, Book 81, 1983.

—— 'Is the Notion of Human Rights a Western Concept?', *Interculture* (Montreal), Vol. XVII, Nos 1–2, Books 82–3, 1984, and *Diogene* No. 120, p. 87, 1982.

Preiswerk, Roy A., 'A contre-courants; l'enjeu des relations inter-culturelles' (textes réunis et publiés par Gilbert Rist), Ed. D'En Bas, coll. *Nord–Sud*, Publications de l'IUED, Geneva, 1983.

Rist, Gilbert, 'Relations interculturelles et pratiques du développement', *Revue Canadienne d'Etudes du Développement*, Vol. V, No. 2, 1984.

—— 'A quoi bonne le développement?' *Philosophica*, 25/1980 (1).

Schumacher, E. F., *Small Is Beautiful: Economics as if People Mattered*, Harper & Row, 1975.

TOES/NA Newsletter, Susan Hunt (Ed.), Economics Department, University of Maine, Orono, Me 04469, USA. This is the organ of The Other Economic Summit/North America.

Vachon, Robert, 'Pour une réorientation radicale des ONG; du développement endogène a la solidarité interculturelle', *Interculture* (Montreal), Vol. XVII, No. 4, Book 85, p. 38, 1984.

Verhelst, Thierry G., 'Customary Law as a Constraint on Agricultural Development. A Re-evaluation', *Cultures et Développement*, Universite Catholique de Louvain, Vol. II, Nos 3–4, 1969.

Zaoual, Hassan, 'La crise du paradigme du développement', *Revue Tiers-Monde*, Vol. XXV, No. 100, 1984.

3. Other important texts cited

Douglas, Jim, *Lightning East to West: Jesus, Gandhi and the Nuclear Age*, Crossroad Publishers, New York, 1983.

Fanon, Frantz, *The Wretched of the Earth*, Grove Press, 1968.

Freire, Paulo, *Education for Critical Consciousness*, Continuum, 1973.

——— *Pedagogy of the Oppressed*, Continuum, 1970.

Fromm, Erich, *To Have or To Be?* Bantam, 1987.

——— *The Anatomy of Human Destructiveness*, H. Holt & Co., 1973.

Garaudy, Roger, 'Pour un dialogue des civilisations', Denoël, coll. *Coudées Franches*, Paris, 1973.

——— *Comment l'Homme Devint Humain*, Jeune Afrique, Paris, 1978.

Gorz, André, *Farewell to the Working Class: An Essay in Post-Industrial Socialism*, Pluto, 1986.

Goss-Mayr, Hildegard, *L'Homme Face a l'Injustice; Libération Non-violente, Spiritualité et Praxis*, Académie sociale catholique d'Autriche, Europa Verlag, Vienna, 1976.

Holland, Joe, 'The spiritual crisis of modern culture', Center of Concern, *Occasional Papers*, Washington, DC, 1983.

——— 'The Post-Modern Paradigm in the Church's Shift to the Left', Center of Concern, *Occasional Paper*, Washington, DC, 1984.

Ki-Zerbo, Joseph and Sizoo, Edith, 'Lomé's Missing Link', in *Lomé Briefing*, No. 7, March 1989.

Max-Neef, Manfred A., *From the Outside Looking In: Experiences in Barefoot Economics*, Dag Hammarskjöld Foundation, Uppsala, 1982.

Morin, Edgar, 'Pour sortir du XXᵉ siècle', Natan, coll. *Points*, Paris, 1981.

——— *La méthode* (t. I and II), Seuil, Paris, 1977.

Partant, François, *La Fin du Développement, Naissance d'une Alternative*, Maspero, Paris, 1982.

White, Merry and Pollak, Susan (Eds), *Cultural Transition*, Routledge and Kegan Paul, 1986.

Index

acculturation, 53-5
Australian Catholic Relief (ACR), 91
advaita, 124
Afar herdsmen, 106-8
Africa, Caribbean and Pacific regions
    (ACP), 147-55
Afro-Fascism, 21
agricultural reform, 18
agriculture, 9, 10, 11, 12, 31, 33, 37, 94,
    107, 108-12, 147, 151
Ahmed, Ait, 21
Alagamar, 47, 76
Algeria, 11, 13; Declaration of, 156
alienation, cultural, 159
All India Trade Union Congress
    (AITUC), 133
Allende, Salvador, 13
American Friends Service Committee, 91
Amin, Samir, 13, 82
Anglade, Georges, 30, 32
Angola, 22
animal draught, 107, 108-12
animal husbandry, 106, 151
animism, 28, 46, 51, 56, 57, 100, 123
anthropocentrism, 62
anthropology, 84, 85, 99
anti-apartheid movement, 98
anxiety, 28
apartheid, 17, 86
apiculture, 103
architecture, 32
Argentina, 15, 40
Ariyaratne, A.T., 30, 104
asangraha, 125, 133, 134
Asia Partnership for Human
    Development (APHD), 100, 123
Asian Cultural Forum on Development
    (ACFOD), 101
atheism, 46, 74
Aurobindo, Sri, 62, 128, 138
austerity, 29

Australia, 91
autarchy, 82
Awash basin, 106-8
Aymara peoples, 57

Bamileke peoples, 27
Bantu peoples, 107, 108-12, 115
Belgium, 86, 91, 94, 123, 147
Belkin, Gerald, 33
Bellagio, Declaration of, 19
Benachenou, Abdellatif, 12-13
Bhagavad Gita, 48, 125, 126, 130, 144
bhakti, 49, 128, 143
Bhave, Vinoba, 29, 134, 136, 137, 143
Bhoodan Movement, 134, 137
Bible, 30, 44, 46
Birou, Alain, 19
Boff, Clodovis, 71
Bokassa, Emperor, 21, 45
Bolivia, 57, 97
Bon Nouvel, 98
Boukman, 50
Brahmins, 134
Brandt Commission, 13
Brazil, 9, 15, 47, 50, 55, 63, 76, 82, 83, 85,
    86, 95, 97, 98, 103
Broederlijk Delen, 91, 99, 123
Brot für die Welt, 91
Buddhism, 29, 30, 45, 46, 48, 49, 53, 72,
    73, 97, 100, 101, 104, 114, 123, 158, 160
Bulletin of African Theology, 100
Bureau, René, 26, 41
bureaucracy, 9, 10
Burkina Faso, 15, 36
Burma, 38, 53

Cabral, Amilcar, 21
Camara, Dom Helder, 75
Cambodia, 53
Cameroons, 15, 28, 75, 94, 95
Canada, 123

Cancun Summit, 20
Candomble religion, 98
Carajas project, 86
Caritas, 123
cash crops, 33
caste system, 128, 129, 130, 132, 134
Castro, Fidel, 10, 46
catching-up strategies, 156
Catholic church, 46, 98, 114
Catholic Fund for Overseas Development
    (CAFOD), 91
cattle breeding, 34
Central Agency for Joint Funding of
    Development Programmes
    (CEBEMO), 91
Central Intelligence Agency (CIA), 17
Centre for Development Co-operation
    (CNCD/NCOS), 91
centralization, 40
Ceylon, 48, 53
Chantilly Conference, 153, 154
charity, towards Third World, 79
Chasle, Raymond, 19, 148
Chavez, Cesar, 44
Chile, 13, 46, 85, 99-100
China, 10, 29, 53, 54, 138
Chinmaya Mission, 132, 134
Chipko movement, 45
Chitananda, Swami, 128
Christ, figure of, 47, 48, 54
Christian Aid, 91
Christianity, 15, 46, 47, 49, 53, 54, 57, 73,
    75, 76, 77, 98, 101, 111, 114, 115, 123,
    129, 132, 138, 139, 142, 145, 160
civil disobedience, 157
civil rights, 15
civil servants, 10
clanism, 39, 56
class analysis, 145
class conflict, 84
class struggle, 104, 136
co-operatives, 12
colonialism, 19
Comissão dos bairros de Belém, 95-6
Comité catholique contre la faim et pour le
    développement (CCFD), 91
Communist Party of India (CPI), 133
community, sense of, 27
competitive spirit, 27
Confucianism, 100
Congress Party (India), 135
conscientization, 15, 16, 18, 20, 21, 91, 95,
    96, 98, 126, 129, 132; of the rich, 143
Conselho indigenista missionario (CIMI),
    97
Cosmao, Vincent, 61, 62
Costa Rica, 40

Creative Dramatics of Cagayan de Oro
    City group, 94
crisis of the West, 67-70
cultural pluralism, 21, 84
culture, 17-23; conception of, 17
Développement et paix, 123
Danechurchaid, 91
Darwinism, social, 11
De Leener, Philippe, 33
debt, 9
decentralization, 39
deculturation, 56, 100, 139, 141, 157;
    resistance to, 39
delinking, 26, 80-3, 161
democracy, parliamentary, 39
democratization, 18
Denmark, 91
dependence, 12, 13
dependence theory, 156
desarrollismo, 12
desertification, 107
development, 79
Development and Interchurch Aid
    Department (DICAD), 102
Development and Peace (Canada), 91
Development Decade (UN), 9, 20
development models, collapse of, 9-16
development pornography, 86-8
development projects, 102-12; criteria
    for, 84-6
development: as concept, 62-4; as Trojan
    horse, 52-7; cultural approach to, 160;
    ideology of, 10; strategies, 19
dharma, 114, 128
dictatorships, 9, 43
difference, right to, 80, 159
division of labour, international, 82
Douglas, Jim, 76
Dravidian movement, 49
drought, 103, 107
Dumont, René, 152
Dupriez, Hugues, 31, 33
Durckheim, Karlfried Graf von, 74
Dussel, Enrique, 49
Duvalier, François, 15, 50
Duvalier, Jean-Claude, 51

ecology, 160
economia de los pobres, 83
economics, 25-31
Ecuador, 97
Ecumenical Association of Third World
    Theologians (EATWOT), 100
education, 12; adult, 34, 95
Egypt, 100
Einstein, Albert, 76

Ela, Jean-Marc, 28, 44, 50, 95
El Salvador, 47, 75, 85, 98
Eluard, Paul, 79
Engels, Friedrich, 11
Entraide et Fraternité, 91, 123
Eritrea, 22
Ethiopia, 9, 46, 87, 100, 106-8, 155
ethnicity, 17
ethnocentrism, 156, 159, 160
ethnocide, 63
eurocentrism, 20, 22, 41, 45, 54, 63, 141
European Economic Community (EEC), 86, 147-55
eviction, of peasants, 15, 55, 103
evolutionism, 10
exposure programmes, 87

famine, 103
fantasy law, 39
fascism, 68
feminism, 152
fishing, 151
Food and Agricultural Organization of UN (FAO), 32
Ford Foundation, 91
France, 11, 69, 86, 106, 147
Freedom from Hunger campaign of FAO, 32
Freire, Paulo, 15, 17, 20-1, 138, 143
FRELIMO, 22
Freud, Sigmund, 28
fundamentalism, 141
funding agencies, 117
funding questionnaire, 118-20

Gandhi, Mahatma, 29, 44, 49, 70, 76, 78, 81, 124, 127, 128, 129, 130, 133, 134, 135, 136, 138, 141, 142, 158
Gandhian movement, 114
Garaudy, Roger, 17, 24
genocide, 97
Germany, West, 91
Girardon, Jacques, 35
Goss-Mayr, Hildegarde, 71, 75
Goulet, Denis, 18
Greenpeace, 69
Griffiths, Bede, 127-9
Group of 77, 13
Groupe de recherche et d'échanges technologiques, 94
Guaymi peoples, 99
Guevara, Ernesto 'Che', 29, 87
Guinea-Bissau, 21, 22
Gunder Frank, André, 13
Gutierrez, Gustavo, 49

Haiti, 15, 32, 33, 42, 50-1, 57, 98, 117

harijans, 134
health care, 9, 12, 95, 151
Henri, Paul-Marc, 67
hierarchy, 11, 26
Hinduism, 21, 39, 45, 46, 48, 49, 100, 101, 104, 114, 115, 123-46
historical materialism, 20
hoe, use of, 109
Holland, 147
Holland, Joe, 71, 73, 75, 76
homo economicus, 25-31, 157
hospitals, 11
housing, 12, 151
human rights, 9, 18, 95
hunger, 25
hydro-electric dams, 11, 86
hygiene, 34

Idi Amin Dada, 21
Illich, Ivan, 19, 30-1, 55
immigrants, 154
imperialism, 146, 156; cultural, 53, 87, 152; fight against, 87; of socialist countries, 87
Incas, 38
inculturation, 53-5
India, 11, 14, 15, 21, 32, 38-9, 45, 49, 54, 114, 117, 123-46
Indians: Brazilian, 97; Quawasquar, 99-100
indigenous culture, 24-32, 83-4, 91, 154, 157; as source of social struggle, 43; conservation of, 102
individualism, 27
Indonesia, 39, 114
industrialization, 9, 12-13
industry, promotion of, 11, 135
inertia, as form of cultural resistance, 112
infant, as king, 28
infibulation, 115
inheritance, systems of, 111
Innovation et réseaux pour le développpement (IRED), 94, 118
Institut pour la recherche et l'action culturelles, 130
Institute for Cultural Research and Action (ICRA), 138
Instituto de estudos da religiao (ISER), 97
Interchurch Co-ordination Committee for Development Projects (ICCO), 91
International Coalition of Development Associations (ICDA), 92
Intermediate Technology Development Group (ITDG), 94
International Foundation for Development Alternatives (IFDA), 19
International Monetary Fund (IMF), 82

International Network for a Society
	Overcoming Domination, 134
Iran, 13, 45, 81
Ireland, 91
Irish National Electricity Company, 86
irrigation, 36, 104, 137
Islam, 46, 49, 53, 100, 108, 115, 123, 145,
	160
Islamic schools, 114
Italy, 147
Ivory Coast, 9

Jacolin, Pierre, 34
Jamaa movement, 111
Jamaica, 13, 15
Japan, 53, 139, 140
Jeyaraj, Mr, 129
jnana, 125, 126, 128, 132, 133, 143
Jung, Carl, 76

Kalinga peoples, 86
Kampuchea, 97
Karen peoples, 38
karma, 125, 126, 128, 132, 133, 143
Kenya, 34
Khmer peoples, 38
Khmer Rouge, 10, 97
Khomeini, Ayatollah Ruhollah, 46
Ki-Zerbo, Joseph, 19, 80, 84
Kimbanguism, 111, 114
King, Martin Luther, 44, 70
Kiongozi, 98
Konate, T., 148
Korea, 53, 57; South, 13
Kothari, Rajni, 19
Kweshi, Oscar Bimwenyi, 61

land ownership, 95, 110
Latouche, Professor, 57
law, 157 *see also* legal systems
law, indigenous, 40, 99
Le Roy, Etienne, 38, 39, 41
Lebret, Louis J., 160
Left movement, 44, 79
legal systems, 38-42
Lenten Campaign, 77
liberation movements, 43
liberation theology, 49, 71, 158
licensing, foreign, 14
Lijjat project, 105-6
literacy, 9, 18, 34
literacy programmes, 15, 20
Lomé Convention III, 19, 147-55

Machel, Samora, 10
Macumba religion, 98
Mali, 38, 148

malnutrition, 9
Manley, Michael, 13
Mao Zedong, 29
Maoism, 10, 104
Marcos regime, 15, 44, 86, 94
market economy, 46
marketing systems, 25
marronage, 42
Marx, Karl, 11, 46
Marxism, 18, 20, 75, 84, 101, 113, 114,
	129, 133, 136, 142, 145
Marxism-Leninism, 31
Masai, 34
Masuika, 108-12
matriliny, 110
Mauritius, 148
maya, 49, 124, 125, 128, 132, 139
Mazgaonkar, Daniel, 134
Mazgaonkar, Hansa, 133-4
Mbembe, Achille, 95
Mbuji-Mayi, 111-12
medicine, traditional, 32, 93, 96, 103
meditation, 76
Mengistu, Haile Mariam, 10
Mennonite Central Committee, 91
Menon, Narayana, 132-3
Mexico, 9
millet, 36, 56
misappropriation of funds, 27
Miske, Ahmed, 19, 42
Miskitos, 17
missionaries, 12, 53, 54, 117
Mobutu, Marshal, 86, 100
modernity: alternative forms of, 56;
	rejection of, 62
modernization, 16
Monchanin, Father, 127
money, attitudes towards, 27
monocultures, 33
Monrovia Symposium, 20
Morin, Edgar, 67, 71, 74
Morocco, 40
*Movimento popular de libertação de
	Angola* (MPLA), 22
Mozambique, 22
multinationals, 18, 85
music, 55
Muslims, 38
mutual aid, 31
Myrdal, Gunnar, 38-9

Nagaraj, Mr, 130
Nandy, Ashis, 19
Napoleonic tradition, 40
Narayan, Jayaprakash, 29, 133, 137
Narducci, Angelo, 149-50
Nargolkar, Dr Vasant, 137

National Secretariat for Social Action
    (NASSA), 123
Nawal, Hassan, 19
neo-colonialism, 11, 38
neo-liberalism, 9
Netherlands, 91
New International Economic Order
    (NIEO), 13
Nguema, Macia, 21
Nicaragua, 10, 15, 17, 46, 47, 98
Niger, 86
Nigeria, 25
Nityananda, Swami, 128
Nkrumah, Kwame, 40
Nomadep, 106-8
nomads, 106
non-governmental organizations
    (NGOs), 11-12, 18, 20, 31, 34, 45,
    77-8, 83, 85, 86, 87, 91-2, 95, 101, 104,
    141, 144, 145, 154, 155, 157; attitudes
    of, 113; Christian, 123
non-monetary culture, 18
non-violence, 44, 47, 136, 137, 141, 143
North-South relations, 12, 13, 69, 80, 118
Novibor, 91
nuclear weapons, 69
Nyerere, Julius, 13

Oikos, 91
open door development, 82
oral traditions, 18
Organization of African Unity (OAU),
    20, 32
Orthodox church, Ethiopian, 100, 102
over-funding, dangers of, 118
oxen, 108-12
OXFAM, 91

Pakistan, 40
Panama, 99
Panikkar, Raimundo, 19, 24, 63, 70
participatory observation, 93-101
Patriotic Front (Zimbabwe), 99
peasant life, valorization of, 94
peasant organizations, 21, 63, 158
peasants, 9, 13, 15, 26, 29, 33, 34, 36, 43,
    45, 47, 48, 55, 79, 83, 87, 94, 100, 102,
    107, 108-12, 129, 157
Peru, 13, 14, 47, 97, 98
Pesantren movement, 114
phagocytism, 41
Pham van Dong, 10
pharmaceuticals, 32, 93, 96, 103
Philippines, 15, 32, 38, 40, 44, 75, 94, 117,
    123
Pipal Tree, 130, 131, 138, 140
Pires, Dom José Maria, 47

Pisani, Edgar, 19, 148, 152
Pol Pot, 10, 97
Poland, 46
politics, 38-42, 157
polycentrism, 39
polygamy, 110
popadums, production of, 105-6
popular culture, 96
Portugal, 91
poverty, 9, 30, 34; creation of, 14-15;
    fruitful, 32
Prebisch, Raúl, 13
Preiswerk, Roy, 18, 82
Prigogine, Ilya, 70
productivity, increases in, 31
Programa de cultura e capacitacion rural
    (PROCAR), 99
progress, validity of, 79
proletarianization, 103
Prometheus, Age of, 52, 71, 72
Protestant church, 98, 113
psychology, 32

Quawasquar Indians, 99-100

racism, 68
rainfall, 33
ram-raj, 135
Ramakrishna Mission, 129, 132-3
Ramdas, Baskaram, 126
rationalism, 75
rationality, Western, 28
re-personalization, 80
Reagan, Ronald, 69
Reddia, Sri Balaram, 125-6, 142
reforestation, 137
religion, role of, 45-51
renouncement, 138
research projects, 93-101
Ricci, Matteo, 53
rice growing, 56
Rich, Adrienne, 156
Rist, Gilbert, 18
Romero, Monsignor Oscar, 75
Rostow, W.W., 10-12, 156
rural extension programmes, 36
Rwanda, 27, 40

Sachs, Professor Ignacy, 160
Sahel, 14, 34, 94, 107
Sarvodaya movement, 30, 105, 106, 133,
    137, 138, 142, 143
Sarvodaya shramadana, 104, 114, 118
satya, 124, 125
satyagraha, 125, 136
Saux, Father, 127
Schumacher, E.F., 29, 94, 104

Scottish Catholic International Aid Fund (SCIAF), 91
secrecy: of religions, 56; power of, 44
self-reliance, 161
self-subsistence, 26
Senegal, 34, 36, 39, 148
Service d'études et d'animation pour le développement, 95
Shah of Iran, 46
shamanism, 57, 100
Shankar, Mr, 126
Shant, Mrs, 131
shanty-towns, 43
Shining Path, 47
Siddharta, Mr, 138
Sikhs, 38
Singapore, 13
Sivaraksa, Sulak, 29
slum dwellers, 96
Société pour l'action et le développement populaire, 129
social struggle, 43-51
socialism, 18, 31, 56, 69, 93; actually existing, 9; revolutionary, 9
Society for International Development, 20
Socio-economic Development Centre (SEDEC), 123
soil erosion, 35
solidarity, 73, 80, 84, 86, 91, 126; forms of, 85; intercultural, 159; international, 87
sophism, 24
South Africa, 13, 16, 17, 21, 75, 86, 98
South West Africa People's Organization (SWAPO), 14
South-North Network on Cultures and Development, 159
South-South relations, 118
spirituality, 46, 70
Sri Lanka, 29, 30, 38, 63, 104, 114, 118, 123
standard of living, measurement of, 29
state, phenomenon of, 38-42
strikes, 133
Sudan, 82
sugar cane, 103
swaraj, 125, 145
Sy, Seydina Oumar, 148
Syriac church, 138

Taiwan, 13
Tamil Nadu, 21, 49
Tamils, 38, 104
Tanzania, 13, 33, 98
Taoism, 73
Tapirape Indians, 63
taxation, 38
technical innovation, failure of, 109

technology, 32-7, 88, 135, 157; imported, 14
Terres et Vie, 94
Thailand, 15, 48, 53, 114, 139
theology, 100 *see also* liberation theology
Theology Exchange Programme, 118
Thich Nhat Hanh, 48
Tigrean movement, 22, 46
town and country, relation of, 25
tractors, 32, 35
trade unions, 15, 21, 43, 85, 86, 142, 158; rural, 103
traditionalism, 159
transnationals, 11
transport systems, 25, 32, 95
tribalism, 39
trickle-down theory, 10
Trocaire, 86, 91
Tshiamalenga, Ntumba, 39

Umbanda religion, 98
underdevelopment, 61, 65
unemployment, 68
Uniâo e consçienca negra, 98
unions, rural, 15
UNITA, 22
United Kingdom (UK), 11, 91, 86, 147
United Nations (UN), 9, 11, 20
UN Conference on Trade and Development (UNCTAD), 13
UN Economic and Social Council (UNESCO), 20, 67
UN Economic Commission for Latin America, 14
United States of America (USA), 46, 93, 98

Vachon, Robert, 45, 72
Vahini movement, 49
Vandervaeren, Charles, 148
Vastenactie, 91
Vedanta, 124, 125, 130
Vietnam, 9, 17, 48, 93
voluntary workers, 12
voodoo, 50-1, 57

wages, 25
Wahid, Abdu Rahman, 19
War on Want, 91
water tanks, repairing of, 104, 114
water technology, 37, 94
Welfare State, 67
West, malaise of, 68, 72
Westernization, 11, 16, 18, 20, 25, 37, 40, 41, 44, 45, 46, 53, 55, 56, 62, 91, 112, 114, 117, 123, 124, 126, 135, 139, 158
withdrawal into oneself, 159

women, 105-6, 134; in market gardening,
94; peasants, 109 (independence of,
110); role of, 45, 138, 152; working
land, 110
women's groups, 15
World Bank, 11, 82, 86
World Council of Churches, 54, 102

Yaoundé Convention, 147

Yin and Yang, theory of, 93

Zaire, 25, 27, 37, 40, 41, 75, 100, 107,
108-12, 114, 115
Zawal, Professor, 57
Zen, 53
Ziegler, Jean, 20, 22
Zimbabwe, 10, 15, 25, 37, 99
Zulus, 38

Reseau Sud–Nord Cultures et 'Développement'

The South–North Network on Cultures and Development was launched following the 1985 EECOD Chantilly Conference on 'The Cultural Dimension of Development in the Lomé III Convention'. The South–North network is open to all those who struggle for justice and the right of peoples to be different; that is to say, to people who broadly share the ideas expounded in books like this one. Acting as a flexible tool for communication, research, mutual solidarity and action between grassroots organizations, NGOs and committed academics from both South and North, the Network joins others in the resistance against the dominant monocultural development model and the quest for new types of solidarity and 'projects'. Activities are: a regular liaison bulletin, international meetings and advocacy.

Network co-ordinator: Dr Edith Sizoo
Research co-ordinator: Dr Thierry G. Verhelst
Address: rue Joseph II 172, 1040 Bruxelles, Belgium
Telephone: 32 2 230 46 37   **Fax:** 32 2 231 14 13   **Telex:** 20718 Jeseur

The South–North Network is now developing in all continents. Currently operational networks: **Asia:** – Mr Siddharta, c/o INODEP-Asia, Indiranagar 1 Stage 902, 560 033 Bangalore, India. **South America** – Mr Rubem Cesar Fernandes, c/o ISER, Cx P 16011, 2221 Rio de Janeiro, RJ, Brasil.

These continental networks and those soon to be launched in Africa, the Caribbean and the Pacific can be contacted via the Brussels-based secretariat. Donations for cultural projects, as defined in this book, may be made to the bank account of 'Reseau Sud–Nord Cultures et Développement', Bank a/c no. 001-0924826-07 at CGER Bank, rue Archimède 21, 1040 Bruxelles, Belgium.

Please contact the Brussels secretariat for any information on the Network's activities at intercontinental, continental and national levels.

Zed Books Ltd

is a publisher whose international and Third World lists span:

- **Women's Studies**
- **Development**
- **Environment**
- **Current Affairs**
- **International Relations**
- **Children's Studies**
- **Labour Studies**
- **Cultural Studies**
- **Human Rights**
- **Indigenous Peoples**
- **Health**

We also specialize in Area Studies where we have extensive lists in African Studies, Asian Studies, Caribbean and Latin American Studies, Middle East Studies, and Pacific Studies.

For further information about books available from Zed Books, please write to: Catalogue Enquiries, Zed Books Ltd, 57 Caledonian Road, London N1 9BU. Our books are available from distributors in many countries (for full details, see our catalogues), including:

In the USA
Humanities Press International, Inc., 165 First Avenue, Atlantic Highlands, New Jersey 07716.
Tel: (908) 872 1441;
Fax: (908) 872 0717.

In Canada
DEC, 229 College Street, Toronto, Ontario M5T 1R4.
Tel: (416) 971 7051.

In Australia
Wild and Woolley Ltd, 16 Darghan Street, Glebe, NSW 2037.

In India
Bibliomania, C-236 Defence Colony, New Delhi 110 024.

In Southern Africa
David Philip Publisher (Pty) Ltd, PO Box 408, Claremont 7735, South Africa.